NORTH COUNTY DUBLIN

A MEMOIR

1935-2014

By

Dan Redmond

DEDICATION

To my parents, my brothers and my sister, who winced and scratched their heads in bemusement.

CONTENTS

ACKNOWLEDGMENTS

Special thanks to Dr Cathy Fowley, whose inspiration and guidance in DCU started me on this odyssey.

And to my nieces Emer, Siobhan, Maeve and Grainne, who laughed at my descriptive and proscriptive efforts while giving brilliant practical support.

INTRODUCTION

I began scribbling in 2004 with the idea of it helping me to become familiar with a computer I had received. I also used it to write short stories, lyrics, and rhymes. Offerings which didn't interest the arbiters, though locally, I did win a prize or two. Anyway, I could not resist spoiling a few blank spaces of this memoir with one or two bits of verse.

In 2011 I enlisted in a DCU course where I hoped to broaden my perspective. There, I met a nice bunch of fellow students who, with nowhere else to go, and hoping for a little intellectual stimulation found themselves stuck with me. They came from diverse backgrounds: Sean was an ex-naval engineer, Nula was in the airline business, Michael was a semi-retired editor of a national newspaper, Teresa was an office manager of a large insurance company, and Ann was from London's Bethnal Green. All were very sociable and helpful. All had stories to tell. I found it a humbling and privileged experience listening to their life adventures and reading excerpts from their memoirs. The brilliant tutor was Dr Cathy Fowley.

The text of this memoir is colloquial; the narrative, unaffected. If any reader is hurt or embarrassed by the content, it is incidental. It is life as I lived it.

A glossary of local, colloquial terms can be found at the end of Part 4.

PART 1

Chapter 1: New Horizon

1946. No matter what the circumstances, being evicted from your home carries a stigma. Our problem arose because of our father changing jobs. He was born in Coolatin, County Wicklow, Ireland, in 1900 and in 1923 moved to the Castleblondin Estate near Castlecomer, County Kilkenny where he was employed as a tractor driver. This was, incidentally, where my brother Lorcan and I were born.

By 1934, our father had decided on foot of a situations vacant ad in the daily paper that his fortune would be better served elsewhere, and found employment with a William Keeling – a decent man, who was a fruit farmer near St. Margaret's, County Dublin. And about a year later and six miles from the city, with a certain Harry I. Usher, owner of the Brackenstown Estate which included horse racing stables.

The split-level, three-storey house which we were allocated was the middle one of three. On the left of our house lived Corky Culhane and his family, with Jack McGrath on the other side of us.

The Culhanes were to move away within a year or two. The McGraths were next-door neighbours and after moving they remained close friends for many years. Our 19th-century houses were situated on rising ground about sixty feet above the Ward River, and at the edge of a wood. The steep drop down to the river was also wooded, as was the rising ground on the far side of the glen which included quite a few huge ancient beech trees providing nesting for about ten pairs of cranes – large, grey, noisy, ungainly birds, though when in flight their great slow-moving wings gave a perspective of regal invincibility.

The three houses were situated on Brackenstown Road, an artery linking the two great north roads with Swords on one end, and Knocksedan (Hill of the Fairies) on the other. The two upper floors of our brick-built house were used as bedrooms, with their front windows facing the road and out across fields as far as the eye could see – fields that were the property of a very tolerant gentleman called Johnny Cuff who occasionally could be seen speeding by our house at twenty miles an hour in his high, two-wheeled gig pulled by a jennet.

What remains vivid of our parents' room, was the ornate iron brass-knobbed bedstead, the same bed in which three of our brothers would be born. The bed had a paillasse and a fibre-filled mattress. It was a fine, airy room; the walls decorated with pale nondescript wallpaper; worn brown linoleum covered the floor. An alcove served as a curtained wardrobe, and a similar one on the other side of the chimney breast with doors affixed was used for storing objects for safe-keeping, such as our father's uniform and army equipment, a Brownie camera, plus our parents' personal bits and pieces, including a hand-written account of the Vinegar Hill incident in its original folder, compiled by an English officer. The document is now in the safe-keeping of the National Archives.

Our room on the top floor was much the same, minus the floor covering. The two plain single beds that lay end to end were also made of iron – the base with its many springs securing it to the frame. Both were covered with a thin, hard-wearing, fibre-filled mattress. We slept two to a bed, one at either end. The bottom sheet was of cotton, homemade from flour sacks. The top sheets, along with the blankets and eiderdown, were supplied 'on the nod' by Alec Sloan's for a few bob per week. Under our bed was a white enamelled pot that, if not washed properly each day, became in no time as brown and smelly as a putrefying kipper.

The beds were a curse on light sleepers – the slightest movement wringing squeals of protest from the many springs holding the thing together. On the mantelpiece shone a Sacred Heart lamp through the dark hours of our nights. These upper windows were dormers and were fitted with shutters, as were all the windows in the house. When not in use, the shutters folded neatly into the casement.

The kitchen and back door of this split-level house was below road level and faced out over the beautiful wooded glen. It was a large, open-plan space with the fireplace filled with a range and oven. Upon the high mantelpiece were the remnants of our parents' wedding presents – two now cracked porcelain dogs, the tea canister, an alarm clock, a writing pad with a pen and a bottle of ink, and vitally, a box of Friendly matches.

Furniture consisted of a kitchen table and two forms which were made by our father, serving us there and elsewhere for about twenty years, a dresser, a couple of shelves on either of the chimney breast, three or four miscellaneous chairs that included a collapsible director's chair acquired by our mother for two thousand Sweet Afton cigarette coupons. Mother's foot-operated Singer sewing machine, positioned under the window, held pride of place, and returned its investment a million times over. On the window ledge, our Cossor radio was parked with a car battery attached.

The floor was tiled with manmade, nine-inch square, biscuit-coloured flags. I cannot recollect any pictures hanging except one of Jesus staring down with eyes that found you no matter where you tried to hide. There were two clothes lines running parallel at ceiling height for airing the freshly ironed clothes, plus a shorter one across the fireplace. There was a sizable compartment for storage that was used mainly for storing firewood and our father's bicycle, largely owing to it being in permanent darkness, being part under the stairs.

The house, as I have mentioned, was at the edge of woods that was also home to a million jackdaws; noisy, gregarious birds the whole year round, especially in springtime. They were tolerable, roosting and rising at civilised hours, and when we eventually moved on we missed them.

Chapter 2: In Retrospect

I have very few fond or precious memories of that early period. My memories are fragmentary, and overlap on occasion, for I don't recall events in absolute sequence. Such as, was I four or five when this occurred? Or seven or eight when something else happened? As far as parental love and joyful experiences are concerned, there are none, except I loved our mother's cooking.

Though I know we were cherished, our parents were not demonstrative. In fact, personal and public displays of parental devotion were over at three or four. I never saw an intimate moment between them, neither did I witness the slightest act of violence. I'm sure there was intimacy of some kind, but confined to the bedroom – the five of us as proof of it.

While now on the subject of love, my first experience of an embrace was on my first day at school. This gruesome event occurred when Mother placed me on the school step and then did a runner. Miss Tighe, the unfortunate teacher, lifted me up, whispering endearments, trying to console this snotty-nosed, bawling creature. But this cuddling business being so bloody alien, I wriggled free and headed full pelt toward the school gate in an attempt to escape. The result was that for the first three weeks at school, I spent my time in third class sitting or standing beside my brother Lorcan.

At home I was punished unmercifully, but deserving of it, for in hindsight I never gave a single thought to the consequences of my impulsive shenanigans. I do recall incidents which affected our simple existence; for example, one winter's evening when I was a six-year-old, we were chasing one another around the kitchen table. Our father and mother were not home from work yet. I threw a small bag across the table to impede my brothers. I recall it striking the oil lamp and dislodging the globe. Horrified, I saw it – I can still see it – slowly rolling toward the edge of the table... We were mesmerised as it slowly tumbled onto the flagged floor and smashed. This was a disaster as they were nigh on irreplaceable.

Light was vital for homework, for Mother's ironing, knitting, washing, reading, and for our father needing to repair shoes, or trim somebody's hair. There was holy murder when they arrived home, tired and worn out. We, the children, were aware of how vital the light was. That fact, and not the hiding I received, reinforces the memory. We had tallow candles that although smelly and smoky, made do for a month until somebody unearthed a globe in the city.

I also remember with amusement the speculations and reveries of Ussher's stable lads, or 'lads' as they were called, on the size of the present their owners would give if his horse won. The odd owner was known to drop a fiver, that's if he had a big bet on, or perhaps if he was drunk. The usual was a couple of quid when the happy event occurred. I also enjoyed the lads recalling the films they saw, especially the cowboy ones. This gang of fourteen- and sixteen-year-old lads, craving a bit of home life, a cup of tea and a warm fire, would assemble in our house between three and four o'clock before resuming their stable duties. This was our tithe home from 1935 to 1946.

Chapter 3: The Ussher Estate

Harry I. Ussher had been a well-known jockey in the steeplechase world, and the lover of the owner of the estate, a red-haired lady called Mrs. Croft. She was, as I recall, also the owner of six or seven cranky Scottish terriers. Apparently before dying, which was I believe in 1938 or 1939, she had willed the estate, which included the racing stable establishment, to Harry for his lifetime – the estate would ultimately be returned to the Dickie Croft line.

Harry, known to his staff as the 'Big Fella', was a large, jowly, unsmiling fellow, and the wearer of slouch hats, shooting jackets and britches. He was seldom seen outdoors without his shotgun and a couple of dogs, even bringing them in his shooting brake up to Mooretown. This was nice flat land of about forty acres, a little isolated from the estate, and personally owned by the Big Fella. He used this land for schooling their horses over five and seven furlongs. The track had a wooden stand to accommodate half a dozen people to view and time the horses. The stand was built by Mick Dooley, whom we'll hear more about later.

The estate, of which about half was under timber, woods laid down by Sir Robert Molesworth in the 17th century, was employing around twenty to twenty-five staff in our time and was important to the local economy. Harry was only moderately successful as a trainer, though he had excellent clients which included Mrs. Dorothy Paget, Mr. Shaw Taylor, Mr. Boyd Rochefort, plus other wealthy owners. Their horses, alas, were seldom to be as renowned as their owners.

The stable accommodated about forty flat racers and steeple chasers in the two adjoining stable yards. The front yard was for horses deemed good; the back yard, filled with the lazy and the no-hopers. The mares and foals were stabled in loose boxes in a remote part of the estate.

At that time Johnny Dooley, a pleasant, placid gentleman, was both secretary and general manager. Jack Augustus, or 'Guzzer' McGrath was a hardy, doughty, low-sized, friendly man who replaced Gerry Hamilton as head lad and was a brilliant schooler of horses. He was the same Jack who used to live beside us, and was now living in a bungalow in the stable yard. The stable jockeys in our time could easily be identified by them wearing jodhpurs. They were 'Titch' Tyrell, Joe Hogan, Tommy Ellis and later, Gerald Heffernan McGrath.

The Tyrells were from East Wall – small, dark-featured lads, always ebullient and confident. There were three of them. Titch, whom I have already mentioned, was by far the best jockey, winning lots of races here and in India. That was where he eventually became a trainer, got married and eventually died when only in his sixties. Billy, the second eldest, was an excellent amateur boxer, competing year in, year out in the national championships during and long after his horse riding days. He was still around up to the millennium. And Jackie, the youngest, didn't stay long at the horses.

Tommy Ellis, an ever-smiling, broad-shouldered, good-humoured lad from out the back somewhere in Meath, was a great character and a fearless horseman. Tommy was also a wonderful singer and yodeller. Indeed, when passing through the woods at night he'd break into a song, his powerful voice echoing through the glen and able to be heard a mile away. He was employed primarily to break horses – the tougher the horse the better Tommy liked it. He was poached by another trainer, but then a year or so later he reappeared. Being naturally heavy confined him to riding over the jumps, and mostly on horses other jockeys avoided. Joe Hogan was in his thirties when we knew him. He was also a gentleman and from a renowned horse-racing family from Limerick. I believe Joe, like Tommy Ellis, was contracted on the understanding that they could ride for anybody if not needed by their own stable.

There were ten or twelve stable lads who were issued with corduroy britches. First year apprentices were paid a half crown a week, and the rest five bob. That included being 'all found' and with a suit of clothes whenever the Big Fella, not you, decided you were in need of one (which incidentally was very seldom).

One particular lad I remember, he was about fifteen years of age in 1942 or 1943, was 'Giant' Martin. I never knew his proper name, but he was a dark-haired, fresh-complexioned chap, observant and polite. He was from either Meath or Kildare and of a horse-racing family. What distinguished him from the other lads was when they were playing 'Beg O' Me Neighbour' and 'Snap', or reading comic cuts during the dark winter evenings, 'me bould Giant' would take the Big Fella's shooting brake into town for a spin (having of course first ascertained by means of Stephen Bradley, the house-boy, that the Big Fella was getting stuck into the scotch). Giant would muster a couple of the lads to push the car out of the garage, past the main house toward the back avenue. Petrol? No problem! For the loosely chained lever of the petrol hand pump on the storage tank allowed enough movement to fill up whenever the car needed it.

Saturday nights in town now became the norm. Though spending money was scarce, girls were more than delighted to hop in for a spin. Giant very generously taught most of the lads to drive, including Joe Farrell. That was the routine until months before its time, the petrol storage tank went dry and the Big Fella went mad. The common consensus was that somebody was robbing the petrol and selling it.

George Naylor, a big, merry-eyed, stout, good-humoured man with a luxurious moustache was gardener. He produced grapes, figs, and peaches, along with all the vegetables the house required. All of those mentioned, except Jack McGrath, resided in the main dwelling house.

Another of the staff was young Pat Barnwell, as opposed to old Pat. Young Pat was a gentle soul, quiet and solemn. Always turned out neat and tidy, spending most of his time in the woods creating charcoal from laurel (of which there was a plenitude).

Paddy Oakes was the travelling lad. He and his wife, both from the midlands, lived with their family in the Naul Road gate lodge on the other side of the estate. Paddy's principal job was driving the motorised horse box, but as petrol was now severely rationed, he was usually driving a horse-drawn unit, again, built by Mick Dooley. This unit towed a two-horse box when racing was local, such as Baldoyle, Phoenix Park or Leopardstown. If there were more than two runners, two journeys were easily achieved. In our early years, Gerry Hamilton, a Scottish gentleman, was head lad in the stable, and to my horror, he and his family moved back to Scotland around 1939.

I was about five at the time and deeply in love with his beautiful daughter Rose, a beribboned, fair-haired girl about my own age. The

Hamiltons lived about a half mile upriver from us, and during our fuel-gathering sorties we would pass their bungalow. Rose would come running out and take hold of my hand, and when Lorcan and Jimmy McGrath continued on into the woods I would stop to play with Rose and their pet rabbit. Some evenings she would hear us coming and run to meet us, and when I'd stop to tie the lace of my runners, or to take a pot-shot at a bird, she'd wait. The biggest test was when the three giggling Dooley girls wearing their silly pixies, leaving them looking like gnomes, would chant, "Aren't they lovely?" and, "Da-han loves Ro-sey." I didn't care, and I wasn't annoyed, and I held on to Rose's hand as if I owned her.

Our father's job, along with Mick Galvin, Martin Tracy, Paddy Mac and one or two casuals, was to look after the gallops and building the hurdles and fences. There were also sheep and cattle to be looked after. Indeed, I often heard our father relate that when a sheep was found drowned in the river or lake the Big Fella would go berserk, but when in bad weather twenty of them followed one another into the lake, he would be quietly philosophical about it.

Before moving on, I must relate a little incident concerning Mick Galvin. In the thirties there was a foot and mouth outbreak. The diseased animals were efficiently dispatched by army marksmen, and the animals buried. A couple of years later another animal went down with an undefined ailment, similar to foot and mouth. Actually, I believe it was our mother who alerted Johnny Dooley.

The Big Fella restocked, aware it was not foot and mouth, and was reluctant either to call the vet or to report it to the Department of Agriculture in case of further disruption. He asked for a volunteer to dispatch the beast, and Mick put up his hand and declared himself an expert on the subject. The Big Fella addressed Mick doubtfully, abandoned responsibility and drove off.

Mick, from County Clare, then fetched a pick-axe, gave a couple of experiential swings and with a mighty swipe drove the spike into the inert beast's skull. The animal gave a horrendous roar, leaped to its feet, and with the pick in its skull, charged into the woods. Mr. 'Buffalo' Howard, the Butcher in Swords, had to be sent for to put the poor beast out of its misery. At the time, Mick was as astounded as his audience and became quite upset. In reality, he was a harmless man who eventually died in 1981, and shares his grave with his wife and son in Rowlestown graveyard.

Martin Tracy was another well-liked person, and in our time, he was employed as a groom tending the mares and foals. And though Martin would admit that he wasn't great at riding horses, by God he was a daisy at backing them! He was a grand, witty fellow from the midlands. Actually, he was our sister's godfather. Martin married Kitty O'Toole from Swords and replaced Gerry Hamilton's family in a bungalow. It was in a beautiful situation down by the river, and remained there until the Big Fella passed away. Martin later joined Aer Lingus and remained there until he retired.

Chapter 4: Terms of Engagement

Though our mother milked eight cows twice daily, we bought our milk from Barnwell's, our closest neighbours. The two Pats lived nearby in their tiny whitewashed cottage. Mrs. Barnwell, the wife of old Pat, had died many years before we came on the scene.

They had a few hilly acres devoted mainly to grazing five or six cattle, which included two cows. Each morning at eight thirty, Lorcan or myself with jug in hand, would knock on their door to be greeted first by a growl from Freefare, their cantankerous black and white terrier, and then politely by old Pat. A loudly ticking grandfather clock also welcomed us into their spotless kitchen with its dresser displaying Delph of all ages, shapes, and colours.

Old Pat, a friendly man, was stooped, middle-sized, aged about sixty. He also was the possessor of a heavy grey moustache, and even indoors was always hatted. He would be dressed in dark trousers, the bottoms tucked in with bicycle clips. On his upper body he wore a collarless striped shirt under a waistcoat which graced a silver watch chain. Black polished or goose greased boots completed his uniform.

Young Pat, similarly attired (though without the clips and watch and the hat), would be there getting himself ready for work. They appeared to be very content, reflected in how politely they addressed one another.

The milk was kept in an earthenware crock on the cold flagged floor and covered with a clean white cloth. The crock would be lifted onto the table and uncovered, and Pat would bend over the crock with cup in hand, his moustache with superb judgement a mere thou from the surface and begin blowing the cream away. Then, with cup in hand, he'd begin filling the jug. This routine continued until we had our measure. He was paid on Saturdays.

Our mother had specific tasks to perform each morning and evening Monday to Saturday, her contribution bringing their joint wage to two pounds weekly. This meant that we, the children, had to fend for ourselves in the mornings, washing ourselves in the same basin of water secured from the barrel outside the back door, and use the same face cloth to ensure that no tide marks were exposed or ears ignored. And we all dried with the same ragged towel hanging from a nail. The mirror, procured for two eggs and a thrupenny bit from a tinker, allowed us to admire ourselves while washing our teeth with the same brush. We would then grab our already wrapped lunches of bread and jam and were ready for the two-mile trot to school. God, how I hated that bread and jam. Jam-soaked bread is horrible. Nevertheless, at break-time we would devour it.

On returning from school we'd quickly eat the already waiting slices of homemade bread and inevitable jam along with a cup of milk, for our chores also waited. Water must be fetched, so equipped with a white enamel bucket (white exposed dirt or insects, unlike a galvanised one) we crossed Cuff's field to the well, usually spilling half of the water on the way back.

Gathering fuel for the fire was another vital chore. Kindling that ignited at first go must be stacked on top of the oven ready for the morning kettle. Lorcan, Frank and myself, and sometimes our mother, maintained a good store of green timber sawn into blocks, but with the exception of ash as it was useless for quick ignition. The enjoyable part of finding fuel was climbing the trees, for there was a challenge in getting at that rotten or withered branch without falling. Cuts and bruises were an added dimension. It was enjoyable, especially when Lorcan devised a brilliant feature... We'd find a tree denuded of its lower branches, either through the tree casting them or the result of our previous sorties. He'd climb up to maybe twenty or twenty-five feet to his selected limb, which ideally would be ten inches thick, and then with our bushman, he'd commence sawing close to the trunk and underneath the limb. Whenever he judged it 'just so', he'd begin sawing the upper side until the limb was nearly ready to break free. He'd climb another five feet, and then yelling like an Apache he'd leap down on the branch, the bough and himself dropping clean to the ground with a clatter and an explosion of leaves setting squawking jackdaws alight for a mile around. God! It was great fun.

We had competitors in our fuel gathering world. A bunch of urchins from Brackenstown cottages frequented the woods, but they were never in our league. They would be satisfied with the odd elm bough, but mostly with green branches about an inch thick and sawn in three-foot lengths. They were then bundled and tied, heaved onto their backs, and away for the mile walk home. They were a noisy and undisciplined bunch, probably blamed for any and every destruction on the estate when the Big Fella went on the warpath, such as nicking fence and hurdle poles for firewood, or doing his orchard, or whatever. When a storm felled a tree where it was difficult for the estate workers to harvest the news travelled like wild-fire, it was then women and girls joined the fuel gathering, they with their ropes and armed with a saw swarmed over the corpse like 'pissin wires'. That was the first time I became aware of the mature women's bare legs with their shins and knees blotched with very pronounced red, map-like markings. I asked Mrs. McGrath if it was a disease; she tittered it was from 'hatchin t'fire'.

Our adventures up near the main house, though not too near, were confined to when the Big Fella was away racing. We were careful to disguise the newly sawn stump by darkening it with clay. Tops gathered and obscured, especially if the tree was near the wood path, because again, if the Big Fella happened this way there would be hell to pay.

Of course, we had learned this procedure from the Big Fella himself, in that it was against the law to fell timber without government permission, and his staff felled a tree every couple of months, coal being so scarce. The downside of these operations was treading through those narrow footpaths in cold, wet conditions, our short trousers no protection against wet stinging nettles or the unnoticed briars which sneaked out, scratching and tearing our legs and our clothes. For hours after, even in bed, we would suffer. It was merely another occupational hazard in our world.

Chapter 5: Our Mother

My mother Brigid Redmond on the knee of her mother, Mary Dunne, her brother
Michael and my mother's cousin.

Our mother, having attended Ramsgrange boarding school in County Wexford in which she had excelled in home economics and animal husbandry, was a marvel as a cook, a seamstress, a knitter, a baker, a jam-maker. She was a competent aide at a birthing, and the laying out of the departed. She played camogie for Wexford in 1922-23. She smoked twenty woodbines a day, and would wager her shirt on two flies climbing up a wall. I believe that same college, with its pupils largely from the farming communities with most of the wealthy farmers owning a couple of hunters and chasers, was responsible for her gambling, a weakness she brought with her to the grave.

Of course, a racing stable was the last place she should have been, because every time a saddle was thrown on one of Ussher's horses the avid stable lad would always give the nod, even if the horse was minus a leg.

Her family had been well off until the twenties with a good farm and a business. Their clients being the establishment, the business evaporating due to the tumult of the age and our grandfather's fondness for hard liquor. The farm was sold in lots until it was reduced to thirty acres. She blamed her personal misfortune on the day she saw a rough-looking bousey with his cap at a rakish angle giving her the eye. Yes – our father.

She had a complex character and was subject to random bursts of rage, annulled with a constant self-sacrifice and acts of warm-hearted benevolence. She was intelligent, compassionate and had common decency by the bucket full. She was also stubborn and naïve, all of which could be verified within an hour when under pressure, which seemed to be most of the time.

She was also afflicted with the Mr. Micawber syndrome, of keeping herself buoyant with the surety that something wonderful (including money) was going to turn up. I clearly recall one morning as she dressed the beds, her looking out and seeing that Tom Tyrell the postman had passed without stopping. She remarked in anger, "Blast him anyway! There goes the shagger without leaving a letter!" As if Tom had a bag full for her but for some reason would not deliver them.

Her childish pleasure and naivety was witnessed in a ritual every Monday afternoon when Charlie Smithers, Joe Farrell, Terry Hayes and Jackie and Billy Tyrell, plus others would gather around our fire after exercising their horses, though too early to feed them and it also being before our mother's milking time. Charlie would relate the film he had seen in Bobby McDonald's, a wood-built cinema in Swords, with the principal man being the 'Chap' and the heroine the 'Mott'. Charlie, in his flat, unemotional voice would paint the most wonderful adventures and acts of heroism, of romance and heartbreak, filling our imagination with astonishing scenarios. Indeed, one particular film titled 'Rosanna of the Seven Moons' had our mother repeating the same for ages afterwards whenever she'd get someone to listen. Charlie, from Whitehall and aged about eighteen at the time, a taciturn, serious, and utterly decent young fellow, was a brilliant purveyor of the art of recalling a film, and art it was.

Our mother, either by accident or impulsive disposition, talked herself into further slavery. It arose when an owner came to view his horse that wasn't living up to his expectations. He was also displeased with the ragged, neglected state of the beast's tack, particularly its blanket; this neglect apparently reflected the horse's position in the stable regime – a backyard no-hoper. Jack, the head lad was embarrassed, as was the manager, Johnny Dooley. Indeed, the Big Fella himself was too, for though these particular clients were not too important, their fees for stabling were. The stable maintenance routine saw that from time to time their blankets were sent somewhere to be upgraded, a prolonged and expensive exercise.

Our mother, on hearing about the furore and to help out 'poor Jack', suggested to him she might be able to do something with them. And she did. Although she could do nothing with their shabbiness, she otherwise left them as new. I remember these events vividly as one incident concerning the blankets relates to the first time I saw the sea.

It came about that the stable had four runners at Baldoyle, and discovering the horse blankets were in shreds, Johnny Dooley pleaded with our mother to do instant repairs. This request was the day before racing. Most of her night was spent repairing two blankets; the fabric with its leather trimming was very difficult to stitch and had to be done by hand. She promised that the other two, partially repaired, would be ready before the horses were paraded. At ten the next morning three of us set off pushing the pram loaded with the blankets and infant Frank, also a parcel of bread and butter sandwiches. Down the path over Dooley's Bridge, through the woods of the estate and out through the Naul Road exit. Our journey took us through Forest Great, Cloghran, and on to Kinsealy, where we met the agitated Paddy Oakes (the travelling lad) who grabbed the blankets and shot away in the Big Fella's shooting brake.

Our mother then decided, for a treat, we'd visit the seaside for our picnic, and about an hour later we found ourselves in Malahide. God!

I couldn't get over the immensity of the sea and how sound carried, the smell of the seaweed, the odd yacht far off. At that time the seashells were so large and numerous they were a hazard for barefoot walkers. I also well remember the five-mile walk home, most of the way with two of us in the pram.

Johnny Dooley was always well turned out, as his position required. A daily white shirt and its detachable collar were imperative to his status. But the efforts of the Blue Swan laundry included tearing your collars to pieces in no time, and returning your shirts buttonless. Yes, our mother began to look after his shirts and collars. Then Joe Hogan's, Joe being a steeplechase jockey. She was then inveigled to do the lads', about a dozen of them. Another opportunity for her to reveal her talent arose when asked by Johnny to upgrade his Harris Tweed jacket with leather elbows, including cuffs with leather trimming. Appeals were made for the turning of shirt collars and overcoats. Lengthening or shortening of trousers and britches became the order of the day. Generally, all this was for nothing. The unfortunate lads had nothing to give, but by way of reward would saw a heap of logs for our fire or go to the well for her whenever she asked. Johnny and Joe would be generous, slipping the odd ten-bob note into her hand. She was a Trojan to work, and intensely concerned with the quality of it.

One afternoon Joe Hogan came into our kitchen wearing a new polo-necked jumper, jerseys which are standard in the racing world.

"Where's the old one, Joe?" our mother asked.

"It's in my room ready to be dumped," Joe replied, adding, "Why?"

"I'll get a pullover for one of the kids out of it," she said. And she did. Indeed, there's a photo somewhere of our younger brother Billy wearing a recycled pullover for his Holy Communion. The unravelling of these garments was always a pain; as our mother unravelled, one of us had to rewind the wool into balls, a tedious, boring exercise.

I clearly recall her, week in, week out in our backyard with a washing board in the galvanised bath – it rocked on a backless chair; she with a bar of Sunlight soap happily scrubbing and singing until her nail-less fingers were raw. Before the whites were rinsed they were steeped in a separate tub with a blue bag added. Her labour resulted in about fifteen-plus shirts hanging on the clothes line, and if a cloud appeared she'd blast it out of the sky. Later the dried washing would be taken inside to be pressed with a couple of solid irons, one heating while she used the other. All that labour for the sum of six shillings which Johnny had negotiated, with half the money ending up in Bobby Savage's, the bookies in Swords.

She was a capable woman, doing so much for the pleasure of it, justifying her efforts by announcing it was a way of paying homage to Jesus for the gift of life. It was a preoccupation that kept her anxieties at bay. Her own mother was of a similar character, renowned for her common decency, hard work, generosity of spirit, and her crankiness. While our mother was religious and very conscious of her every act and word being monitored by Jesus, she was not a zealot. Though in our school days during the season of Lent she would dragoon us into saying the rosary every evening after tea – all five decades. God, it was so boring and uncomfortable kneeling on the flagged floor of our kitchen, and no way of avoiding it. She was generally involved in this novena or that one. Still among her belongings are the hand-written prayers. To sum up, she was of a generation of genuine believers, and inculcated by those generations into always doing the decent and honourable thing.

She'd make a collar for your shirt
And she could turn an overcoat
Knit and darn and or Singer sew,
A superb cook and baker – her griddle bread evoke
Forgiveness in your heart for her verbal blows.

My mother (Brigid Redmond) waiting to go to the Bingo.

Chapter 6: The Environs

We had been living in Brackenstown for about two years when, one summer's evening, a disturbing event occurred. Beyond and above the wood and on the opposite side of the river from where we lived was a large field used for schooling the horses over hurdles and jumps. We could actually see the activity through our kitchen window, the horses and their riders queuing up to learn their trade. On this particularly bright evening at around eight, the lads turned up along with Stephen Bradley. Stephen was the hyper, red-haired house-boy. They were equipped with a ladder and ropes, and began to climb the huge beech trees to where the cranes were nesting. Amid an awful racket of squawking and screaming birds, one by one their nests of many, many years were destroyed. It was a frightening and dreadful act, but we assumed the birds may have been upsetting the horses. That night the birds flew away never to return.

There were two artificial lakes on the Ussher Estate, one a coffer. It was used to store water when the main one was having maintenance done. Both were used to generate electricity. The multi-talented Mick Dooley was the mechanical and electrical engineer. To us he was always Mr. Dooley, and to the estate he was whatever a situation demanded – be it smithy, sawmill operator, carpenter, plumber. And he was a wonderful neighbour, as was his wife Mrs. Dooley, mother of Jean, Margaret and Patricia.

Mick had manufactured our bushman saw from a tubed bicycle frame. He built the stand in Moortown, and made the unit for towing the horse box. He was of medium height and build, though very strong – he had to be to control the young horses he regularly had to shoe. He was also the brother of Johnny the secretary/manager of the estate, and of Alice Dooley, manageress of the main house.

Mrs. Dooley would appraise us with an amused, tolerating smile no matter what devilment we got up to. Mick and his family lived in the Mill House, a large two-storey building with basement, incorporating the sawmill, the turbines, and Mick's workshop. Several times a year Mick would put his life at risk when flash flooding would overcome the generating room. He would have to submerge himself up to his shoulders in cold fast-flowing water to manually adjust the bypass valves, there being no automatic controls to the system.

In the dry seasons when water levels became low, a large petrol combustion engine was brought into action to charge up the battery banks, its eight-inch exhaust protruding from inside the mill and backfiring great puffs of smoke out over the lake... also firing our imaginings of Errol Flynn or Tyrone Power on a pirate ship attacking a port in the Indies.

The flooding brings me to a defining point in my own character analysis, one which I still struggle with. When the river was in spate (this happening many times a year), up to ten feet deep and a raging torrent, we would be told, "Under no circumstances go near that river!" Not even the two hundred yards to the bridge further down in case we might fall in. Where did I go? Yes, to the river. I could not resist it.

After a storm, this foaming, turbulent, living mass of water often uprooting fully grown beech and elm in its frenzy as the water poured off the hills and roared through the woods seeking the tranquillity of the estuary a few miles further down. I received many violent thrashings for my impetuous misbehaviour, and when the river flooded again, I went down again to be part of it, and again paid the penalty.

On one very memorable occasion during the war, rice was on the evening menu. Rice was a food we had only heard about. Sweetened and with raisins added, it was a wonderful treat to which we looked forward. Unfortunately, it coincided with a flood which resulted in an unmerciful hiding and no rice.

Another little experience connected to the river happened when we were out gathering kindling and I slipped and fell in with the water up to my neck. Lorcan and Frank pulled me out, but what were we to do having been told to keep away from it? Lorcan noticed old Jimmy Mac (McDonald) – though crippled with arthritis, struggling up the back avenue with a bundle of kindling on his back. He was also puffing his pipe. Lorcan intercepted him and spun him a yarn about our father looking for a match. Jimmy in his decency gave him a couple. We lit a roaring fire, hanging my clothes around it. Wearing only Lorcan's waistcoat, I was hovering as near to the fire as possible.

Underwear? Other than a vest, during the winter we did not have any, nor pyjamas. I cannot remember ever hearing that word. We had two shirts each, and the same with trousers; one for this week, and one for the wash. You slept in that shirt, which made short work of getting dressed each morning, and only removed it under duress on Saturday nights when being washed in the galvanised bath and checked for 'boushies' (head lice). Our parents wore underwear, witnessed by the John Ls and bloomers hanging on the clothes line.

I digress. I had been wearing knee stockings, which indicated the weather was cold. Anyway, the stockings were hung over the fire, high enough to ensure they didn't burn. Gradually, it being near tea time and my bits of clothing deemed wearable, my stockings were retrieved. I was growing relieved by the minute until I attempted to put them on to find they had become petrified, melted. As soon as I touched them they dissolved. There was murder when we got home. As a recalcitrant, I got the worst of it.

Chapter 7: Holidays

Do not walk by a proffered hand
Nor give the quid as if it were a toll.
But give it with compassion and then understand
The confraternity of love; the confraternity of souls.

It was when I was about seven and after a few more uncivilised episodes, that we were dispatched to New Ross, County Wexford for a two-week holiday and into the keeping of our mother's wonderful people. We were billeted in the farmhouse belonging to Grand-uncle Johnny and Grand-aunt Katie. Our unmarried uncle Michael and his sister Kitty, both quiet, gentle people, also lived with them.

Uncle Johnny was around seventy at the time, a big hardy fellow with a reddish moustache. He walked with a stoop as if searching for something, or constantly in deep thought. As far as body language there was none that I noticed. Never any fidgeting. No change of expression. Just a blunt yes or no to a question – the terseness signalling 'slan leat'. He was very tolerant toward us, but then he and Katie had no children. The only time he relaxed was at night while sitting in the alcove surrounding the fire chatting with the neighbours. He'd be leaning forward with his hands joined and forearms resting on his knees, expressing opinions and responding to questions only to the fire.

Aunt Katie had her own peculiarities; a tiny woman with her greying hair severely drawn into a bun, and ever attired in a long brown dress, topped with a buttoned-up cardigan. She had a serene, unlined face, totally focused on whatever she was engaged in. With her feet not visible, she appeared to float about the place, darting here and there like a wraith; a restless creature and a great housekeeper. Occasionally, she'd suddenly cease her duties to float to her little stool near the fire, a tin of snuff fetched from somewhere within the folds of her dress. A pinch offered to her nostril, then with a smile offered it to us. I tried it and it did make me sneeze.

Michael, who would eventually inherit the farm, would take us out of an evening on long walks up through the hills to see the raths, sometimes taking us for a spin around the roads in their pony and trap. God, what a civilised way to travel! Though I had often seen traps before, I had never been in one. It was so intimate – so beautifully constructed, and the jingle of the harness and traces, the clip clop of the trotting pony, the hum of the iron shod wheels on the stony road was hypnotic. Other evenings we would go up the hills to gather wild strawberries.

The kitchen of the farmhouse was marvellous. It had a huge hearth within an alcove, with a wooden bench on either side for seating. The fuel for cooking was mostly withered furze which burned fiercely, though there was also a supply of turf to maintain the heat when cooking. A wheel equipped with a handle for turning it was positioned near the fire which on investigation turned out to be a fan. A selection of blackened hooks to facilitate pots hung over the fire, attached somewhere up the chimney. In the kitchen itself, great junks of bacon hung from the exposed joists of the high ceiling. Needless to say, this home cured bacon was our fare for breakfast and dinner and tea six days per week, with kippers on a Friday. The home-cured bacon was so salty it was nearly inedible. Another minus worth mentioning was the homemade farmer's butter – ugh!

There was yet another serious drawback in the homestead. A cupboard in my bedroom was inhabited by what appeared to be a hundred mice. They spent all night long squeaking and rustling among paper. I complained, and Uncle Johnny and Aunt Katie did look and act concerned, but the mice were still there the next night, and the one after.

Our Uncle Pat (Dunne) was a tall, fair-haired, and ever-smiling man. He lived a mile away in Myler's Park on our grandmother's small farm with his wife and family. He offered to bring us to the sea, Campile being the venue. All that night I dreamed and looked forward to a day picnicking and splashing about in the briny. But instead of the side car or at least a pony and trap that I was expecting, an ass and cart turned up with a load of our cousins on it.

The distance to where we were going was about ten miles, though at the time it seemed more like a hundred... And with the ass needing a breather every now and again. Indeed, every time we met a hill we had to get off or he'd stop. It took us half the day to get there, and on arriving at Campile the tide was out revealing mud flats. The ass was un-yoked and given a nosebag. We ate our bread and butter sandwiches, re-yoked the ass, turned around, and spent the rest of the day going home.

During the return journey I mentioned the raths to Pat. "A few years ago," he began, "I had this fierce dream. I dreamed there was a pot of gold under one of those rath stones, so I told a few of the lads in the village and that very evening, armed with spades and shovels we went up the mountain. All night we dug... rooted under every stone. One of the lads even had a ferreting bar and drove into the ground under the stones."

"What did you find?" I asked excitedly.

"Nothing," he dolefully replied, giving the ass a skelp, and resumed plodding. "Though I often wondered, was it the correct rath we dug up?" he mused. Be gobs, I might have another go one of these days!

Our Uncle Pat had a large family and never found gold, but found treasure in that family who went into business, nursing, and other professions. Pat himself struggled in vain to make a living on his own holding, and eventually sold up to become a steward on a neighbouring estate. And each year thereafter, he visited us during the Dublin Spring Show week where he presented cattle on his employer's behalf.

Our Aunt Kitty at that time was a skinny, good-humoured girl, never without a woodbine in her gob. Her role was assisting Aunt Katie with the running of the house. This included looking after fowl, feeding the pigs and churning their butter at times when the men were busy milking their couple of cows. She had a boyfriend called John who was employed on Uncle Johnny's farm. They eventually married. I elaborate on their situation to illustrate the conditions of a farm labourer at the time, though Kitty and John were a sight better off than most, having a flock of turkeys to supplement their income. But for the ordinary employee it was very different.

The conditions of the farm labourer's verbal contract (which excluded the winter months) were as follows: Each working day he dined with the farmer and his family. This benefit ensured the man had the energy to work, or as the joke suggested at the time, 'an empty sack won't stand.' In the forties he earned a notional ten shillings per week, though only paid twice a year – in August and at Christmas.

All farms at the time operated mixed units with cattle breeding and fattening, pigs for breeding and slaughter, and of course, they all kept fowl. The wealthy farmers usually kept a few hunters for amusement and eventual sale. In this lowland area, I recall few sheep at the time. The main provider of income was the cabbage, potatoes, barley, wheat and oats they grew. During the lean times, generally caused by late frosts or a particularly wet June or July, was when the farmer often lost his main crop. This meant come August there was little or no income, so the farmer, to do the decent thing must borrow from the bank. Many did not and let his man suffer.

During the labourer's indenture, his wife and family must negotiate credit in the rural shop on the promise of settling when her man was paid. They existed on the bare essentials, such as tea, flour for bread making, oatmeal for porridge, sugar and salt. As for clothing, I do not know how she managed. But no matter how these unfortunates scrimmaged, life was desperate.

When her husband was paid, she part-paid the shop, holding on to a pound or two to exist for a couple of months. When her funds were gone it was back to the shop to beg. Yes, to beg for credit to carry them through to Christmas. I learned about these unfortunates through Aunt Molly, and through those I witnessed coming to her shop who were treated with nothing but the utmost deference. These were the voiceless forsaken, and in their thousands, they must migrate to find emancipation in GB. There, in the coal mines, factories and building sites, most accepted without distinction. Our Aunt Molly and her clientele would find confraternity in their mutual prayers for a good harvest, and then all would be well. Molly swore if she had a tenth of what she was owed she'd have been a millionaire.

Kitty eventually married John and had a family of one son, also a John. They too lived in a labourer's cottage and like me, never got rich. From the couple of times I visited in the early 1940s, I never saw Kitty again.

Before I consign those wonderful people to history we, my brothers and sister, particularly remember Pat with the greatest love and respect.

His humanity revealed in a million ways, particularly for the compassion he tendered our mother when she went down to Wexford in that tragic year of 1948 to attend their mother's funeral. As she stepped off the bus in New Ross, Pat, seeing the threadbare and obvious poor condition of her coat, hurried her immediately to a draper and purchased her a new one, an expense he could ill afford. You are remembered with fondness, Pat, every morning and every night.

The odd year we would be sent to Wicklow to our Aunt Molly and Uncle Jim's for the last week of our holidays, where we were always, and are still, welcome. I recall in certainty that when reaching the age of seven or eight, holidays were no longer holidays, but were spent working on farms in the North County Dublin, weeding, picking potatoes, peas, rhubarb and strawberries, and thinning turnip and mangle. I didn't mind because it was a sight better than school.

Aunt Molly (my father's sister) and uncle Jim Carroll outside their shop.

Up to this point of our lives the word beautiful was only used when referring to the Blessed Virgin, or a sunny day. I never experienced anything I'd call beautiful. Our parents were not patrons of the arts. That role was confined to the rich and educated people. Consequently, we knew nothing about art, nor were we made aware of things that were beautiful, though many a kitchen wall of a poor house or cabin such as ours sported a print or copy of a bygone pastoral scene. In 1943, beauty to the peasantry was a big funeral, a cake of freshly baked bread, a new suit, or a bicycle. One did not set off walking of a Sunday to go sightseeing, or to admire the scenery, but to visit friends or relations to pry for news or scandal.

I would agree that the great buildings of the city were admired, not for their architecture but for the power they represented. A bridge across an estuary silhouetted against a sunset was not viewed as a wonderful creation of human endeavour, but just as a great way of getting to the other side.

In the early 1940s, the great unwashed were not attuned to classical music, or indeed any music. Though when mucking out the pigs, or thinning turnips, those possessing a wireless at home could he heard humming an aria from some opera or other. Bloody nice it was too, but you daren't tell him so, but instead sneer at a mammy's pet, or call him even ruder names.

My awakening to beauty was in a Wicklow bog in 1943. We had been dispatched to our Aunt Molly's for the last two weeks of our summer holidays after working for the earlier weeks. On arriving in Tullow, we were then transported by pony and trap to Ardoyne, where Uncle Jim and Aunt Molly had a shop and farm, there to be warmly greeted.

Several of our uncles and aunts lived in the locality. For instance, Uncle Bill and his family lived in Coolkenna, where they too had a farm and shop only a few miles away. A few days later we made it known we would like to visit Bill and his family. Aunt Molly agreed, but warned us on no account touch the biscuit tin under Bill's bed. Apparently, Bill didn't trust banks and stowed his money in this tin, taking the further precaution of connecting an electric wire to it. Having taken notice of this we were transported to Uncle Bill's.

Bill, about fifty at the time, was a restless, active man, lean and hardy. Though his sharp lined face always gave the impression of suffering, this prospect would instantly change to merriment with a bawdy joke or comment, or an earthy yarn.

He'd been a commandant in the revolution of 1916. This fact gave him great pride, and an unfortunate belief in his superior business abilities. His shop was successful. He was good at accounting. But his business was untested, the nearest similar shop being three miles away.

Shortly before our visit he'd been to an auction where the local pub was for sale. At the end of the bidding, Bill's offer was accepted, or so he thought. Rather than go through the formalities including paper work and financial necessities, Bill and his supporters celebrated with glasses of the hard stuff. The auctioneer then informed Bill that in the absence of the highest bidder the premises had been sold to the underbidder.

On the day of our arrival I felt we were not entirely welcome as they seemed to be vacating the homestead. We unfortunately had come on the day they were going to the bog to harvest their turf. The transport was a gig – a high-wheeled, shallow cart pulled by a light horse.

When Bill's mob climbed aboard, followed by three of us, there was no room for Bill himself. The situation was resolved when Larry, Bill's eldest lad, mounted the horse and away we went. The bog was in a glen only a couple of miles away. It stretched away for about a mile until it climbed up out of itself. The turf, which had been cut in May and stacked in heaps to dry, was now ready to be brought home. We all got busy running to and fro, and at a torrid rate throwing sods up into the cart, most bouncing off Bill who was trying to build the load. He then stood up with his forearm defending himself, and told us three to "Shag off!" or words to that effect.

It was only then I took any notice of the surroundings. Climbing the side of the glen I looked down on a sea of gleaming green rushes bowing and waving in the breeze, creating the most beautiful sight I had ever witnessed. The rushes bending and holding for a moment, and in unison straightening resembled a wonderful seascape. In 1985 I returned to relive the moment, but the bog had been drained and fenced, and where once turf was harvested, sheep now grazed.

Psalm 6

When wolves begin to gather I sense danger looms
And fear and foreboding is my mood.
A battle being inevitable; one which could spell my doom
If I cannot find a refuge; however crude.

Chapter 8: Purgatory

In 1939 our family had increased by one more, William, called after our Uncle Bill who had been called after Willie Redmond of *Redmondite* fame. Our Billy was never well, and was always on the puny side; a little fair-haired boy whom our mother cosseted. Yet when he was four years old, like us, he went barefoot to school, and came with us fuel gathering, always just tagging along.

What was memorable about that time? I hated school! The teachers with their thirty-five to forty pupils were impatient and pressurised. I recall being in second class and taught, along with other subjects, religion. Before proceeding, I must acknowledge that our teacher was a kind and compassionate person. The lesson was on how to receive the blessed host. For this she would produce a small box in which were about forty brown cardboard tablets, each about the size of the host, and would go through the process of placing one on each of our tongues, maybe collecting them and repeating the routine for the benefit of those slow on the uptake. She'd even use one of her pets to demonstrate in front of the class. When satisfied, she'd gather the tablets and return them to the box, satisfied with a job well done.

Another year and class we were taught by a different female. She, as I recall, did not cane us, but had developed a wonderful alternative – using a penny between the fingers of her clenched fist to thump you on the head. It was excruciating.

They all had their individual idiosyncrasies. I recall going into fifth year and finding our teacher and school principal, Andrew Hamill. While most had monikers, Mr. Hamill was universally known as Andy. He was a warm, sociable man, stoutly built with greying hair and the wearer of horn-rimmed spectacles. His preference in suits seemed to be for thorn-proof grey.

From day one we discovered he had a natural interest in us. We could feel the tentacles of his humanity reaching out toward us.

"What kept you?" Andy would enquire. And before the student replied he'd suggest, "You were out picking mushrooms, weren't you?" And again, before the stuttering pupil replied he'd again suggest, "Did you get many?" The crime forgotten as a story developed with confraternity and trust building all the time. When Andy caned a pupil, it was not for neglect of attention in class but for some act of vandalism or disrespect.

Andy was a brilliant communicator, whether it was religion, geography, or history. His narrative style woke the stultified and inspired the dreamers. I travelled with him and Jacob on our camels from Beersheba to Bethel then on to Mesopotamia where Jacob was to visit his uncle, the wily Laban, and to eventually marry his two daughters Rachel and Leah. I was with him and Cais Julius when invading Britain in 42 BC. Again, I was with Andy and Julius Agricola for the last major stand of the Celts in Anglesey in 70 AD.

As a motivator Andy was a genius, awakening your interest in the annals of the past, infusing your dreams with scenes of great events and glory. For the first three months of fifth year I enjoyed school, for Andy enlarged the subject with human beings, explained in geographical and historical terms. For history was fact. History was knowledge. History was learning.

Returning to school following Christmas, I was shocked to find Andy gone and a mirthless Mr. Keane commandeering the principal's desk. Through the following twelve months I learned little, but Andy had sparked the flints of curiosity and lit a little fire which as yet has not gone out.

There were few joyous schoolday events, but I suppose the teachers must maintain a sense of the serious; keep children involved in the subjects at the expense of fun. Though there were one or two unforgettable incidents. One was when a teacher arranged a flower competition with a thrupenny bit for the winner. The next morning, the school lane teemed with eejits carrying bunches of daffodils, narcissus, cowslip and primrose, all easily available in the woods and estate entrances in the locality. Of course, we had a bunch of something or other, but immediately knew we were out of the running having carried ours the two miles, probably dropping them a couple of times on the way. There were two outstanding offerings. One was a bunch of daffodils proudly carried by Michael Hughes, widely known then and now as 'Bats'. The other, a bunch of beautiful tulips carried by Liam Heron, an excellent student and a favourite with all the teachers. Bats knew he was beaten, that's if Liam presented his offering. "Giv'us a smell," Bats pleaded, and of course Liam proudly offered up his bunch. Bats buried his head in them and ate half and damaged the rest. Neither of them won, though Bats was punished.

I clearly recall another incident when I was about nine years old. It being winter I was wearing boots... second-hand boots secured by our mother from God knows where. They were so oversized that even stuffed with oaten straw I still never had to undo the laces. Twelve o'clock was lunch time and most of us, having devoured our lunch at first break, moseyed out into the playground to stand or sit against the school wall in the wintery sun. A mouthy fellow happened to glance down at the boots and ran off hollering delightedly, "Hey lads, com'ere! Yer man has his boots on the wrong feet." A glance down agreed I had. Without stooping, I switched them. And when your gills turned around and advanced with his expectant tittering companions, I could glare at them with suitable disgust.

Other than the hardship of inadequate clothing, cold feet and hands, chilblains and boils, and the odd wetting, our school punctuality was good. There were those who took the odd day off, coming in the next day and using the same excuses such as, "I was minding the house, sir," or, "Me mother slept it out, sir!" or, "The clock stopped, sir." There were others who were genuinely sick, as was poor Joe O'Rourke.

Joe was from Drynam, a village about two miles from our school. Joe, like me and ninety-eight percent of the class, was of a poor family. He could be described as a harmless boy, his smiling round face, black straight hair and childish sleepy eyes disarming the most vicious bullies. At break-time, even though he was of stocky build, he would never join in the chasing games. Joe is remembered as standing with his back to the school wall, and in keeping with the weather, either froze or fried.

Like the majority of the pupils, he wore what was called a gansey and short trousers. These invariably brown ganseys, costing little, were popular. It was a long-sleeved cotton jumper with a collar, and after a couple of washes hung around the wearer like a maternity bib.

It served as an excuse for clothing, it being utterly useless for preserving warmth.

Like most of us, Joe went to school barefoot. In that year of third class, Joe began to go missing. He would turn up after a day or two's absence, smiling apologetically and offering no excuse except to hand a note to the teacher. At times on his arrival at school, his eyes would be encrusted, leaving him to squint at the blackboard. Other times, sitting at his desk he would doze. The teacher would no more than bang his lectern with his cane to keep Joe and the rest of us awake.

In the spring of that year and after a week's illness, poor Joe died. On the day of his funeral and in a mark of respect, the class marched the half mile to the church for the funeral mass, and afterwards congregated around the grave. As the priest led us in prayer, and as was the ritual of the time, the grave was filled. Hands were shaken, and obsequies offered. Fags were lit as the crowd began to disperse. Then there was a scream, as a distraught Mrs. O'Rourke flung herself on the grave with heart rendering cries of, "Joe. Joe. Joe." It was a horrific scene, the poor sobbing woman clawing the red earth until her also poorly dressed neighbours and relations helped her to her feet. I was shocked, for I had never been exposed to such naked anguish. It was a silent procession back toward the school; we turned right, the poor mourners turned left, making their way by foot back to their village. I felt that poor woman's grief for many a night afterwards.

The poor children, who were in the vast majority, were easy identified by their garb of trousers patched, some well, most adequately patched. Worn jerseys and shirts ditto, which by Friday were not too clean, for all the kids had chores besides their ekker. Clean, worn and patched clothes had a currency of their own, as had repaired footwear. Those with their jacket cuffs and elbows replaced revealed the silent statement and standards of their parents; tears and rips stitched and patched in such a way it displayed the artist, the gift.

I never heard of any child being teased or taunted for the state of their being, either by teacher or pupil. Though one year as the new term started the teacher picked Dan Doyle out of a bare-footed bunch of us, had him stand on a chair to laud his cleanliness and his general appearance, stating that this was the standard she wanted to see for the rest of the year. Poor Dan, an electrician, died a few years ago. RIP.

The well off, or those a little better off than the rest of us, came to school by pony and traps or floats, the float being a low-bodied flat bed. The upmarket model was one with pneumatic wheels, suitable for transporting milk without it being churned in transit. Some of these farmers were most generous. The Watsons and Duffs for instance, brought cartons of milk to be distributed among the needy. We never needed it but there were quite a number who did. The teachers would gather them near the fire and share whatever with them. If a lad arrived with an apple instead of a lunch, or it was the result of a morning raid on somebody's orchard, he'd also have two or three pupils around him begging 'butts on ye'. I have another 1945 memory of the excitement generated by the oranges available in Savage's shop. They were for those who had tuppence to spend, which eliminated most of us. These were Jaffa oranges, very large and by all accounts very sour tasting. I recall some of the kids diving on the cast away skins and chawing the white inner of them.

Jaffa? That image of a little Palestinian town stayed with me for many years until eventually I got the opportunity to see it. It was hard to find – even the Jewish people I asked had to ponder before explaining it was where I was standing, a rundown suburb of Tel Aviv. St. Peter's Church was closed for some reason, and there were no orange groves in sight. It being Sunday we found another church close by with a Filipino priest and congregation, and enjoyed a wonderful mass in English.

Chapter 9: The Path to Freedom

The only thing I liked about our school was the path out of it. At three thirty, leaving through the school gate, the air miraculously revived me. The first house on the right of the school lane was where Miss Tighe lived, as she had been the higher and lower infant teacher. A hundred yards further on was a small community building from where a Diddley operated, and where half the mothers of town and districts saved a tanner or a bob each week for Christmas. The last building on the corner and facing the main street was Mary Ryan's sweet shop. She also served tea and buns, being very popular at night with Ussher's stable lads, they after leaving Bobby McDonald's wood-built cinema further down the street.

Here, just opposite was Art Agnew's cobbler shop, we crossed the street. Further along was Tim Clarke's emporium, with huge sides of leather hanging from hooks on either side of the entrance. There were galvanised buckets, baths. There were mops, yard and sweeping brushes, mop-pots and pans. Every utensil needed for the kitchen and yard of house or homestead. There were head collars, bridles and britching for farm horses. Mr. Clarke, or Tim, was a large, dark-haired man with a heavy moustache, and one of three in the town who owned a motor car. The other two were Canon Kelly and Jack Savage. Though people were heard to say that Tim's motor was more often parked in some ditch or other than outside his shop.

The recalling of the cobbler Art Agnew reminds me of an evening coming from school when a dramatic incident occurred further up the street. As we crossed a great hue and cry arose with women and children running in all directions as a runaway driverless horse and gig came charging down the street. Out of another cobbler's shop beyond Savages grocery charged a young man still in his apron and running alongside the galloping horse grabbed his bridle and skidding along in his hobnailed boots for fifty yards brought the animal under control. Along with the relieved and cheering bystanders, the shop keepers and staff came out to laud him and he with an embarrassed grin immediately hurried back into his place of work. God! It was the bravest thing I ever saw. I cannot remember the man's name but I thought I heard May Savage shout, "Good man, Pauric!" As we hung around the red-faced owner or driver appeared and climbed onto the gig then proceeded to absolutely thrash the unfortunate animal with heavy stick and turning the gig headed back up the town still beating the poor beast. Moments of valour followed by utter disgrace.

Returning to our odyssey, O'Keefe's Pub was on the corner as we turned toward the river and Gallow's Hill. Opposite the pub was McGowan's corner, McGowan's being grocers. On our right we passed the wooden gates of the partly ruined castle. It was where we knew there was an orchard, and where once a Bishop lived. The castle was built by Bishop Comyn at the end of the 12th century. It was assaulted by Edward Bruce in 1316. I believe the castle's purpose was as a refuge for the townspeople whenever the district was sacked. In those times it was garrisoned by a sheriff and number of soldiers.

Coming to the bridge which crossed the little river and on our left, was a water mill. It was owned and operated by Mr. Paddy Pentony, and during the early forties, very active in crushing oats and milling flour. I would become fixated with the huge wooden wheel grumbling round and round, and the water spilling off it. Opposite was the Quarry field where Paddy grazed a few sows. I recall one evening on our way home when a schoolmate Kit Kenny clipped one of them with a stone, and then running for his life with an enraged Paddy after him.

Opposite Pentony's was, and still is, a pub called The Pound. There may have been a pound there once for stray animals, or one's subject to the courts. After crossing the bridge, we climb to the junction, and parted company with the kids bound for the village of Rathbeale. We turned left for Brackenstown.

The first bungalow on our left belonged to a very tall, good-humoured man by the name of Tom Finnegan. Tom had migrated to Australia in his youth where he found work on a large fruit farm. He often amused us with the same joke that when picking apples, he would pick twice as much as the others, because he didn't need a ladder. We got to know him from when he passed our house while he was out walking. Our mother would send him down the odd cake of bread and by return delivery he'd send her back two bob. Tom could not readjust to our cooler climate and returned to Queensland where eventually he died.

Next was Tom Tyrell's bungalow. Tom was enormous and moustached, and was also the morning postman. I never remember him without his hat which he always wore with his uniform. Tom, after reaching the furthest point of his round, would on his way back pull in and park by our house and have a cup of tea. After seating himself, a newspaper would be fished from his bag and his pipe ignited. He then would proceed to slurp his tea, draw on his pipe, and squirt great gouts of brown spit onto the floor. Our mother warned him several times, first providing a heavy folded sack which he endeavoured to miss. She then provided a bucket. Eventually she lost patience with him and told him to, "Feck off and get his tay somewhere else."

Next point of interest on our daily journey and still on our left was the walled and dwindling Protestant enclave. On our right, all huddled together is St. Columba's Church, a 9th or 10th century round tower and a square clock tower. The round tower is one of sixty-five still standing in Ireland with the ruins of a dozen more here and there. There is one in the Isle of Man, also two in Eastern Scotland. As to their antiquity, it is suggested, though they are not identical, that they were reproductions of the then existing campaniles of Ravenna and Padua. Anyway, it is also suggested that in troubled times the round tower was where the church or abbey secured their valuables. They were built for a purpose. They were built to overlook the forested landscape of their time, to see and to be seen. Perhaps with so many of them visible to a neighbouring one. Without being presumptuous I imagine the towers were used as either watch towers or light houses. As light houses, especially during Christian festivals. The Paschal unifying light of the Jewish calendar adopted by Christianity and exemplified by St. Patrick's fire on Croagh Patrick down to the tiny candle we light for a prayer to be acknowledged. One can visualise the cardinal point openings of the tower reflecting not a beam but the unifying glow of a lantern or lanterns offering sanctuary and confraternity and an awareness of our mortality. Alternatively, they were used as watch towers to summons help during times of local unrest and from the now established Danish redoubts along the coast. Perhaps sometime in the future local historians might, out of curiosity, test the light house theory with solar lighting keeping in mind the light pollution that now exists. Indeed, if the experiment was to be positive perhaps a permanent fixture might be installed, creating the first beaconed tower in over a thousand years. At least unlike bells, ever-present light would be non-intrusive. History has recorded some towers being vandalised, some during tribal disputes, a few by the Danish marauders, but with so many towers surviving it appears they lost interest and concentrated on pillaging the churches.

The age and purpose of the square clock tower is debatable. It was always free standing, and perhaps built after the reformation by the new order to negate the round one. Not that it matters in our now unified Christianity as both towers are milestones in our local history. Actually, it's recorded that in 1500 the first clock tower in Ireland was in the walled town of Youghal. Is the Swords one that old? Perhaps by identifying the clock maker a clue might be found. Anyway, with the tower crenulations it might be the chancel template for all the following Anglican churches, with some of them also with clocks. There appears to have been an annexe built against this tower probably used as a temporary church while Mr. Johnston was building the new one.

St. Columba's Church was designed and built by Francis Johnston in 1792 for £2,500, and built over the ruins of a previous Catholic one. The original church was where Brian Boru was waked overnight before the cortege marched on to Armagh for the interment.

A few yards further on and falling away to our left is the Well Road, which acquired its title from St. Colmcille's holy well. It is recorded that this well is likely to be pre-Christian and the same well or spring, 'Sord', that gave the town its name. It now appears to be used as a feature of a recently built block of apartments. On one of the steps leading down to the well, nature created an imprint resembling a human foot. Local legend said that it was St. Colmcille, who created it when he took one step from his church to the well, a distance of a couple of hundred yards.

The waves that once engulfed this land – each have scarred and left their mark

Marks to show who now commands on river ford and foreland scarp

But the Celtic tribe who built this tower – their fervent wish – our legacy

Cometh your hour preserve our tower for old Fingall.

A long wall on our left and steep embankment on our right gave the effect of a sunken road for about a hundred yards as we approached Doctor's Hill. In our time somebody had made a large hole in the wall, giving us the grand prospect of the town below. Had we been looking through this hole three hundred years earlier we would have witnessed the last battle fought in the town.

The defenders had raised a barricade, and when attacked by the forces of the crown they stoutly resisted until they were overcome. They then retreated into the glen beneath us where two hundred of them were massacred.

Time is marked by gross events – crosses in serried lines – ancient mounds,

Testaments of intransigence to a new creed or despotic crown.

No cross or cromlech marks the Hollow's deep – nobody comes here to grieve and pray

And only wondrous Nature weeps in its own enchanted way.

When up from nearby woods arise a host of Starling in a symphony of wing

In exquisite harmony they contrive a silent requiem.

And that solitary Heron pondering its shadow on the Pel

Silently preoccupied; serves as a grieving sentinel.

At the crest of the hill we'd loiter for a moment to catch our breath. Here on our left, a narrow grass-covered lane dives down into the glen. A hundred yards down that lane were two cottages. One was Doughty's, I forget the name of the other resident. The chimney of one house was a little below our road level. I clearly recall one evening on our way home from school, and with a bunch of bigger kids in front of us engaged in using sods to take pot-shots at the smoking chimney. To our horror they got lucky for out of the house charged the enraged occupant, and with a table knife in his hand. Instinctively we raced home, though to turn back would have been the safer option but would have meant an hour's detour. As we raced along we could see this fellow scrambling up the steep grassy slope to the road, but in his haste, he slipped back a few yards, thus saving us.

The only good thing was, we had seen him but he couldn't see us. Nevertheless, we were ever so careful afterwards, passing on the pathless side of the road.

It was on another evening by that same long wall overlooking the glen we overtook Brendan and Peter Walshe, two comical brothers of our own age. Their father Pop was a wonderful father to them. His wife, the lad's mother, died young leaving Pop to rear six of them on his own, and hold down a job. Anyway, Peter had this rhyme he'd picked up from somewhere, and went like this.

There was an ould woman God bless her

She threw her leg over the dresser

The dresser was sticky an stuck to her mickey

There was an ould woman God bless her.

We thought this was hilarious, and I remember the following Sunday morning Frank coming down the stairs of our house singing the rhyme while passing our parents' room. Our mother bounded out in her nightdress and demanded him to repeat it. Frank obliged, and she too laughed at the good of it.

It was from along this wall we often saw the mitchers from school splashing about in the Jacko, a swimming hole in the river – with Bats in the middle of them. A couple of hundred yards further on our right, past a public water fountain was a cul-de-sac where there were about eight council cottages. As we were not tribal members, we quickened our pace for to loiter was to be a target for a dig in the snot or to be used for pot-shots. Though one evening there was an animated atmosphere. Mrs. Monahan who had lived in the second house had died and was being waked. Three or four young lads of our age beckoned us to come over to the door. They said it was all right to go in. Indeed, they had a proprietary bent on proceedings. The bravest lad, Noel Hoey if memory serves, went in and after a suitable length emerged as if he'd been to hell and back. I went in with him to see an old lady sitting in the hall praying. My man dragged me into the room where poor Mrs. Monahan lay in her bed, her hands bound in a rosary. I knelt as instructed, said a hail Mary, and then hooked it. It was a shock, for I never considered death. Anyway, it was not near as shocking as poor Joe O'Rourke.

To return to our odyssey, a further couple of hundred yards along the main road were two more council cottages. These were of an earlier age with quoined windows and doors. A family of Gannons lived in one, decent honourable people. I recall one Sunday morning getting a cross bar on my father's bike to eleven o'clock mass, when passing Gannon's cottage their daughter Maisey flew out their gate and the brush that followed her nearly knocked us into the ditch. A half mile further on the left was Coleman's abode, a small, ramshackle, mud-built farmhouse. There were no fowl or farming paraphernalia to be seen, though I do recall a couple of young men coming and going. But when they vanished the place quickly fell into ruin.

A half mile further was the Cradle house, so called because the upper storey was only half the length of the lower. This house belonged to a Johnny Cuffe and was used by his herder (a man employed to look after cattle). Johnny Cuffe was a wonderful character, and once a huge land owner. One of many yarns about him was when in the pub and finding himself short of ready cash, he'd advise the barman to "Put it down to Johnny Cuffe." Several times afterwards in different pubs around the town when a new barman was employed, some smart fellow when thirsty and short of money would loftily instruct him to "Put it down to Johnny Cuffe." It worked a couple of times, but the cant is used to the present day.

At another sharp, right-angled corner was Mansfield's bungalow. Though Mansfield had left for England in 1938, the house was now occupied by Sonny Callahan and his wife and her sister. We now could see our own house; if there was smoke from the chimney our mother was home from milking. If not, she'd have left a few slices of bread and jam out for us.

My first communion is only remembered by the collection, though not the church collection. With Lorcan as my minder, I set off to exhibit myself around the six houses in the vicinity. Six bob was the total, having been topped up by two shillings from Joe Hogan. I think our mother bought me a pair of socks with the proceeds.

Communion also meant that every fourth Saturday we had to attend children's mass. This included a fast from midnight the night before. I recall one cold morning feeling extremely peckish and covertly pilfering two Marietta biscuits, and later stuffing them into my gob. It wasn't worth it for I suffered agonies of conscience for years afterwards.

The only pleasurable school days I recall were when showers of summer rain fell on the hot road leaving large steaming pools. God, it was ecstasy slopping about in them in our bare feet! We'd tear through them, splashing one another until saturated, arriving home late to receive a few clouts of the dish-cloth for delaying Mother's milking appointment. Another brilliant though rare event was a lift home in Canon Kelly's car when he chose our road for a spin. The canon, a little old gentleman, is fondly remembered.

Psalm 90

It's wonderous being human; great to feel the surge of life

And to hear the birds singing at dawn

To appreciate your marvels; to kiss our child good night

Thank you Lord for the miracle of being born.

Chapter 10: A Miscellany of Ghosts

There was good trout fishing in the lakes. Indeed, Jack McGrath, the head lad in the racing stables, was an expert angler. He seemingly never missed a night sitting among the reeds, the midges tearing lumps out of him. You would never know he was there until he croaked a "Good night." He said he caught twenty or thirty trout in a season. His wife Mary, a lovely soul, used to wear an otter pelt around her shoulders – apparently Jack had caught the beast and had the collar made.

Mary, now ensconced in their bungalow in the stable yard, also loved a fag, and was seldom seen without one in her gob. Whenever she ran short of a puff she'd emerge with a plaintive cry, "Era butt, Jack?"

And Jack, before relenting, usually replied, "Ah, go to blazes, Mary!"

Jack and Mary had three children, and with Jack at work and Mary gone shopping, Maggie, just to tease Jimmy, would bundle him out the door and lock it. She'd then put Gerald sitting at the window eating buttered Marietta biscuits, and school him into making faces of extraordinary enjoyment, with Jimmy outside fit to be tied.

Jimmy was a comical chap and later employed as a stable lad. He was a lad in every sense. He used to bunk off, occasionally bringing a couple of other apprentices with him, the remaining lads having to exercise and feed their horses. Jimmy remained tending horses most of his life, though not in Brackenstown but a few miles away in the Cloghran Stud Farm. Maggie, his sister, worked in Dublin City and eventually married there, leaving Gerald, a successful apprentice with brilliant hands and style, winning a lot of races. He too eventually left Brackenstown and went to a stable in England. Last I heard of him he was working in a car assembly plant in Birmingham.

Lorcan, our eldest brother, with his pal Bobby Dow, would put down baited night lines in the river and were often lucky, providing us with trout for breakfast. Bobby? He was an only son, and consequently was a bit spoiled. He was a burly built chap, one of those individuals whose muscle was concealed with flesh giving him an overweight appearance. He was from Swords where he lived with his mother and two sisters in their lovely little cottage down in the hollow, a picturesque area by the river.

Bobby's father, being a lifer in the British Army and I'm sure pretty busy at that time, it being 1942, came home occasionally, and after a few days would be gone again. Bobby was an adventurer, perhaps a little bored in that he attended the Protestant school where there were few male pupils of his own age, so interface with similar lads was seldom. His interest in football and hurling was non-existent, as was ours at the time with no football or other kids to play with. Bobby began to visit of an evening, joining us while we gathered firewood. He would slowly climb the odd tree then strut around as if he'd conquered Everest, the same tree we'd shin up in a minute. He claimed he was an expert at everything, as normal thirteen- or fourteen-year-olds do.

He had a throwing knife on this particular evening; a knife which he'd fashioned himself. During his long, loud and detailed description of how he nearly killed a rabbit and entailed him waving this knife about, the blade flew out and stuck in fast between my toes and in the root of a tree. It never drew a drop of blood. Instead of relieved apologies, Bobby explained he'd aimed to obtain this result. I was not overawed.

Another evening our father was in our garden with a few of the stable lads including Sean Moylan, leaning over the fence chatting with him. Then Bobby happened along and, without being asked, announced he was an expert gardener. Our father in devilment asked him if he was any good to fight. Bobby took the bait and stated he was an expert boxer. "You'd never bate Sean!" our father proposed. Sean, low-sized and a couple of years older than Bobby and with the arms of a blacksmith, smirked at the prospect. The fight began immediately with Sean giving Bobby a clout in the gob which knocked him over. Bobby, in tears, gamely regained his feet and said it was not fair, so Sean gave him another. By this time our mother had been alerted by the cheers of Sean's supporters and rushed out to rescue him, also giving our father an earful and the lads their walking papers.

Bobby was then brought inside and mollified with a mug of tea and several scones, until a knock at the door interrupted proceedings. It was a delegation of the lads offering their profuse apologies, and announcing that Sean too was terribly sorry for giving Bobby a 'sly one'. So, after further admonishment by our mother, Bobby's prestige was restored and the lads rehabilitated.

Our mother liked Bobby mainly because he was so polite, particularly at the table, such as, "Could I have another slice of tart, Mrs. Redmond?" Or, "May I have another scone, another cup of tea?" We liked him too for he was non-threatening and only came to the woods to live out his dreams.

His mother was a wonderful little person, bespectacled and extremely talented. As a confectioner, she had no equal. Indeed, when invited to little parties in their cottage where we were the only guests, we cleaned her out of her delectable tiny sweet-meats, her feather-weight pancakes with their wild honey filling and another delicacy called and n****rs pudding. It being black and served hot with custard it – it was delectable. Then tea from China cups, cups with handles and *saucers*!! Her prowess as a seamstress was illustrated in the magnificent patchwork quilts and cushion covers about her sitting room and bedrooms. The combination of colours, fabrics and geometrical patterns were absolute works of art. God, I so envy and admire those Mrs. Dows of the world, who so quietly and unassumingly can give voice to their soul!

For several years Bobby was part of our lives, indeed enriched by them, until circumstance left us living where our paths did not cross. Bobby eventually married and became Verger in St. Columba's Church, Swords, living in the lodge where he eventually died, may he rest in peace.

Three of the O'Tooles from Swords (Cles, Johnny, and Cal) were also excellent fishermen who frequented the lakes. There were others who came to hunt; one fellow to ferret for rabbits, another select group to shoot... That's when they got the billy that the Big Fella, the estate owner, was away. They all wheeled their bicycles through a wicket gate situated at the end of our houses and parked them in the shade, and then would be invited in for a cuppa by our mother.

One inhuman incident stands out, it being similar to the cranes episode... Christian Brother John, a weedy, myopic little fellow wearing glasses, accompanied by a couple of others turned up about twice a year. On this occasion, having had their shoot, he was in the highest of spirits as he took from his bag a most beautiful milk white bird with the tips of its neck feathers delicately touched with gold. I remember it being about ten or twelve inches long as he proudly laid it on the table. He'd shot a golden owl, an extremely rare bird even in those days. His intention, he told us, was to have it stuffed and exhibited in his All Hallows college refectory. We thought it was him who should be stuffed. Anyway, it was a horrible thing to do. I've often wondered, was it the last of that species of owl, or are there still one or two meandering in the twilight down by the river?

Another episode of note occurred around this time. One evening Frank and I were in the garlic-covered woods gathering kindling. I was eleven years old with Frank being eight. *Red Cloud*, a terrific book about Native Americans which I had been reading in school, must have been on my mind when a super idea struck me. Why not camp here in the woods, just like them? I sat down on an old tree stump to ponder on the concept and couldn't find one negative reason as to why not. I don't think I consulted Frank for his opinion or his advice, or dwelled on whatever opinions our parents might have on the subject, but immediately engaged myself in selecting a campsite.

The spot I chose was nearby and remote from casual strollers. It was also where two ancient walls met at a right angle, the area surrounded by dense elm and elder trees. Of course, a camp must have a fire, so I raced home the three- or four-minute trot to where Lorcan was engaged in sawing timber into blocks and babysitting our infant brother Billy, our mother being away milking and father out working. Furtively, I secured a couple of matches as well as two empty tin cans – well, we needed cups! – and immediately returned to the camp where we got a great fire going. As I busied myself making the camp snug, I decided for continuity's sake that I would train Frank to be a soldier.

Should we need supplies we could borrow from Mrs. Shields who lived on their farm about three hundred yards away, or from Mrs. Dooley who resided three hundred yards in the other direction. Most of our food would be foraged from the Big Fella's henhouses, apples from his orchard and the remainder from Tom Tyrell's strawberry beds.

When engaged in these momentous plans and decisions, half the district's population was out looking for us, especially around the lakes. As it grew darker, and the resident jackdaws were settling, I deemed it time to make the beds. While in the process of gathering moss and leaves, we heard somebody climbing the wall. It was our father! "What the bloody hell d'ya think you are doing here?" he angrily demanded, as he stamped out the fire. "You're in for it when you get home," he emphasised with a shake of his head, then climbed back over the wall to his bicycle. Yes, I got it right enough, though being used to it I don't remember, with my only regret that but for our father cycling down the Brackenstown Road and getting the whiff of wood smoke, the North County Dublin would have had its own Red Cloud.

Chapter 11: Our Father and His Family

My father Miley Redmond holding my brother Lorcan.

Late in the 19th century, our grandfather Lawrence Redmond nailed his future to a dodgy mast. When tested, he remained true to his employer as a steward to a certain Luke Bolton, a surgeon in the British Army. Luke was from his father's estate of Island, near Oulart in County Wexford. Luke, having served in Egypt and about to retire from the army bought a farm in Coolatin, about forty miles further north, bringing them into South Wicklow. Here he gave Lawrence the option of several acres wherever it suited him, and then had a house built for him. It was also where our grandfather got married and eventually reared his family. After the 1916 uprising, I believe Luke sold up and left. It was from Luke our grandfather received the Vinegar Hill document.

On Luke's departure, our grandfather went into the transport business, securing a number of horses and carts to be driven by his four sons. It was in this business our father was employed for about eight years. The business was to provide cut stone, kerbing, lintels, quoins and sills from the granite quarries, mostly for the Wicklow County Council road maintenance and government building programs. Though Lawrence became blind, he lived into his eighties. Our grandmother Margaret claimed direct descent from Fiach McHugh O'Byrne – King of the O'Byrnes. Fiach's territory was the objective of the two renowned Red Hughs, O'Donnell and O'Neill, when they escaped from Dublin Castle. Margaret died in her bed shortly after Lawrence, though only sixty-seven years old. Poor Fiach was not so lucky, having his severed head spiked on the gate of Dublin Castle. Our grandfather, our father and his brothers were Parnellites and later Redmondites, and eventually members of the IRA for which they paid a price.

It was in an internment camp in Wicklow our father was imprisoned for two years and where Frank Lemass was his commandant. Our father was delegated camp barber, a skill and pastime he learned in the camp. And whether he liked it or not, he was to be local barber wherever he lived for the next sixty years afterwards, charging nothing but he would accept a tanner – rising over the years to two bob a skull, if you had it, which most didn't (or said they didn't). He loved the chat as he trimmed and snipped away with his hand clippers and scissors.

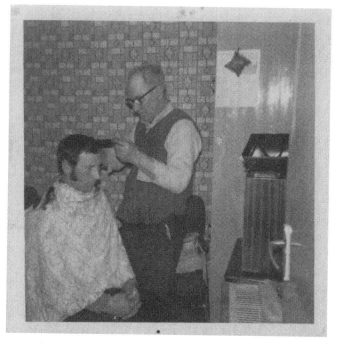

Our father (Miley Redmond) giving Lorcan a trim.

As a father, I remember an intelligent man satisfied with his lot, envious of no other, and absolutely at peace with the world. Actually, in many ways, he was the complete opposite to our mother. If he was ambitious or ambitious for us, he certainly kept it under wraps. He was exceptionally good living. I can never remember him going to bed without spending five minutes on his knees and likewise every morning. He was taught to drive a tractor in the Castleblondin Estate in Kilkenny. When he moved to Dublin in 1934 he had no car but he had a bike and later a motorbike. He never mentioned any desire to own a car (though Lorcan used to loan him his car every year for his holidays). He could recite poetry which he learned in a hedge school and would do so when old comrades turned up and compared memories. But his abiding love was seeing stuff grow, for his time farming — along with it being a business was a form of expression. Hay, for instance, mowed when green and ripened on the ground; turned, raked and cocked in straight rows without a stalk out of place. Hay, which when saved in rick or barn, would eventually be loaded on horse-drawn carts for the market in Dublin's King Street in such a way as to reveal the pride and skill of the farmer. The hay rolled in perfectly formed layers on the cart, the same carts returning to the farmyard loaded with manure from one of the many urban stables, dairies and piggeries in the city.

In those days the farmer himself was very much aware of his position in the community, obligated by his conscience and a social interest, and the fact he was the main provider of employment through the operation of a mixed farming system which then was labour intensive. During harvest time he gave ample employment. As I recall around our bailiwick, the elderly Mr. William Keeling, Willie Sneyd and Patrick Kettle, Frank Wilson were gentlemen of a more genteel age who would never be wealthy, but who possessed honour and dignity exemplified by their righteous standards. Indeed, that same honourable Patrick Kettle, who each year on the anniversary of C.S. Parnell's death, would drive his pony and trap into O'Connell street, secure the pony, and then for a couple of minutes stand to attention in front of his monument.

Our father left all the rearing to our mother, including chastisement, though he helped in many ways such as using his 'last' to fix our footwear with leather heels, and the soles carved from worn car tyres. He was a marvellous provider and was also a stoic, who only complained when our hens got into his garden. His life was otherwise content – as long as there was a packet of Gold Flake beside his cup every morning. On occasions our mother would have to bully him to affect something or other.

Now in the forties, like most men in the district in answer to the emergency, he joined the defence forces, serving in the Swords LDF, setting off spick and span to Gormanstown and elsewhere for target practice and manoeuvres. He had had some experience and was an excellent shot, coming second in a big competition with the other units in the county. Why I mention this is because these soldiers brought their weapons home. Our father's brass-butted 303 Lee Enfield, bandolier, bayonet in scabbard, helmet plus uniform, a pair of leather gaiters, a bull's wool great coat – which incidentally was brilliant for going over the bed on cold nights – and his gas mask, footwear and cape were all neatly stored in that alcove in their bedroom.

Many the early afternoon, to ensure we didn't get up to devilment (like going down to the river) our mother would lock us into that bedroom for an hour while she dashed to the town on our father's bike for a pound of rib or round steak for the dinner, and maybe a pound of suet for rendering into dripping. While she was gone, the gun and bayonet were unearthed – and we were soldiers. I still often observe that it was only for the grace of God that we didn't gut one another.

Uncle Paddy, our father's youngest brother, would visit occasionally. He was in his late twenties then, a dark, wavy-haired lad with a permanent mischievous grin lurking on his good-humoured face. He was a restless, fidgety fellow who seemed to find it difficult to relax. At this time, he either owned a lorry or was employed as a driver. His job had him trucking grain up from the docks to the flour mill in Phibsborough. Passing up through Gardiner Street one night at around ten o'clock, a row outside Killeen's public house distracted him – a Garda had been floored and was being subjected to a vicious kicking by several lousers. Paddy jammed on the brakes and leaped from the lorry armed with the starting handle. With a half dozen swipes he cleared the footpath, pulled the Garda to his feet, and bundled him into the cab and delivered him to Store Street barracks a short distance away. Paddy, when later being interviewed by the superintendent, let it be known he had twenty-one summonses against him (mostly for no driving licence and mostly earned at Binn's Bridge). These were instantly dismissed, and Paddy was given the freedom of Dublin City. After the war Paddy remained in the trucking business, first in Birmingham, then later in London where in 1983 he died aged sixty-nine. May he rest in peace.

There were two other brothers; Bill, the eldest (who I referred to earlier) was a successful shopkeeper and farmer, and Jim, who inherited the family home was a great raconteur and generous man who lived until he was ninety-six, preceded by his lovely wife Bride by only a couple of years. There were two sisters whose families we often visited when they were alive, and still occasionally keep in contact. Aunt Molly married a local farmer called Jim Carroll, an utter gentleman. They also had a grocers' shop in Ardoyne. They reared three children who have rewarded their parents handsomely by the success of their own children as business people and as servants of the state. Liz, who married Jim Wolohan, an undertaker for the Rathdrum town and district, had two daughters who still manage their farms and the business.

In the dawn's cold eye behold! and find clarity
In a naked world exposed to a fundamental eye,
See the minuteness of your life; see the futility
As man strives to compete and unfulfilled he dies.

Uncle Jim Redmond and my father Miley Redmond.

Our father, Miley Redmond.

Chapter 12: The Effects of the War

We were only aware of the horrors of war by the number of soldiers camped around the Big Fella's woods, their screams of terror when, as late-night revellers, they returned from the pubs in Swords, often staggering off the wooded footpath and down a steep bank, and sometimes into the river. A bonus for us was that we were never short of soldier's caps.

Another incident occurred at eleven o'clock mass one Sunday morning in Swords – the anti-aircraft guns were aroused in Dublin Airport as an intruding German plane came scampering in off the sea, and the ack-ack let loose. Well, there was a panic-driven rush for the church exits, old ones wailing and praying. Of course, we didn't join them, we couldn't! An old gobshite near the end of our seat, intent on joining the rush, slipped and fell, blocking the way. The plane had well and truly gone before we finally got out, though the artillery kept banging away for ages until all the lads had a go.

We kept a dozen or so hens – Rhode Island Reds, if my memory serves me right, but we didn't have the means to contain them properly, and the woods was where some nested. Though they still turned up at feeding time, rooting in our garden and getting us blamed for it, and then had the effrontery to roost in our shed at night. The eggs were a godsend. Food fit for a king was a half dozen slices of homemade bread fried in beef dripping, then dipped in egg.

During the Emergency and consequent rationing, we gave up having sugar in our tea but got it in scones, gingerbread, tapioca, apple tarts and dumplings, rhubarb tarts, blackberry jam, crab-apple jelly, and custard. We ate like kings. A sack of flower was enough for weeks of baking, and when the quality of flour became very dark, my mother had a muslin cloth with which to sieve it – a worthwhile but time-consuming exercise. Two empty flour sacks with seams unravelled and then re-joined made wonderful, long-lasting, perfectly white sheets.

When in Brackenstown, we were the only family with a radio though Dooley's had a gramophone. Our radio was a Cossor. Where it came from I do not know, but it was energised by a dry battery until our father unearthed a clapped-out car battery which we used to charge in Mick Dooley's workshop. Whenever a big race was broadcast, our kitchen would be full, mainly with the stable lads and a few neighbours, our mother providing them with tea and scones. Of an evening 'Dick Barton, Special Agent' was not to be missed. Then later, 'Big Bill Campbell and his Rocky Mountain Rhythm'. 'Round the Fire' was for the Come-all-ye's. Sunday evenings were for Joe Linnane and his live social interactive programme in the different towns around the country. The Sunday night play followed at nine, and was seldom missed. Our cultural requirements were pandered to by this or that quintet or ensemble which seemed to go on for ever. The most popular songs of the time were the cowboy ones, with Gene Autry singing 'A bridle hanging on the wall', and 'South of the Border'. I cannot recall ever hearing a match being broadcast, or a crowd in the kitchen on a Sunday.

We used to get the buttermilk for baking from old Pat Barnwell when he churned, though there was competition. Most women baked, but my mother (craftily) would give Pat the odd cake of bread, thereby getting the inside track. Gerry Hamilton, the Scotsman, sent one of his children up to old Pat for buttermilk and Pat, ever honest and forthright, agreed he had some but said it was for a 'party'. Gerry, on being told, remarked he'd heard of all kinds of parties but this was the first buttermilk one he'd heard of.

When the war ended there was no great hullaballoo. It had little or no effect on us except a few of the lads returned, Billy Woods being one of them. He remarked that his worst experience was witnessing an incident in London where an unfortunate fell under a bus, his screams to that day still haunting him. Billy served with a northern regiment and saw service for three years with Montgomery's army in Europe. It was around this time we acquired new neighbours – Mr. John O'Conner, an extremely good-humoured, friendly man from County Meath, along with his wife and small family. John had been employed as herdsman.

Psalm 90

Why is life ephemeral, Lord, why must we grow old?

Why may we not live forever more?

We know paradise is promised, as your prophets have foretold

But I still would rather hang out as before.

Chapter 13: On the Brink

We, the children, were becoming more demanding... needing more supervision which our mother could not offer due to her milking duties. Indeed, her short temper was now on a hair trigger in trying to keep all the balls in the air, and us from murdering one another. She swore many times that she was having stalls made for us to keep us apart. At this point my father, to remedy the situation of his motherless children, applied for employment elsewhere and found a job with another farmer. The wage was two and sixpence more than what the Big Fella paid, but minus our mother's cow milking and washing activities. Father gave a week's notice. The Big Fella tried to dissuade him, pointing out that he and our mother were vital to the estate, and that we must, among other perils, vacate the house even though our father had offered to pay rent. Nevertheless, he commenced his new job with Colm Lawless of Rathbeale.

The county council could not provide accommodation, nor would they advise on how to attain it. Kips in Dublin City were advertised and suited financially, but were never considered. Our uncle Paddy Redmond, by now living in Birmingham, advised giving serious thought to packing up and joining him there. At this point our parents were desperate and extremely agitated with the shameful prospect of being turned out at the side of the road.

A fairly large farm adjoining the Ussher Estate was sold, and the new owners advertised for a tractor driver with wages much better than what Colm Lawless paid. Our father applied and was employed; the extra money he said, would allow us to rent something half decent. At this point the Big Fella went to law and we were summoned to court where the inevitable occurred – immediate possession was given to the Ussher Estate. Outside the court the Big Fella very kindly assured our father he would not be calling the bailiffs.

In 1946, sitting in front of me at school was Tommy Murphy (a thoroughly decent chap) who lived three miles from school and was often late. When challenged by the master, a Mr. Keane, he was always excused. One day in school I heard Tommy whispering to the chap sitting beside him, "Don't tell anyone, but we're moving to live in Swords and Dad is going to open a bicycle shop." I raced home and told our mother. When father came home and had his tea, he cycled to Murphy's house. Mr. Murphy was more than decent, for within minutes he volunteered to accompany our father that very evening to meet the owner of the cottage, a fussy Mr. Halpin who resided in Rathfarnham, about twelve miles away. There a deal was made, the rent being ten bob a week with a week in advance.

I suppose we were excited but not euphoric, realising we would miss, and I sometimes still miss the river, the glen beneath Pat Barnwall's, and the seclusion of the woods. There were now five of us – John (Jack) called after John Redmond of the Redmondites, was wheeled in a pram the three miles to our new home. It was the same pram that had been brought from Castlecomer with its large Swastika (Hitler's stamp) indented on either side. Though mind you, only a keen observer would notice Jack under the bits and pieces which represented our most valuable goods. These included the oil lamp with globe and shade, and a Sacred Heart lamp, the Cossor, a set of Delph with a number of the cups with handles missing, plus six pullets with wings and legs trussed, one or two of them to our mortification escaping and fluttering about the road of the village until caught. The remainder of our chattels came by horse and cart driven by our father. A collection of poorly dressed, snot-nosed kids had quickly gathered to watch proceedings, heart-warming in their affinity, though they told us later they thought we were tinkers.

The ancient whitewashed cottage in Pickardstown was the end one of three. They were built of mud and stone and had a slated roof. It was a four-room affair of which two were bedrooms, one a kitchen at the back, and a front parlour. There was also an unexplainable windowless space about six feet wide and ten feet long in the centre of the building. Actually, it was a dark, dank hole – I could never figure out what its purpose was. The house was without electricity or running water, similar to most of the county, though there was a reliable village pump a hundred yards away.

Our mother insisted on a rainwater barrel to provide soft water for washing clothes and the like. The tar barrel, unearthed, was positioned at the rear of the cottage. Accommodation was also provided by a chalet in the garden, as Mr. Halpin had stressed with great import. On inspection it wasn't so hot, all right to look at, but too cold, old, draughty, and rat infested. Mr. Murphy had used it as a workshop in his bicycle repair business. There was also a small hut in the garden with the word LAV scrawled on the door. We thought our cottage had a side entrance until we attempted to use it, but apparently it belonged to neighbours.

The Boot before the extension.

Martin Tracey (L) and Billy Moylan (R) standing in front of the chalet in the garden during a visit with my father (Miley Redmond – centre).

Chapter 14: Our Neighbours

There were ten buildings in the village which included a shop and a pub. Our adjoining neighbours were the Smiths – decent, good-living people. Mr. Smith, a tall gangling man, was a bus driver. He was also highly energetic and amenable to new ideas which would improve their standard of living. So, when our father suggested they build two adjoining pig sties, thereby saving a wall, Mr. Smith was all for it.

It was actually at this time that Mr. Smith had acquired a portion of bog somewhere in the Dublin mountains. He had a blacksmith make him a slay, an elongated spade for digging the turf. On his days off he'd head for the mountains on his bike and spend twelve hours digging and stacking the wet sods. He had kept up this routine for months, until the day he hired a lorry to bring it home. Yes, this man was a worker, one who didn't drink or smoke, had a house full of children, yet had a wonderful sense of humour. Building the concrete sties at the bottom of our long gardens took a couple of weeks. The cement had hardly set when there were two Bonhams in each sty.

The Daltons were our neighbours on the other side. They lived in a brick-built county council cottage with an acre of garden. Mr. Dalton, a tall silent man seldom seen without his hat, was employed as a carpenter with the ESB, a well-paying and secure job. We were living beside them for only a short spell when Mr. Dalton died, from what I never knew. This left poor Evey, his lovely wife, to rear her six children on her own. Luckily, Evey's brother Paddy Duggan lived with them, a man who was a 'Godsend' to them. All the kids called him Duggy. They were nice people and good neighbours, and Evey's children were never a burden to her.

When our pigs were small we had no trouble acquiring feeding for them, which was the scraps the Daltons gave, plus our own scraps. As the pigs grew bigger we, with a farmer's permission, would gather the hazards after the main crop had been harvested. These hazards were the smallest of the potato crop. Not much bigger than marbles, they were too small for seed, and too expensive to harvest for the farmer's own piggeries. It was an awful job; we'd be picking for hours trying to fill a sack, but it had to be done. Mr. Smith used to bring home bags of swill from the CIE staff canteen to feed his animals. On many a trip, he arrived home with more of it over himself and his bicycle because of a leaky bag. At the time there was no such thing as plastic bags.

Old Mick Condron was another man of note. He lived with his wife 'Nana' and his mother 'Lammie' in an ancient whitewashed cottage at the penultimate end of the village. A brick-built house in the garden was where their three sons had an apartment.

Mick was employed by the county council, and allocated a six-mile stretch of road to maintain. His tools were a bill hook, a shovel, a brush, and a spade. He was a most conscientious man; a man who took his job seriously, as reflected in the perfection he sought and achieved. I'd venture a fortune on the fact that there was not a stretch of road in the country that was maintained to the same high standard.

Personally, Mick was a low-sized, moustached man who always wore a hat. He was a reticent, and would avoid conversation when he could. When cornered, though always polite he would seldom engage in frivolous discussion. He had three sons much older than we were, with one married and another working in construction. Eddie, the youngest and a good-humoured chap, left for Britain a few years later. This left Mick's eldest, also Mick, living with his wife Bess and family in the third of our whitewashed row of cottages. They too kept a few hens along with a Bantam cock – the noisiest hoor in Christendom. At four in the morning he'd begin, and I often marvelled at how he didn't bust his gut with this persistent crowing, a racket which only ceased when he had all of us out of bed.

Beyond young Mick and Bess Condron's house was Maxwell's, their house was a two-storey affair from which they operated a shop. This was a boon for the villagers and the wider area. The barn and yard of their premises was once a forge, now converted into a cowshed by their son Eugene who operated a dairy. They were a decent, generous, and good-living family. The eldest members migrated to the US before siblings were born, and those siblings were in their teens when they all eventually met. All the family prospered, with two of the sisters, Bridget and Teresa running the shop.

On the other side of the road facing our house were two county council cottages. Not as well built as Dalton's, but much better than ours — ours being mud and stone built, and less commodious. Of course, over time we all became electrified and had running water plus bathrooms. In one of the cottages lived Jack O'Connor and his family of four sons, three of them carpenters, the other one in a good constant job. The O'Connors were highly respected in the parish for their principled involvement in the revolution of 1916.

The father, Jack, was a tallish dark-featured man with a marvellous head of now greying hair. He was easy-going, engaged principally as a wheelwright in his workshop a half mile from the village. They, observing Smith's and our successful pig venture, opted to keep a couple. But judging by the pigs' constant squealing, Jack quickly lost interest in them, and between their pigs and Condron's cock, they subjected the villagers to the ghastliest daily concerts. Jack then began to dig and till the garden, but his interest faded in that too, as it quickly returned to the wilderness it was before.

Adjoining O'Connor's cottage was Madden's, to be later inherited by Drey's. They too were wonderful neighbours. Old Ned, a widower, had two daughters and three sons. Dinny, the eldest son, remained with the one employer all his life. Young Ned, a smart-looking lad, had a varied career between working for farmers, in construction, and for a year or two, in the car rental business. Then, like me, he emigrated to Britain. Paddy, or Whacker as he was better known, was the youngest lad. I was always fond of him, maybe it was because of the thrupenny bit, and the odd time tanner he gave me for cleaning his bike. He even rewarded me with a bright yellow wallet, an unwanted present he got for Christmas. It has survived to the present day, being too bulky for pockets. There was nothing in it when he gave it to me. Still nothing in it. Whacker too had a diverse career. In his youth he was with dairy boys, then farming, and later spent most of his life in pubs employed as a barman and manager. There were two sisters; Molsey who was employed for many years but never married, and chose to remain at home, and Lily, a handsome girl who married Kieran Drey, an ex-army man and now a professional driver. As Ned grew older, the Dreys were invited to come and live in the cottage as an aide to Molsey in looking after old Ned, who incidentally lived into his eighties.

All these lads and lassies were never idle; they were never on the dole. A different mindset existed then, for to be idle was seen as being lazy, a stigma recognised by every employer in the district. Fifty yards beyond the village was another labourer's cottage, as council houses were described by the authorities. It was inhabited by an elderly widow by the name of Mrs. Fields, and by 1950 her family had married and moved away. Her house appeared to be ok, but in fact it was very damp. Indeed, when we as children were sent with a message to Mrs. Fields, on opening the door the damp odour was first to greet us. All her family were talented and industrious. When they left the village, it was for their betterment. If I may add, we bought the cottage in 1958.

At the other end of the village was the pub – The Boot Inn, the focal point of the hinterland. It was a haven for the journeyman where he paused for an hour before returning to the city. It was a place of rest for the returning drovers and their collies; likewise, for the carters and those who had the eight pence for a pint of Guinness before making their way out into the country. It was a place of respite for those engaged in construction sites, especially on Friday evenings, stopping for an hour before continuing their journey homewards. Actually, in 1946, we, the newly arrived in the village, were often awakened around seven o'clock by the chatting O'Hara brothers, Martin and Mick, they with two others pedalling onwards to their place of work, a building site in Rathfarnham, having already cycled from Rowlestown, six miles further out.

The pub was where dreams were shared; where football matches were replayed. It was where the lonely found voice. One such character was Mickey or 'Manager' Berigan, as he was known. He cycled in from the neighbouring village of St. Margaret's which was two miles away. He was a tiny man of about four feet ten inches, invariably dressed in a raglan-style light overcoat, with a dark-coloured suit beneath it. A hint of an old-fashioned collarless shirt was to be seen, and on his head a greasy flat cap. We would see him sedately passing our house on his old black bicycle around five thirty each evening, and four hours later wobbling homewards. I believe he earned his nickname because he was more often to be seen in the pub than the owner himself.

In the pub, Manager seemed content to be by himself. Though on weekends, if somebody sponsored him, he could be quite loquacious, and give a rendering of the only song he knew – 'Going to the woods to get broom'. Manager would end the song convulsing with laughter, so it must have been funny. From our point of view and owing to his unfortunate harelip, we hadn't a clue what he was on about.

On summer evenings he'd often sit on the stile in the centre of the village and doze awhile before setting homewards. One evening while lounging at the stile the question of damp houses arose; Manager related his experience. Apparently, their house had been damp, and on enquiring here and there for an economical cure, an expert was found. This fellow insisted on tarring the interior walls, and when the job was completed he suggested they light the fire so as the tarred walls would dry, he also recommended that they should all retreat to the pub to celebrate for a couple of hours. When they returned and opened the front door, they met the tar running out.

Manager bore the scars of his bicycle journeys without complaint, an occasional limp, scars and abrasions on his face and hands. They were never enough to dissuade him from his tipple. Many wondered how he survived. Others suggested he knew how to fall. My brother Frank, on his way to St. Margaret's one evening via Barberstown Lane, came across an abandoned black bicycle by the side of the road. On looking down into the ditch he could see a body. On closer inspection it turned out to be Manager. When awakened, he became quite temperamental, denied he'd fallen in, and swore he was only having a rest. And furthermore, he could cycle this road any day of the week with his eyes shut.

Manager was an inoffensive man who lived into his seventies. Whenever I think of him I see him unobtrusively sitting near the window of the public bar, and only when addressed would his two little birdlike eyes light up in recognition, giving him life for an instant before fading into the nonentity of the wall behind him.

This pub was where young fellows assembled before cycling off to dances in the towns of the north county. During World War Two, this pub was the focus of American troops stationed in Northern Ireland. They'd be taxied down for a good meal and a bit of 'How's yer father' with the quare ones who trundled out from the city.

The atmosphere wasn't always idyllic in those bonafide years when the city pubs closed at eleven o'clock. The bonafides were pubs three miles outside the city limit who remained open until midnight. This circumstance certainly increased the clientele turnover, but quite a few were unwelcome. Drunk when they arrived, they would become noisy and belligerent. They came not so much for drink as to have the 'rare up'. This resulted in not a lot in the till, and the odd row resulting in damage to property, never mind the injuries to staff trying to eject them.

On the eight o'clock Sunday evening closing time we would witness the shenanigans, though we were strictly banned from going anywhere near the pub. I recall one evening a particular bunch had with great difficulty been pushed out on to the path and the pub door slammed shut. In their zeal, the bar staff had pushed the proprietor Mat Weldon out along with them. He, with nowhere to run, gave an admirable exhibition of the Queensbury rules, walloping left, right, and centre before escaping through the reopened door.

Mat Weldon was a thoroughly decent, good-living man. Some would say "a man ahead of his time," for he was forever chopping and changing the pub interior as if striving to find the absolute in ambience. He was entirely correct in his choices. Well, except for one minor fact – before his clientele could enjoy these newfound comforts and make it their personal watering hole, Mat would start pulling the place apart again.

A half mile down the road from the village, Mat formed a coursing club. This, for several years, was a very successful venture. We and the Dalton kids benefited by acting as flankers during the coursing meeting, i.e., keeping the hare running straight up the coursing field to the hare escape. For about five hours' duty we'd get five bob each – a fortune for ten-year-olds! Alas, a coursing club was formed in Coolock, and bigger prizes offered. Mr. Weldon refused to compete, and viewed them as interlopers. He ended the enterprise in 1950 or thereabouts.

We also had casual neighbours. These were unfortunates who for one reason or another found themselves homeless. They were housed in a couple of small cabins a hundred yards from the village, and belonged to a very charitable local farmer called Mick Monks. One reason for their misfortune was they never married, staying on in the family home until ousted by a married brother or sister. Another reason was drink, and being over fond of it. Then there was the elderly, leaving an isolated home in the anxiety or fear of dying alone. The first poor fellow we got to know was Paddy Cahill, a harmless man from God knows where. Then there were the two Fagin brothers, two fine big fellows. And there was Nicholas Lockeran. There was an elderly fellow known as Kildakey. Another was McDonald, better known as Ramsey. They certainly were not lazy because they worked through the spring and into the harvest. During autumn they would snag turnips or wring mangles or do whatever employment was offered. Mick Monks housed them rent free, and Mick Monks and his family often fed them. And often at Mick's own expense, bury them.

Lastly, Mick and Mary Kane were beholden to Mick Monks. For a number of years, they lived in one of his tiny houses. Mick Kane, a veteran of the Boer War and fourteen years in the British Army, was elderly when with his wife they came to our village. A five shilling a week army pension was what they subsisted on – at least it was constant! Mick Kane would often sit on the village style and regale us with yarns from his experiences. They eventually left the village to end their pilgrimage in a care home.

Psalm 17

By our thoughts and deeds you know us Lord

And by the integrity we hold throughout our lives

In our nakedness you measure us – in conflict and accord

And by such we will be appraised.

Chapter 15: New Experiences

That year of 1946, while now living on one of the main arteries into the city, we experienced totally new activities. I remember after our first or second week, being awakened at around three o'clock in the morning by a frightening rumbling or drumming noise, and the odd cry of a human voice. Looking out the window we witnessed a herd of forty or fifty cattle being hurried along the road; the leading drover trotting ahead leading his bike, apparently closing gates, his dog guarding the gaps in the hedges. And a second drover and his bike and dog behind ushering them along – all bound for the Prussia Street market. This short-horn breed, suitable for transport, would probably be on the sea for Liverpool before the day was out.

It struck one as a pitiful; with another six miles to go, the poor beasts – with their drooling mouths having come in from the Naul or Garristown, a distance of fourteen to sixteen miles trotting on unforgiving stone roads, were by now numbed with soreness, thirst and exhaustion. The beasts created little mess, their bowels and bladders long emptied. This was the routine of the age, and would continue for many years until motorised cattle trucks took over.

Other mornings, convoys of two and three hay-laden carts would crankle by. Others laden with straw to be used as bedding in the urban dairies, piggeries and stables, for other than buses and trams, most of the transport in the city was horse-drawn. These farm carts would on the road all the year round, supplying the market with potatoes, turnips, and cabbage. The cabbage was beautifully loaded in a ridge-shaped form. These farm carts had a peculiar cranking sound as they rolled along on their iron-bound, wooden wheels, with the carter marching alongside his horse, an Irish draught – a wonderful, obedient, intelligent workhorse, used in practically every farm function.

The cabbage carter had a difficult task, for when he reached the market his load would be auctioned, and instead of a heel-up outside a large shop or central city greengrocers, half the load might be bought by a greengrocer from Kimmage, the other half perhaps by a shop in Irishtown. The only incentive was the screech, the delivery charge of a half a crown – it wasn't mandatory, and many a miserable grocer gave nothing. The carter, up to now still walking and, after the delivery of his cabbage would then set off to maybe Stony Batter or the Coombe, or back to North King Street, to load up with horse, pig, or cow manure, and eventually home.

Those horses, in their traces from perhaps five in the morning, would get the odd breather during the day. Perhaps while hip shod waiting to be dispatched from the market they would have time to nuzzle their nosebag and slake their thirst from a bucket though there was no shortage of drinking troughs about the city. There was one particularly handsome granite trough at the Parnell monument. Actually, there still is one positioned nearby, seen against the Rotunda wall. If memory serves me, there was another trough at O'Connell's monument, it also provided drinking water for the public through a fountain spigot. There was a trough in Drumcondra and at the Five Lamps, and another at Phibsborough. We would see the teams returning from the city in the late afternoon to be unloaded, the cart cleaned, and often straight to the field to be reloaded with cabbage for the next morning. We got to know most of the carters and the farmers – our neighbours, the Monks, Joe and Charlie Barnwell, Eamonn Lawless, Pat Shields.

Some of our neighbours might have a tray of strawberries or a chip or two of blackberries, even mushrooms, for transport. The carter, usually for nothing (or maybe an eventual pint), would make a space and deliver them to the auctioneer early, thereby beating the bus people and getting the highest price (for the purchasing grocer didn't want to hang around the market waiting for bargains).

Chapter 16: Work – An Introduction

Employment of a kind began when we were about five or six years old, whether it be gathering dry fuel for the morning fire or going to the well for water, or perhaps peeling potatoes for the evening meal. During the summer, work was picking blackberries for jam making and crab apples for jelly. The daily chores were compulsory and included having as much ready for when our parents returned from vassalage. Instinctively, our mother was preparing us for life. A life she saw as duty, trust and servitude. As we grew older we would go farther afield for firewood, and afterwards spend our 'leisure' hours sawing the boughs we had brought home into blocks. At least we came to know what burned best, with ash the winner by a mile. The sight of neatly piled sawn blocks in the fuel store gave her great reassurance, for we'd have a month's firing stored, and though each Friday the turf man still knocked, she seldom had to part with a penny.

Paid employment began when I was about eight years old. The event happened on a morning in June of 1942 which coincided with our parents' landlord and employer, Mr. H. I. Ussher, being in Galway for a few days at a race meeting. Our mother inveigled Mick Galvin to do the morning milking of the cows. At eight o'clock she put Frank in the pram along with a parcel of bread and jam sandwiches, and a sixpenny lemonade bottle full of milk, corked with a rolled-up piece of paper, and off we headed. We were going toward Mount Ambrose, a farm a couple of miles away where she'd heard there were pea pickers wanted.

We arrived at the farmyard at around nine o'clock, and joined other family groups which included Mrs. O'Rourke and her three children of Paddy and Denis (universally known as Spider). There was also a sister whose name I forget. They were from a village of twelve cottages called Rathbeale, better known as the 'Twelve Apostles'. Mr. Jones, a friendly, smiling man welcomed us and said we were waiting a while to see if there were more pickers on the Leas Cross bus, the terminus only five minutes away. This gave us the chance to ramble around the yard. Over near the back of the house I spotted a great pile of clay and rocks. On investigating, I discovered a huge hole in the ground. Before further examination, a roaring man burst out of a nearby barn shouting, "Get t'hell away from that feckin' hole or I'll kick t'arse off ye!!" It was Jim Markey, who I later knew as a gentleman. Apparently, he was an expert at digging and lining wells, and here, accompanied by Frank Sheils, they were nearly down to the water table. Hearing the commotion, our mother promised me a few clatters when she got me home.

At this moment we were joined by the bus people, a noisy, gregarious bunch, elated at the prospect of meeting, examining, and having a snigger at the local culchies. Already, there was a horse and cart in the field and bundles of pea sacks being offloaded. A sturdy set of weighing scales was already set up on the headland for weighing full bags. Mr. Jones announced that we'd be paid one and threepence per picked bag.

We were given two drills to pick, while Mrs. O'Rourke and her brood were allocated four drills. Mrs. O'Rourke was dolled up in an apron made from sacking. This 'get-up' we thought was terribly funny. Each group were given a wicker basket and empty bags galore.

After half an hour I discovered this pea picking lark wasn't near as easy as climbing trees or hauling home heavy boughs. Several times I examined the basket to see if there was a hole it, it being so slow to fill. Again, by lunch time, we had filled three bags, the O'Rourkes had six. Our clothes had dried on us, but the green stain remained; the wet was from the dew-soaked stalks, and stain from the chlorophyll.

At one o'clock the picking began again with the O'Rourkes euphoric, knowing they were top of the class. They were brilliant, deft workers, naturally athletic and good-humoured, Spider forever giving short answers to the mother, accompanied with his hyena-like laugh of 'heh-heh-heh' which could be heard and enjoyed all over the field. The bus people tried and failed, but also in a good-natured manner. Among them were three mouthy fellows who in the forenoon had filled only two bags. Now they were running to the scales every ten minutes. The man at the scales, finding one bag too heavy, began to remove surplus peas and discovered nothing but stalks underneath. On tipping the bag, rocks spilled out. They were dismissed immediately.

We did better in the second half and filled five bags, leaving our mother quite happy with her ten bob. Incidentally, during the picking we came across wheat stalks growing up through the peas and were told wheat used up all the minerals in the earth. The sown peas restored nitrogen through their stalks. Mr. Jones was pleased with us, and invited us to the next day's picking to which our mother agreed. That was where she got our bus fares to Wexford for two weeks' holiday.

The following year, 1943, was the year our elder brother Lorcan, a sturdy lad, had got a job pulling rhubarb, or rubob as the city kids called it. His employer was a farmer called Mr. Keeling whose farm was about two miles upriver from our house.

Our mother inveigled Lorcan to bring me with him on the chance of a job. The farmhouse was on top of a hill. It was a fine, ivy-covered residence, though I thought it creepy, it being next to a graveyard. The farmer was a man about seventy leaning on a stick with his other arm behind his back. He was of stocky build and wore a faded dark suit with waistcoat that was graced with a watch chain. An impudent grey face glowered beneath a bowler hat. A winged white collar was attached to his stripy shirt.

He grunted to Lorcan's introduction, while staring at me without comment, then turned around and began hobbling down a car-road to the fields, muttering over his shoulder, "Com'on." I, dressed in jersey and short trousers and with a pair of canvas runners on my feet, meekly followed, though I didn't like being separated from Lorcan. One side of this lane was walled for fifty yards, and on the other side a hedge. My employer stopped at the end of the wall and pointed his walking stick at the overgrown butt of the wall where weeds, including nettles, grew in profusion. "Weed'm," he said. I was a bit confused and wondered should I ask for a hoe or a spade. "Tsk, tsk, tsk! Are ye goin' to do anything?" he said crossly.

I stooped and began to pull the weeds and sods, avoiding and leaving the nettles, and after about ten minutes I say, "I want to go to the lav, sir?"

"Tsk, tsk, tsk," he muttered in annoyance. "Ye can go behind the wall." I didn't want to empty myself, but I needed to find something to help me with the nettles.

About fifty yards away I see Lorcan with another young man among the rhubarb. When I emerged, they straightened with questioning glances. "I'm looking for something to weed nettles," said I.

"Nothin' here," Lorcan said, stooping and dismissing me. The other chap, a fair-haired lad of about eighteen, gropes in the little orange box he was using as a table to tie the bunches of rhubarb. From it he pulls a small, light bag, removes his newspaper-wrapped lunch from it and motions with his head. "Just put your hands in the bag and then pull them." I had just met Pat Mullaly, a decent, honourable chap. I returned to my weeding and by using my foot to bend the nettles I could grab and uproot them with my bag-covered hands. My boss stayed for half an hour then hobbled back to the house, and occasionally would appear in the distance to make sure I hadn't gone to sleep.

Next morning, coming near the farmhouse I became aware of a fluttering noise and discovered it was a windmill, or wind charger. Later I was told it was for charging the battery banks which provided light for the house. That same fluttering noise I came to hate, associating it with my bondage. That second day he had me weeding the front garden, and progressing toward the front door, the maid came out. I knew her. It was Nanny Bulger from Forest Great. She barely spoke before she was summoned inside with, "Don't be keeping that fella idle," and who appears but the divil himself. "Com'ere," he orders. I went to the door to find him pointing his stick at a solidified mess on the brass surround of the door-mat. "Clane that up!" he said, pointing his stick at a cloth and a small bottle of petrol. "It was stuff we put down to catch a rat," he offers my puzzled expression.

"What's them things sticking up out of it?" I queried.

"Agin we caught the rat he was stuck solid," he giggled. "Them are his legs where we had to cut him off it," he tittered. I nearly got sick when I heard that. Nevertheless, I spent an hour rubbing, not being allowed to scrape in case I'd scratch the brass. Then it was back to the weeding, and late in the afternoon he reappeared. There was a low but overgrown privet hedge on both sides of the path that led from the road to the front door. "Get the clippers and tidy up that hedge," he orders. "Napoleon is coming home for the weekend, and

I want the place looking nice." Though I'd never seen hedge clippers before, he didn't complain when I'd finished but stood looking at it for a while. Then he pointed to the end of the hedge next to the door. "Sit on that," he ordered, pointing his stick. I thought he was going bonkers, and stood looking at him. "Sit in it!" he irritably repeats. Still staring, I was getting ready to run when he said in a milder tone, "Napoleon used to sit in the two of them." I got it, and duly sat and made an impression, then formed as best I could the two seats. He left me alone after that. The Napoleon he mentioned was his youngest son, who at the time was away studying medicine.

The third morning at nine o'clock as I waited to be detailed, he announced, "I want-cha to go to the bottoms an' cut ragwort." Here, again, I didn't know what ragwort was. "Go into the barn there," he said, pointing his stick, "and get a slash hook." I fetched the hook. It was heavy, so I put it on my shoulder and marched out the gate and down the hill. Dismayed, I could hear steps and the stick following. I climbed the gate and began to walk off. "Open that gate, ye pup ye," he roars.

"I thought you weren't coming, sir," I said.

"Well I am comin'," he swore, and before I had dragged the little-used gate shut he'd found a high spot overlooking the river and had made himself comfortable. "Never mind the nettles," he said, "it's the yellow weeds that needs cutting."

Well I did my best for an hour, but at nine years old and trying to swing this bloody hook, it tired me out in no length. "I'm going for a drink of water, sir. I'll only be a minnit," I said, hoping I could find something lighter in the barn.

"There's a river o' water," he said in exasperation.

"Tis dirty, sir," I said, climbing the gate. Well, I wasn't long, and found no smaller hook and headed back down, and who did I meet on the way up but himself, and he with the face of a demon passing me without a word.

I returned to find that after the respite, the hook hadn't got lighter. Within thirty minutes, Lorcan appeared; he too was angry. "You're sacked!" he said.

It was the afternoon when I sat beside the river and ate my lunch wondering what I was to do. Home at this hour the place would be locked, our mother away milking. One way or the other I surmised, there would be a hiding waiting for me. In a depressed state I spent the evening following the river home, trying to think of ways to redeem myself. Ways that turned into daydreams as my mind tried to avoid the inevitable.

They were all sitting around the table when I entered, my father with a fork in one hand, the evening paper in the other… lowering it a trifle as way of acknowledgment. That was the only sign of sympathy I got from among the accusing faces of the additional family.

Next morning, still a half mile from the farm, that damned windmill fluttered to mock me. I entered the gate to find himself staring at me. I approached to within a yard of him and declared loudly the words that had been forced upon me. "I apologise for my impudence yesterday, sir, and can I please have me job back?"

Still staring at me, he said, "G'wan out to Pat an' he'll tell ye what to do." He turned around and hobbled into the house and never spoke another word to me.

I went out to Pat who put me in another field to weed strawberries. There I stayed, working for two bob a day until we were sent down the country for the last week of our holidays. I clearly recall those events as a crushing initiation into the world of servitude.

The following year I worked for Mr. Keeling's son William. His farm was adjacent to his father's, or perhaps it was land that had once been his father's. My job was picking strawberries at three and six per day. If the day was rainy there'd be no work. On the dry days there would be up to sixty pickers mostly bussed out from town, the transports paid for by William. Some of the pickers were totally unsuited. They came with the vision of getting money for nothing. They'd only be picking for thirty minutes and begin to complain of a sore back, or stop to cadge, "Era butt," or, "Giv'us a drag," sharing the same quarter-inch butt among four or five of them. More often than not they'd be gone within an hour, leaving them to walk the six miles back to town. To keep them from running, William used to lock the gate, but some were determined escapees, traipsing through wheat and grazing fields, creating gaps, leaving gates open. Most stayed and earned their money, for William was not niggardly, and rewarded the best.

Following the year of 1945, I returned to Killeek to find old Mr. Keeling had died. In reality he was a decent man, as long as you didn't challenge him. I always felt he was lonely for the sons and daughters who were too wound up in their own lives. Anyway, the farm now belonged to his youngest son, Napoleon, a hard taskmaster, a doctor, and an ambitious farmer.

My job this particular year was assisting Cockles McCormack, who was from Swords. He had been employed by the Doc to glaze the newly built, double bay glasshouse. I assisted in this endeavour by puttying the frames, and handing up the panes of glass. Cockles was a great workmate, never subject to moods, always upbeat, always singing. His favourite song, his only song was 'The rich mac-a-raga of le whooch cha cha cha'. He'd sing that line a hundred times a day. The only drawback was the million cuts I earned handling the glass.

After three weeks the job was done, the Doc then offered Cockles the job of digging the houses in preparation for tomato plants, so for the same wage we spent another week digging and manuring. The Doc invited Cockles to remain on for the planting, but he declined.

I was then deployed to general farm work such as hay making, which was awful. Then picking potatoes, which was awful. Weeding rhubarb wasn't too bad, though easy after the sun dried you. Neither I nor the other kids had rain gear, and when a shower came, we'd run to where the giant yew trees of the graveyard were overhanging our field. Actually this was the only time we'd meet, for the Doc in his wisdom or cunning had us working on opposite sides of the field, with some going up the field and some down. This stroke was to keep us from talking. Being young lads, we'd make the best of it, though the most serious warning was when we'd get within talking distance, "For Jasus' sake don't lerim' see ye' laughing!"

When in residence the Doc got very annoyed when we ran for shelter, and with the first few drops he'd dash out of the house, shouting, "Get back to work or you won't be paid!"

He was a startlingly handsome and affable man, though subject to terrible rages which at times lasted for hours, even days. These were the times when the Genghis Khan element emerged. The only one unaffected and invariably treated with the utmost respect was Pat Mullaly. Pat, a solitary person, smiled a lot… smiling within himself, content in some serene world of his own. Pat spent his youth and most of his adult life working in Keeling's.

With the Doc being away doctoring until late afternoons, he employed a steward. From the beginning, he insisted on being called 'Mister'. He was from Donegal, and during these early days I often wished he'd stayed up there. He was average height but his thick neck and broad chest, along with huge arms, gave the impression of great strength. His hair was brown, sleek, and quiffed; his attitude was cold and unfriendly. A barn in the yard had its upper storey converted to two rooms. A newly employed bunch of late teenagers from Kilkenny, all from Tullaroan, lodged in one. The other room was the steward's. The ground floor was the kitchen, though I forget what type of cooker it had, if any. Having had to stay late a couple of unpaid evenings waiting for a sow to farrow, I saw Cisse, the new maid, leaving out a meal for the steward, though nothing for me. The meal must have been a condition of his employment.

That converted barn and loft that now was living quarters was the same one I'd been in earlier. It was where I saw an old black bike with two flat tyres, and had asked the Doc if I might buy it. He thought for a moment, then abruptly said, "No, I want it." I asked Pat what happened the bike. He said everything went to the dump.

I recall one morning, going out to weed a particular nettled and thistled strawberry field, I had taken the precaution of wearing light-weight sacks around my bare legs. When the steward with his hands in his trouser pockets and a fag wagging in the corner of his mouth saw my get-up he growled, "What's them?"

"Leggings," I said.

"Well get them off ye. We want none of your own f***in' inventions here." He was cranky.

His fellow lodgers told me he went to the greyhound track each night, I concluded that he wasn't backing winners. Old Mr. Keeling would have loved the steward, for while he didn't shout, he retained a constant petulant expression and had two very suspicious, accusing eyes which I found threatening. When the time came to draw in the hay, all hands except Pat were assembled. We, the kids, were withdrawn from the weeding. The Doc must have taken a week off work, for he never left the haggard where the hay was being saved. The farm had two bogies. These were low, flat trailers, specifically made for transporting loads of hay. From William's farm up the road, they had borrowed another horse and bogy. The three bogies were driven by the Kilkenny lads.

The steward was positioned in the hayshed with me and three other kids. Our job was to collect armfuls of hay and carry and stuff it against the back of the shed. I'll never forget those two days, for between the fog of dusty, musty hay, and threading backward and forwards across the rising bench – the Doc standing in the yard frantically urging us – it was absolute slavery. The farm's horses, bony and aged, were being urged to a trot. William's, though, in better condition, was better able. The steward, now stripped to the waist, was forking the hay up to us. The higher the bench grew, the higher he had to fork it.

As soon as one of my brave companions climbed down the ladder the Doc pounced, demanding, "Where the bloody hell d'ya think you're goin?"

"A drink o' water, sir," me man croaks.

He was reluctantly allowed to drink. But the Doc would not let his bone drop, muttering so as we could hear, "I'm not payin' ye' to drink water."

The steward never urged us – he obviously had a human side – because I'm sure on those two days he discovered Doc was only using him too. Ever after, the steward was polite and uncritical of us, though neither was he friendly. He seemed to have acquired a remoteness, or was it disillusionment?

Arriving to work one morning soon after, one of the Kilkenny lads told us a horse had died. Apparently, this chap had been sent to the field to collect the animal in preparation for to grub drills of rhubarb. The grubber had the frame of a plough, but instead of ploughshares it had tines to tear up the weeds. At lunch hour we went out to see the dead horse. Its skeletal corpse lay with its mouth open. It still wore its britching, held together with wire, the reason for this being it took ages to yoke him in the mornings, so they left it on him. His companion was standing nearby, his head hanging, he too wearing a busted wired-up head collar. And that's the way he remained until a journeyman harness maker arrived on his annual visit.

He was a tiny man with a harelip, who parked his bike in the hay shed and removed a small bag. In the way of tools, he had very few. There was a selection of curved needles, a gimlet and a rasp, a ball of hemp, and a cobbler's hooked knife. He also had a lump of brown shiny material, which puzzled us, until seeing him hold it over a stump of a candle and then draw the hemp through it, creating a wax end.

He stayed for two days, sleeping in the hayshed, having his billy can boiled in the kitchen. His work was superb. The old head collars were now stuffed with straw instead of fibre; the britching and winkers now repaired by cannibalising old bits and pieces of harness. The straddle too had been stuffed again with straw. Before he left we stood around admiring his work. Though pleased with the attention his only comment was, "The harness is rotten, and t'won't last jig time."

This year was my last year at school. About a month before our holidays my younger brothers Frank and Bill and I were returning from school when a big, flashy car pulls up. It was the Doc. "How are ye lads?" he said, with his brilliant, winning smile. Then focussing on me he said in a plaintive voice, "I'm desperate for a good man to work in the glasshouses; the hoors I have are no use at all." I was thirteen and this attention made me feel terrible important.

"I'll hav'ta ask me mother," said I.

"Tell her I'll pay you three and six a day," he said.

"That's the same I got from Mr. William at Easter," I innocently replied. His smile vanished and was replaced with instant anger.

"Three and nine pence," he growled, "an I'll get you to do a bit of grubbing with the horse."

"Alright, sir," I said, for working the horse was man's work – the very idea was fantastic.

A couple of young fellows from Drumcondra had been coming to work for the Doc during their holidays. Purcell was their name. They told me their father was a surgical bootmaker, and at that time was making arrangements to emigrate with the family to the USA to join up with his brother. By this time the eldest chap, Sé, a lad of about sixteen, was working full-time for the Doc, along with an extremely polite young man and family friend of the Doc's called Tommy Marr. Tommy was a beautiful singer with his favourite song 'Sweet Sixteen'. Apparently, the Doc promised to make glasshouse specialists out of the two of them. Sé was a nice, well-reared lad with a benign or fatherly attitude toward us. He also had a Doc-induced self-importance, which wrung all the fun out of him. The Doc did rely heavily on him for getting the crop pruned and tending the plants, monitoring the temperature, and watering.

While I walked to work, his brother used to catch on me and give me a lift on the crossbar, Sé having gone earlier. My first task in the glasshouse was pruning the plants so that the growth would be into the tomatoes and not into superfluous runners. After a week or so I began to see myself as a specialist, that is until one day I was expelled to join the other skins picking strawberries. It was a bit of a downer, with the other lads now delighted at my demotion, asking me what I done wrong. Then I'd say, "This lark is temporary," and that I'd be working the horse in a day or so. Gleefully, they told me the bloody horse had died six months earlier.

Some of the pickers were runners from William's farm, hoping for a more easy and profitable passage here. As they passed the road gate they were cajoled to enter, and when it was estimated we had enough the gate was locked – not to bar other fortune hunters, but to imprison the eejits he'd already captured. Here the procedure was the same as William's – to get money you had to work. Though most made the best of it, there were those who cried bitter tears to be freed.

The mob in the field, including me, were encouraged with, "Pick the ones you see. Then pick the ones you don't see!" or, "Half of them are not ripe!" and, "That punnet is not full enough!" This agitating was continuous, like, "Ah com'on outa dat. Com'on te bloody hell outa dat." It was so humiliating – not the work, but being among amateurs. The most hurtful element was that they were on task work, such as being paid by the punnet; good pickers were earning more than me. The harvest lasted about six weeks, though there were still pickers retained to pick the spent plants of their last berries. These retained staff were known as the 'jam maulers', because what they picked went straight to the jam factory in the city's Kings Inn street. My Killeek period so ended, not as a glasshouse specialist, but a specialist in weeding and picking strawberries. Several times afterwards the Doc tried to inveigle me back.

The following year I left national school and spent the holidays working for local farmers. It was in a hay field I met Pat Barnwell, better known as Dingers; this moniker earned because he was a top-class worker. Dinger was about twenty-two at the time, an ever-smiling lad who loved a joke and a yarn. He was a tall, wiry fellow with his cap precariously perched on the side of his head. He had an effortless method with a hay fork, a rhythm that set the standard that any employer would give his eyeballs for. Dinger was renowned, and others in the same field would not be found wanting. I thought we were working for about one pound per day, that was until after two days when getting paid I found Dinger had set the rate for three pounds per day. I had six pounds – more money in my hand than I ever had in my life. My mother allowed me to brag for a while before relieving me of it. Dinger was seldom idle, and was of great value to buyers and sellers at the cattle markets where he could judge the breed and health of an animal, the weight and value of the beast to the nearest pound.

When the chips are down.

Only fools stick their necks out; glory hunters volunteer
But some don't get option to decline
It's when you decide the demise of one you held dear
Compassion changes worms into lions.

It is torment to be appointed—to be the vital man
With a life at stake and you are called to choose
You must conceal your sympathy though know and understand
Your decision means other friends you lose.

A test of your integrity is to meet a challenge straight and true
To stand square when justice cannot be found,
By being loyal to your comrades when the odds say you will lose
Prove you are a man when the chips are down.

Be at ease with your conscience by being always overt
And consider well before issuing decrees
For its when nobody owns you it is then you may assert
My guiding light is my integrity.

Chapter 17: Highs and Lows

1945 saw Lorcan, my elder brother, employed as an assistant in the antique dealers, Lawlor and Briscoe's, their premises being on the quays. This left Frank, Billy and me to trot the three miles to school. It was downhill in the morning, yet we seemed to be always late. After the first week of the usual excuses like, "The kettle fell inta' the fire, sir," and, "Me mother slept it out, sir," or, "I hata' to mind the house, sir," wore out, the headmaster began punishing me with three severe slaps on either hand every morning we were late, which was two and three times a week. We always left the house on time, but poor Billy couldn't keep up. I then began bullying him, slapping him with a switch to leave him crying and myself in tears of frustration. This went on for months. My dilemma was I was responsible, couldn't, wouldn't, abandon them. I was doing my duty and being punished for it. I despaired at the unfairness; the Murphys, though they cycled, were never penalised. The walk home was more leisurely, though there were the same chores waiting. Firing had to be found, not in woods, but in overgrown hedgerows and ditches of the fields around the village.

Of course Billy complained, but there was nothing our mother could do – she was pregnant again with our sister Margaret, and she had no bicycle. She could not be expected to walk the three miles down and back twice a day. She did write a letter to the principal, who incidentally was my teacher, but with little effect. The result was I continued bullying poor Billy as the teacher kept punishing me. Frank was more relaxed and apparently had a more tolerant teacher. This went on for twelve months while Billy's condition worsened, and he remained at home. That was 1947, the year of the big snow, and the year I left national school.

There were not many high spots in that preceding twelve months except that we still had to find work during the Easter holiday periods, mostly weeding or planting potatoes for local farmers. Notably, at the egging of Lorcan, our mother and father formed a

Gaelic football club with the name of St. Colman's, the club room being our kitchen. I have one grim memory of the time, of a particular evening when the house was full of young fellows of around my own age. In the kitchen I had a log across a chair, and was sawing it into blocks when my mother, infuriated with the babble, tore into me with a vicious clattering. I don't know which hurt the most, the force of the blows or the humiliation of being made to cry in front of the other kids. The oppressing thing about it was that I wasn't the source of the noise. Ever afterwards, whenever I see a child or indeed anybody being bullied, it fills me with loathing of the persecutor.

Anyway, the football team was successful beyond our dreams, particularly with the aid of Mick Monks – a local farmer kindly loaning us the use of a field for a football pitch. This allowed us to compete, with our team winning several important underage competitions. In the initial stages, three of us played on the first team but had to give way to flyers such as the Cronins, the Monks, the McNallys – Ginger and Louie, Pat Dowling, the Brady boys from Finglas, Pat Grace and Busty Byrne from Cloghran, and the O'Connor boys from St. Margaret's. God, they were exciting times. Indeed, I retained from my mother's effects one or two of the objector's letters of matches won and lost over unregistered players, and over objections not being on Irish watermarked paper.

St Coleman's GAA, The Boot, Cloughran. Front L-R: Sean 'Junk' Martin, Timmy Cronin, John Cronin, Mick Dalton, Pat Crosby, Busby Byrne. Middle L-R: Frank Redmond, Peadar Connor, Pat Doolen, Dessie "Bucksy" Connor, Mick Cronin, Dan Redmond. Back L-R: Johnny Fitzsimons, Pat Grace, Jimmy Monks, Brendan McNally, Louie McNally, Austin Monks.

Great credit must go to Richard (Dick) Barnwell, a haulier from Leas Cross, who every Sunday ferried us and our supporters all over the north county on the back of one of his lorries. These acts of decency continued for three or four years when we hadn't a bicycle between us. Our club eventually affiliated to St. Margaret's, where all our players were welcomed.

I must relate my first and last horse riding venture. A large farming family, the Monks of Forest Great, good friends and neighbours, used to ferry their children to school in a pony and trap. It was usually driven by their older brother, Jack. On this particular morning, they had a workhorse in tow, it being brought to Swords to be shod in Matt Donnelly's forge. During the school day Austin, who was in the class behind me, asked if I would I ride the horse home which I, like an idiot, delightedly agreed to. At three thirty I raced up to the forge to collect the nag and was amazed at the height and girth of the beast. Matt gave me a leg up, where I found my legs barely made it across his back. Matt slapped the horse on the flank and out on to the street we trotted to be greeted by a gang of bouseys from Rathingle – a small village on our way home. The horse, with me like a leprechaun on his back, waddled up the street with this unruly gang in tow. It was most uncomfortable and frightening. I knew this bunch would not be satisfied with just walking alongside of us, and I was correct.

To up their entertainment they started throwing stones at the brute, and he broke into a lumbering trot. Never before or since have I felt such fear and suffering. The more I begged and threatened, the more gleeful became my tormentors as I bounced up and down with every stride until we eventually reached the village of Forest Great, by then sea sickness having added to my discomfort. I was unable to walk properly for a month afterwards.

Our mother wanted us to 'get on', to learn a trade or something, because there was nothing but farm work to be had at the time, and *they* only wanted you when their need arose, which was sowing and harvest time. So, in 1947 and a month after I left national school, the bus dropped my mother and me at Gardiner Street and we walked on until we came to Bolton Street Tech school. Here, my mother demanded to meet the principal. After a spell, a Mr. McAuliffe turned up – a small, quiet, bespectacled, grey-haired little man – and my mother began to stun him with visions and descriptions of hardship that would have made Charles Dickens weep.

The principal explained that we were too late, as entry exams had already taken place a month earlier. But noting we were a deserving cause, he agreed to have me do the entrance exam there and then. The room he brought me to was on the first floor and overlooked the street. It did not have a fireplace. It also lacked the mouldy smell of old lunches and damp clothes that pervaded my last place of confinement. Built into both sides and halfway up on the outside of both windows were iron rings. They baffled me until months later when I saw the window cleaners in action, using the rings to secure their safety harness. It was now eleven o'clock and my exam paper would be collected at twelve thirty. This was also lunch time, and apparently the principal forgot about me. At two o'clock he rushed into the room, exclaiming, "I hope you ceased writing at twelve thirty!" Naturally, I told the truth and three weeks later began classes.

The bus service through our village to the city ran three times per day; at twenty past eight in the morning, at quarter to seven, and at ten to midnight. This meant getting to school was no problem, but getting home was – the last three miles I would hitch-hike, often successfully. Then, there developed a serious bus strike which meant me hitching into the city by a milk float driven by a gentleman and dairy boy, Larry O'Toole. Or perhaps in Eugene Maxwell's milk van. These merchants were known derogatorily by some as 'Dairy boys', and were scoffed at for their lack of land ownership. Though at the same time, they were envied for their cash-in-hand enterprise. Anyway, my journey to town meant stopping to make deliveries at cottages here and there along the road.

After a couple of weeks of the strike, army lorries began to assemble in Cathal Brugha Street – one particular route which would leave me to the city outskirts, that's if I was allowed on board. A number of times I wasn't, which meant walking the six miles.

I recall the strike lasting six or seven weeks during which I never missed a school day. By this time, quite a few of my fellow pupils were poor attendees. On Wednesdays, a ritual had developed in our class. A certain number of pupils would not return after lunch, and there seemed to be no penalties. A couple of them began to paint pictures of their adventures down in the Docklands. Vistas were created of giant cranes offloading ships with all kinds of goodies. Tales of their lifting nets bursting and the goodies spilling out on the ground, there, for anyone who wanted them! I was inveigled to join them, and I took just that one and only half day off. But the only ship being offloaded on that day was a collier, and all I got was filthy dirty.

I must say I found it interesting watching the Hackers (self-employed carters) with all kinds of horses, ponies and their carts, and drays coming and going, ferrying a skip of coal to the various coal yards, and returning with an empty skip. The dockers down in the hold of the ship were absolutely black with coal dust, and I'm certain banjaxed from shovelling the extremely lumpy coal into the skips, thus engaged while the crane would be lowering an empty skip or lifting a full one. Somebody remarked that these dockers were temporary, and that the Button Men (the unionised) wouldn't be seen dead near this lumpy coal. Next day at school there was holy murder – three-quarters of the class had bunked off. The principal done his nut, promising to write to all the parents.

I didn't get into trouble at home because there was another priority; Billy had taken a turn for the worst. Indeed, he was moved to Temple Street hospital which incidentally was only a ten-minute walk from Bolton Street Tech. His medical problem I never understood, but it involved fluid leaking through the membrane into his lungs. They kept him under observation while continually draining his lungs. I was able to visit him every day for around a month. Indeed, the nurses very kindly used to give me lunch. Billy himself never looked or felt better – he was eight years old and probably for the first time in his short life had a bed to himself and a few decent toys, which included a train. Our parents were summoned and were told that as he was, he had little chance of survival. They were asked for permission to operate, and our parents agreed. We all went to mass that morning, then Lorcan away to his work, and I to school. At eleven o'clock the principal came into our classroom, looked around, whispered something to our tutor, put his arm around my shoulder, and propelled me out into the corridor. Lorcan, a stoic like our father, was there, a muscle throbbing in his face. With no words spoken, I followed him out onto the street where he jumped on his bicycle and began pedalling. Me, with bag under arm, bawling, ran after him up Bolton Street toward the hospital. It was March 1948.

Coping is an art; the art of making do
Of adjusting to a changing circumstance,
It is the estate of the matriarch who without ado
Must get on with life with just a backward glance.

Coping is to survive while dealing with her loss-
Losing that loved one of her own
Striving to be resolute though heavy is her cross
Bearing our anguish as she mourned.

Chapter 18: My Bovine Experience

A death devastates, particularly when it is a child. His vacant place at the table. His plaintive voice missing. His pitiful pieces of clothing a constant reminder until all physical traces of him disappeared. My memory and prayers for him never lapse, for he is alive in spirit… ever reminding me of my unkindness toward him.

I returned to school until the term ended in July 1948. I sat the exams, the results of which reflected little of what they had strived to teach me. But I did well enough in the trades. These were closed trades, closed to all but those who had a father or uncle already a union member, one who would be your sponsor. It was unfair, but without union membership, an employer wouldn't touch you for fear of causing a strike.

Two vacancies appeared on the school bulletin board. One was for an apprentice fitter in the Grand Canal Company. That made me smile, because on my journey home each evening I passed their basin at the rear of Mountjoy Prison, it being connected to the main canal. It was a graveyard of rotting, half-submerged hulks, now abandoned among the mud and weeds of an also totally abandoned canal.

The other vacancy was for an assistant in Todd Burns of Henry Street, an emporium of high-class house furnishings. My mother insisted on accompanying me to the interview, pushing herself into the office where my interrogators awaited. There were three of them – all male, two youngish and one elderly. They had themselves positioned so as to view me from all angles. After a brief introduction, one of them pushed a chair toward me and, just as I was about to sit, a hard, disparaging voice rasped, "For your mother!" About one minute later we were pushing one another out the door. I had failed the first test.

A certain rotund, bald-headed Mr. Cecil Rathbourne used to deliver our milk of a morning. He was the owner of a nice farm and dairy. On the Monday following my Todd Burns interview, my mother with jug in hand, boned Mr. Rathbourne for a job on my behalf. To our surprise, he invited me to start work immediately. My job, which began at six thirty in the morning, was helping to milk the cows. Having no bicycle, I had to cross several fields to shorten the two-mile walk. Georgie Boshell, a gentleman, was my immediate boss. Georgie, a freckled, fairly tall and energetic man, dressed in overalls and with his cap turned back to front, and Wellington boots which apparently was his choice of footwear the whole year round.

It being July, the cows were out on the land, and when near milking time they would gather unbidden at the gate of the milking paddock. There were about thirty of them, a Hereford and Short-horn cross. They were big, slow, harmless animals whom I got to like.

The milking apparatus was a Dimplex mobile unit, which could milk four cows at a time. The Dimplex had been towed to a concreted area where there was a power point and a four-cow stall. As a cow was milked, it was released straight back out to the grazing field, its place quickly filled by another. My job was washing their udders. This activity along with the warm water made their udders bulge with the need to be milked. After each cow was milked, I emptied the contents of the milking module into a large ten-gallon churn. It only took an hour or so to complete the herd, each one delivering eight to twelve pints of milk twice per day. When milking was completed, Georgie would remain to sterilise the milking equipment while I towed this truck with its three or four churns into the quadrangle adjoining the back of the fine Georgian residence of the Rathbournes.

Most of the barns were or had been stables, with all of them now converted to suit modern requirements. The dairy was one. Another was the quarters of Major Rathbourne. The Major, a blocky gentleman and invariably polite, was now retired from His Majesty's army. He was also a most willing helper during the milk cooling process. The milk was siphoned from the churns to an overhead six-gallon container from which it spilled down over a specialised cold water-filled radiator, and into a new churn. This was where the Major came in. He, for another hour, circulated the cold water into the radiator by means of a hand pump. This allowed me to get on with washing the churns inside and out and turning them upside down on a drainer. I enjoyed the routine, and being trusted with this chore;

work that was without somebody bullying or unexpectedly turning up to suspiciously glare.

After a break there were chores, feeding calves, and the pigs. Their quarters had to be mucked out and bedded daily. There were a couple of horses stabled remote of the quadrangle. I loved and still love the smell of stables. Davy Callahan, the steward, used to look after them, using them to plough, harrow and sow. About twenty acres of the farm which were devoted to tillage – not a lot of tillage compared to some farms. Throughout the summer, and for about four hours per day, I would be drafted to pick spuds, make hay, thin turnip and mangle. This was boring work, toil I did not like.

Joe O'Brien, a man prematurely aged, was another very loyal employee. He was a gnarled old codger; cranky at times. He was also terribly serious, a man who couldn't see the amusing side of anything. If I cracked a joke he wouldn't laugh, and when I explained it to him he'd just grunt and stump off. Joe's wife, Allie, was a wonderful, good-humoured, and exceptionally generous person. They lived in their own home – what I presume was once the lodge of the Rathbournes. I asked Georgie if Joe and Allie had many children, his curt reply, "So many he has them hanging from nails on the wall."

It took me a month to become familiar with the routines and tempers of those I worked with and for. Cecil had two sisters; one about forty, bespectacled and pushy, the other feeble and elderly, who for a time I thought was his mother. There was also a good-looking twenty-year-old niece living there. They had a maid – a beauty. She was a girl of stocky build about my own age. Marie Kerwin was her name. God, she was a stunner – her in her uniform which included a tiara-shaped cap. On some of the warm sunny evenings, they used to emerge through the back door of the farmhouse into the quadrangle, the old birds giggling and waving to embarrass me. Of course, Marie had to titter too, lending support to their idiocy. This caper always left me feeling like a gargoyle. I saw Cecil joining them, though he tried to disguise his sniggers. I never got the joke, nor had I the chance to meet Marie, though the odd morning I'd see her arriving on her crock of a bike, I, at the time like a mule dragging the milk truck toward the dairy.

Cecil himself was generally polite and good-humoured, that is except for one morning when he returned from Merville Dairy in

Finglas where he sold his surplus milk. He had a very serious expression and a rather curt tone as he pointed at a watermark of unwashed milk on the inside of a churn. His solemn, "Be more careful," cut me to the bone.

Georgie was a good-living man with a large family, and at times seemed to be burdened. While he retained a mannerly or respectful attitude, I could perceive a remoteness which didn't encourage conversation. This left me feeling I'd done something to annoy him, so communication gradually receded to monosyllabic. In hindsight, I think he had grown to like the solitary life of working by himself, and I was a distraction.

The first Thursday of every month, the Major religiously went to town to collect his pension. This mission included the 'rear up' with old comrades in the ex-serviceman's club. He then would return on the evening bus and walk the remaining mile until he came to O'Brien's cottage. Allie would make him a pot of tea and leave him in the quietness of the parlour where he'd sleep for a couple of hours. Thereafter, he'd feel his way home to his billet. His reserved polite manner never changed. He neither encouraged conversation nor cut a nuisance short. He was universally respected. Isn't that much better than being loved?

It was an August Saturday which meant we were finished the early milking at about ten a.m. This also meant we were free until two thirty p.m. As I entered the quadrangle with the intent of lugging my trailer of churns to the milking paddock, I was amazed to see a horse-drawn hearse in the yard. It was directly outside the Major's quarters. He'd shot himself. Apparently, he'd been depressed for a time. May the honourable Major Rathbourne RIP.

There is no light like the life-giving Sun
No sweet accord as the singing of the birds.
Miracles to remind me whenever I review
The embodiment of beauty that is you.

Chapter 19: I Fly the Nest

I got wind of a vacancy in another dairy. This was a live-in situation. The pay and the hours were much better than Rathbourne's. I applied and after an interview conducted on my new employer's kitchen doorstep, I was appointed. The herd was much bigger, the system more efficient and no toil for me other than the dairy work.

It had its drawbacks. The Jersey cattle were mostly gentle animals, but there were one or two contrary hoors. One was called Mossesa. Along with having short legs and being cantankerous, her udder was so low the milking apparatus could not be applied until we persuaded her to place her back feet on a four-inch-thick plank. The problem was solved. Indeed, ever afterwards, she would opt to stand on it. Another feature was that every cow was named, and had its personal stall. If a stranger heard us discussing Melba, Myrtle or Mosessa's tits, I'm sure they'd imagine us as maniacs.

During the spring and early autumn milking times when they were out grazing, these intelligent animals would return through the open door of the parlour into exactly their own stall. The reason for their individual names was to record the amount of milk they produced. This was my chore. I weighed, recorded and emptied the container, keeping pace with the two lads who were engaging and disengaging the milking appliances. Another reason for the record was to evaluate the particular Jersey strain, as quite a lot of the cows had been purchased on the island of Jersey.

I had three workmates, Johnny Daligan being the steward. He was a small, good-humoured, rotund character from Tipperary. He lived with his wife and family on the top story of this large, four-storey Edwardian house, a wood-built fire escape giving access. My quarters were a one-room extension built under this fire escape and was about fourteen feet long and eight wide. It was furnished with a table and two chairs, a single bed, and a hot and cold wash basin. The concrete floor was bare. The window allowed linear bands of daylight through the stairs. It was draughty and always seemed cold. In other words, it was beautiful. At last I was free from the order and discipline of family life.

Cyril was a workmate, a tall good-looking fellow of about twenty-four at the time. He was also very intelligent and never ceased to let you know he was. He was a lovely singer and during the milking would sing songs of the great musicals of the time, including Oklahoma. Cyril had been unlucky; when young he was discovered to have TB. He was hospitalised for three years and fully cured, though minus a lung.

The third workmate was Paddy Madden, or Whackser as he was known. I knew him quite well, as he lived opposite us in the village. He too was in his early twenties, a low-sized, dark curly-haired chap, always in good humour. He was a bit of a hypochondriac, ever asking us how he looked, or complaining of a pain here or there. He'd wonder aloud if he looked pale, or if we thought he was losing weight. He loved a gamble, confining himself to the toss school which operated around midday of a Sunday at the stile in the centre of the village.

This stile was only a few yards from Whackser's house. Whackser was lucky, and Whackser was smart. When he'd have a run of luck, like when tossing the halfpennies and he'd get a sequence of heads, he was known to take out his hanky and mop his brow. On the button, Molsey, his elder sister, would come to the door and shout, "Yer dinner's on the table, Paddy." Of course, when picking up the winnings Whackser would make profound apologies before scarpering. I remember one particular Sunday as Whackser was about to do a runner, this after having rooked Jimmy Bulger, an innervate gambler. In a blinding act of generosity, Whackser proffered Jimmy two bob. Jimmy looked at it in disgust and told him, "Keep it and get a mass said for yerself." Whackser was devastated.

Up to this time I had progressed from reading comic cuts to *Treasure Island, Coral Island, Kidnapped* and other classics. This taste had been encouraged by that school book, *Red Cloud*. Now I was a reader and a signed-up member of the *Wide World Club*. This was a magazine that catered for eejits like myself who spent too much time daydreaming. The stories were supposed to be true adventures, and introduced me to the wider world. They were about the wartime ordeals experienced by soldiers and sailors. There were also stories of lost cities found, and then lost again. Anyway, I never secured the door of my cell during the day, as Cyril and Whackser would have their tea breaks in it. It happened that I had left my *Wide World* membership badge and scroll on the table and Cyril came across them. What a slagging I got. He told everybody I was an eejit, and furthermore, that I believed in fairies. I was annoyed, but I knew he was only baiting me. Anyway, I was never smart enough to get even. That was 1951, the year I bought a bicycle.

I open my eyes and sense the earth's singing vibes

Leaving me replete in its redolence and hues

And making me so aware that a God of life abides

And how marvellous just to be alive.

Chapter 20: Resolution

Thursday and every other Sunday were my days off, so twice a week I would catch the bus into town and go to the cinema. Thursday night, I'd go to where the best film was showing. I recall on Eden Quay one night, running after the departing bus. While sprinting by the Del Rio café and pulling my hand from my pocket to grab the platform bar, I heard something clanging and disappearing down the grid into the basement. It was the key to my room. At midnight, I had to break the window of my room to gain entry, leaving it dark and dismal as a result of the cardboard I used to block the hole.

On Sunday nights I would go to the Regal Rooms, all the other cinemas having been booked out. I'd be in the queue early and be entertained by the doorman marching up and down bellowing, "Standin' room only now at wan an ate." This standing room was on the balcony which ran around and above the seated area. I believe it was in the Regal Rooms that I was introduced to Jacque Thati in the wonderful Mr. Hulot's Holiday, a film without dialogue, and the funniest film ever.

Lorcan, our eldest brother, had by now a new job. It was in a car assembly works. He had also bought a car, an Austin Ruby which cost him thirty pounds. It was beautiful – small and square, with a light brown colour and the inside beautifully upholstered. It was a four door with the edging around the doors elaborately filigreed in gold. This being 1951, the car was a 1936 model with no self-starter. That function was achieved by a magneto, activated by the rapid winding of the permanently fixed brass starting handle. The car engine, probably due to age, had developed an unfortunate habit of cutting out when held up in traffic or slowed down for any reason. In other words, there had to be a co-driver. This important function was allocated to me whenever I was available, which meant me leppin' out smartly to wind the handle every time she conked out.

Lorcan also had a girlfriend, and I used to feel a right eejit with them in the front chatting and me sitting silently in the back, ready like the spare wheel for whenever my services were required. Indeed, every time I'd cycle home for a freshly baked cake of bread or my laundry, Lorcan would pounce like a vulture with, "Are ye in a hurry?"

I remember one evening he invited me to the cinema. "Great picture," he promised. "It's on in the New Elec and I have tickets," he enthused. I was gravely suspicious but, studying his deepening frown, for personal safety I thought it best to comply. Of course, then he tells me Anna, his girlfriend and future wife, was also coming.

It was raining and after several unscheduled stops along the way, we arrived and parked in Talbot Street. "See ye here when we come out," said Lorcan, turning up the collar of his beautiful gaberdine, about to do a runner.

"What about me?" I whinged. "Ye said ye had tickets."

"Oh yeah," he said lamely, "they're for Anna and meself." Then, turning his back to me and groping in his pocket, he perused a few coins. "Here," he said, turning around and handing me eight pence, "that'll get ye into the gods."

Anybody who had the misfortune to experience the gods in the New Elec (with trains at regular intervals making their way in and out of Amien Street, now Connolly Station, on the overhead railway) will be no stranger to earthquakes. The film, They Died with Their Boots On and starring Errol Flynn appeared to be very good, though it shuddered a lot and I could hear nothing. When it was over I raced back to the car in the rain. There was no Lorcan or Anna. They turned up a half hour later having gone for tea and buns in a nearby restaurant.

Sullen and silently I took my seat in the back, and sullen and silently responded to His Lordship's commands when the engine faltered the five or six times on the way home.

Afterwards, and whenever I intended to visit home, if in the distance I saw the car parked outside our cottage, I'd turn around and go elsewhere. Anyway, in the absence of co-drivers he sold the car a few months later and bought another, this one with a self-starter.

Lorcan and Anna Redmond at a Dress Dance in the Metropole, O'Connell St. Dublin c.1953/4.

Around this time my brother Frank, who was fourteen years of age, three years younger than me, left school. He acquired employment with a local farmer called Jackie Donaghue, a gentleman and an excellent employer. Frank, on this particular day, was spraying weeds with a leaking backpack. Having completed the task, he decided to reward himself with a fag. The moment he struck the match he was afire, and only for his presence of mind and a nearby huge water trough, he might have died. His arms were badly scorched, and he had no eyebrows for a couple of weeks, but he completely recovered. The only highlight of the day, as Frank admitted afterwards, was learning how to swim.

It was 1952. The war in Korea ebbed and flowed, and it was there the Ulster Rifles earned high praise for a tactical retreat, allowing a US regiment time to readjust their lines. King George VI died, and by the extent of the mourning, he apparently had been a well-loved monarch.

That same year brought me to the brink of a life-changing decision, again largely influenced by the books I read. I decided I was going to travel the world. I also believe that the isolation from other young fellows of my own age was probably another cause – it prevented me from developing and sharing normal ambitions and dreams, or perhaps from following the same star as other lads I knew. I believe that socially this isolation affected me in a negative way, leaving me inhibited and introverted in certain company, unsure of what to say or how to react. Though loneliness never entered my lexicon of emotions, real empathy would only be found with those of my own working class. Another abnormality, though I have had wonderful friends and workmates, once our paths diverged I would never keep contact. It was the same with girlfriends, even when I'd later heard they had enquired about me.

I digress. These books I read awakened a desire to travel, and not to just anywhere, but all over the world. In short, I bought a globe and an atlas and I, after careful analysis, decided to walk down through the continent of Africa to Cape Town, and then by ship to Argentina. I would then cross the Tierra del Fuego into Chile. From there, northwards all the way up the pacific costal highway to the United States. To secure a visa, I went to the Argentinian embassy, a bungalow in Dublin 4, in or near Leinster Road. Fortunately, I had no passport, though recalling the patient, condescending, pitiful manner in which they tolerated me, I doubt I would have been granted a visa.

There was huge unemployment in Dublin at the time, and when I divulged my plans to my parents they were astounded. "Is it stone mad ye are?" my mother bawled, and she persuaded me to change my mind. So I adjusted my destination to Manchester, Lancashire, though I didn't know a soul in it. As a matter of fact, at the time I probably knew more about Timbuktu.

Lorcan considered joining me as the car assembly works were on a two-day week due to oversupply, and a slow uptake of their product.

To satisfy my mother's concern, I climbed three floors of a dingy recruiting agency in Stephen's Street, but I was the wrong sex – the vacancies were for maids and female kitchen staff.

It was October 1952 at seven o'clock in the evening. I caught the boat train to Dun Laoghaire and in the drizzle, joined the embarkation queue and eventually boarded. Most of the passengers were young and from the country. Travelling in groups, they were loud in bravado until the ship left the shelter of the harbour. Then they became quiet, busy dealing with sea sickness. Sitting on my suitcase on the open deck, the ship was halfway across the Irish Sea before I realised I was now truly on my own.

Psalm 113

Why did the sun never seem to shine on me
Or was I deemed to exist in the shade of taller trees?
I've felt denied when I could not emphasise my entity
As a flower which cannot bloom in the gloom of a canopy of leaves.

Life will exist in the shadow if it strives,
Willed to persist -shall thrust through the leaves
For all life is endowed with the instinct to survive;
And unbowed compete with the tallest trees.

PART 2

Chapter 1: Tentative Steps

It's a primal trait, you know? That cave, a Nave
A safe place; that place you call your home.
It's where you unwind; feel safe to recline
Immune in the womb of your comfort zone.

In Livesey Street, Manchester, at six o'clock that winter morning of 1952, I found myself sheltering from the rain under a railway bridge having blundered there from the boat train. The clogged feet of early starters echoed on the wet pavement until they saw the drowned rat that was me, then diverted their passage to the other side of the street to disappear in the rain.

An elderly passer-by wearing a beret and raincoat stopped and kindly asked if I was alright. I explained I was looking for digs. "Number fifty-one," he pointed. "She takes in lodgers and if she is full she'll send you somewhere else."

I hung around until nine o'clock before approaching the door, which by then was ajar. As I knocked, I became aware of the odour of stale sweat, cigarettes, and fried bread escaping on the humid air. "Come in," squawked a voice. I shuffled down the passage toward what turned out to be a kitchen-cum-dining room, and where an old, grey-haired lady was kneeling at the grate cleaning out the ashes. "How are ye, son?" she smiled, bringing her hand from the grate up to her nose and back to the grate, leaving a glittering string of snot. She was my first landlady, the widowed Mrs. Armstrong.

Half a bed for thirty bob a week was the deal, and as rationing of food and clothing prevailed, coupons must be secured. Mrs. Armstrong directed me to the labour exchange in Salford, a mile or so away. It was also where the coupons and maybe a job would be procured. As I remember, six ounces of meat plus four eggs provided your weekly protein needs. Marge and white bread were plentiful enough, but butter, tea, meat and sugar were severely rationed.

On my way to the labour exchange and a hundred yards from Strangeways jail, I passed a large warehouse-type building. 'Yates Wine Lodge' was the logo on the front, but the notice underneath was the one that caught my eye. It read, 'Vacancies. Apply within.' Bearing that in mind, I continued on my way to the labour exchange where, without any bother, I secured coupons and a social security card. On my way back, I speculated on a tenner a week job. That was the wage that would allow me to save a few quid. At Yates and first through a hatch and then through the door, a receptionist invited me into the office where I met this friendly, sympathetic man. This gentleman put paid to my tenner a week. Firstly, he wouldn't believe I was eighteen and suggested I was fourteen and had run away from home. The next shock was when he offered me a job at a fiver a week. I was disappointed but I accepted it, thinking to myself it would do until I found a better paying one.

Livesey Street, where I now resided, was one of thousands of similar Manchester streets with rows of terraced three-up and two-down, brick-built houses. Most of the streets had one or two corner shops providing the bare essentials. Mrs. Armstrong had five lodgers. I was the sixth. Two main bedrooms had a single and double bed. I shared a bed with Tommy White, a grand, big, fair-haired chap from Ballyhaunis. Chris, a dark-haired, short, stoutish lad from County Meath, had the single bed. The room was about eight feet wide and fourteen feet long, with a wardrobe and one chair – the chair which Chris had commandeered for his fags and matches and for hanging his towel. The dark shiny linoleum covering the floor completed the furnishings.

Chris was a pleasant enough fellow, though he had this peculiar habit of blowing his nose and clearing his throat into his towel. The excretions were intently scrutinised and the towel briskly chaffed and hung back on the chair. Needless to say, we took no liberties with Chris' towel no matter how bad the condition of our own. I later discovered Chris was classified as Cock Lodger.

I didn't sleep well that first night nor many a night afterwards.

Unfamiliar noises intruded. Over our street and hundreds of others ran a mainline railway. It wasn't so much the odd train rushing by, but the shunting which continued for hours every single night. The second disturbance was what I thought was a burglary, a persistent hammering of the upstairs window at six thirty a.m. Neither Chris nor Tommy moved so I thought I'd take a gander. Looking out the window, I saw further down the street a lad with a long pole tapping an upstairs window. I later found out he was the knocker up. For a few pence a week, this fellow would go from street to street in his manner, awakening the residents at half past six. Though I often wondered, I never enquired how he managed if a client wanted to rise at half past five.

Three other Mayo lads shared the other large room. It was also a single and a double bed. The thirteen-year-old niece of the landlady used a small room off the first landing. The landlady herself used the front parlour as a bedroom.

All the Mayo lads worked together on the lump, and were digging trenches by the square yard for the electrical authority. Charlie McLoughlan, a big, black-haired, gruff fellow, appeared to be the boss. Charlie was astute, for he was the one who made the deals with the main contractors, assessing the quality of the ground to be excavated and then striking a price.

It was Charlie who classified Chris as Cock Lodger. It was because Chris, from County Meath – a short, stout fellow, was longest there, and was trusted by the landlady. Employed as a bus conductor, Chris never got drunk, well, hardly ever, and he was always polite and reserved. The landlady would discuss her problems with Chris, and Chris diplomatically passed on whatever displeased her.

From the outset, Chris made me aware of the primal structure of the lodging fraternity, and gave me the number one warning – Cock must ever be regarded with respect. One must be ever so polite to Cock. One never complained within earshot of Cock, for a casual derogatory remark could have devastating consequences. Cock fulfilled many roles – he spied, advised, and blackballed to ensure his personal comfort and domination.

A potential rival was rapidly blackened. Clever Cock, not as yet sharing her bed, was ruthless. He'd create a friendly atmosphere, then subtly comment on the quality of the digs to draw adverse opinion from an honest whinger – the victim, who in no time would find himself on the step with his bag.

Then there are the aspiring Cocks. They are easily copped. He was the one who compares the amount on your plate to his. Less meant a possible loss of position in the hierarchy. He's the one who smarmily lauds the landlady, after she serves up crap. He, the one who makes silly suggestions in her presence such as everybody should make their own bed, or help with the washing up. He'd say anything to ingratiate himself. A word in the real Cock's ear suggesting he's being undermined had two beneficial ends. It distracted Cock from us as he demolished his ambitious opponent. Of course, Chris never saw or was aware of himself as Cock, and most certainly was not in any of those categories.

This Yates building where I was now an employee was their main wine depot. It was where the wine was stored in giant vats allowing it to mature, though under strict customs control. This was before being bottled and labelled, eventually to be distributed to the company's many pubs and restaurants around Lancashire and Yorkshire. The staff later told me that the customs were reaping more profit out of it than the company through the duty they charged.

My job was as a helper on one of their lorries which provisioned the outlets. Monty was my driver – an ever-smiling sixty-year-old and extremely decent. And as his name suggests, a living image of Montgomery himself. The truck was a normal Leyland diesel in which I froze in that first winter, the cab not equipped with a heater. The truck, a flat back with a badge front and back signalling max speed of twenty miles per hour. The wine we transported was in cases with twelve bottles to a case. There was Tarragona from Spain, plus ports and sherries from Madeira and the Canary Islands. The Australian whites and reds were less expensive, though were extremely popular. I didn't drink so I cannot comment on the flavours. Actually, I was just learning to smoke, so there – I was already on the road to ruin!

Chapter 2: Learning the Ropes

Tea time in No. 51 was chaotic – four starving Navvies and myself all clambering to use the cooker, with Chris and Mrs. Armstrong always being AWOL at this hour. A good job too, for language was choice and tempers short as pots and pans boiled and bubbled. Turn your back for a second and your pottage was gone, and someone else's in its place.

Here, Charlie was also the boss, not by a cuff or a kick, and neither by rude language, but when he stalled for a moment with pot in hand waiting impatiently for me or you to remove your pot from the gas ring, he nudged, pushed and tut-tutted until you retreated in exasperation. One learned either to dine early or wait until the heavy gang had finished.

The tiny kitchen area consisted of a couple of cupboards and this ancient gas cooker. A square brown shallow earthenware sink with a cold tap served all purposes, including washing and shaving. A toilet existed outside in the tiny yard.

The Mayo lads seemed to have the inside track at the butchers, judging by their fare – fatty, bony meat nearly every day, while I existed on powdered egg and sliced pan. That was my fare until I eventually heard one of Yates' drivers had a source, and had become an egg smuggler. Every Saturday he supplied me with a dozen eggs. Each night these Mayo lads bolted their dinners, washed and shaved, and then disappeared to some pub or other, though I never, ever saw or heard them returning rowdy or drunk.

That was the kitchen routine, with few exceptions. A coal fire was alight in the grate and the radio on the mantelpiece available to those, like me, who could not afford to go out. In 1952 there were few TVs available, especially for lodgers, though in nearly every place I lodged there was a piano which apparently nobody played. All in all, No. 51 was good digs.

Mrs. Armstrong was second-generation Irish, and had lost her husband and brother in World War One. In the Second War, one of her two sons, an Irish Guard, lost his life in Malaya. Her remaining son, a fine big fellow who was married and living nearby, was also a victim, suffering from nerves. She bore her cross without whinging or whining, accepting it all as the will of God. Whenever she got an audience, photos would be unearthed and proudly displayed. As a landlady, on a scale of one to ten I'd give her nine for common decency.

A funny thing about skins beginning their lodging careers. They tended to regard them as home – a refuge and an escape from the realities of this different culture. A foolish mistake, for digs were a business venture contrived to make money. The most successful lodgings pack in the maximum for the least cost. If the area is booming, there's always a clamour for digs. Consequently, no parlour for Paddy – it's the bed or the pub!

Landladies, as I was to discover, came in many categories. The brutally efficient, whose only objective was money, producing a fare which could be predicted a year in advance. Meals devised so as leftovers were recycled daily. Meals served within the hour and with no appeal for latecomers.

The second were equally rapacious, but without the efficiency of the first. The remainder were mostly housewives supplementing a low or irregular income by taking guests with as little intrusion as possible. Good digs, or digs termed as 'mighty' were discussed in reverent tones.

A man in good digs was recognised instantly by his relaxed, contented demeanour, his superior confident gait, and the cleanliness of his clobber. The contents of his lunch box too, was a positive sign. Good digs achieved more in stabilising wandering Irish migrants than a million sociologists. Often, he married his landlady or her daughter, or perhaps a suitable neighbour's daughter would be found for him.

If you were one of the lucky to be selected as a lodger in a one-guest house, life was bliss – good food, access to the parlour, your wet clothes dried, a hot water bottle secreted early, your pyjamas aired before bed. Many's the lad in this euphoric state gave up carousing, even at the risk of being accused as being 'Englified' by jealous, scornful, former boozing pals. Putting your name down for the next vacancy was a waste of time. Nobody left good digs. If his profession or vocation required him to travel, his bed was sacrosanct. No way would he be supplanted. After a week's exposure to common fare he'd return, slavering for attention.

I remained as a helper with Yates for six months, a job which I enjoyed. It gave me an understanding of what the poor unfortunate Mancunians had gone through from 1939 to 1945. The amount of bomb damage was frightening, and yet there was little complaining about their lot. There was one particular ruin that I can never forget. It was in Salford I saw the remains of the great court of the Assizes, its columns lying awry like prints I saw of Rome after the vandals sacked it. It more than any other must have undermined belief in an indestructible establishment, yet what could a civilised people do but carry on.

It was here in Livesey Street we celebrated the Coronation with a street party, as did all the streets, although not all on the same day. The tables were laden with cake and tomato sandwiches, with sweets for the children. But not as much as a bottle of stout or a light ale was in sight.

I liked the Lancashire people, they were friendly and witty, pulling your leg while repeating Irishisms. The lorry would bring me to Blackburn and Bolton one day, Blackpool the next, Leeds and Bradford on Wednesdays. To Liverpool on Thursdays which was where the decent manager provided us with a slap-up meal in their high-class restaurant. Fridays were confined to local deliveries. I recall those summer days when delivering to pubs in semi-industrial areas, factories with their windows open and hundreds of voices of the women and girls on assembly lines or on sewing machines singing to *Music While You Work* on the BBC.

At a fiver a week I was just getting by until the manager of one of the local pubs asked me if I would do a bit of night work at weekends, such as collecting glasses. This also included the cleaning up of the ullage, the spillage, and broken glass… all created by inebriated customers when making their point, or during the struggle with bar staff prior to being flung out the door. I'd get a couple of quid, but I was missing the films in the couple of local cinemas, so I gave up the overtime. One feature I came to dislike was the fog. Absolutely filthy, I used to regurgitate soot – soot that blocked my nostrils and left my clothes filthy. Like everything else alien, you accepted and got on with it.

One day I didn't go to work but caught a bus to Chatterton, a district of Manchester on the Oldham road. It was a large building project which had aroused my interest, seen when passing in our lorry. It was a coal-fired Chatterton power station, I learned later. As I entered the site that morning, I saw a row of builders' huts.

Stopping at the first one, I knocked. A small elderly man wearing a hat and with a pipe in his gob opened the door, and we eyed one another. "I'm looking for employment, sir," I announced.

He continued to stare at me, still with the pipe in his mouth, and after a minute muttered, "I'm Jack. C'mon down the road and meet the lads."

That's how I met Jack, aged about sixty. An engineer and a gentleman. He was site boss with International Combustion, a huge engineering company who gave me a job at the lovely wage of eleven pounds per week, sometimes thirteen. That, of course, included working on Saturday and Sunday. The work was much more physical than Yates, with a huge amount of climbing involved. That, I enjoyed immensely, though it was without safety harness or net.

Many a fright I got when astride a pipe thirty or forty feet above ground, struggling to get my spanner to tighten a remote nut. One scare gave me nightmares for years afterwards. This work involved installing heavy, two-foot diameter piping, each length no more than four feet. Joints had to be sealed with gaskets. What went through these pipes I never asked, but I assumed it was powdered coal. Anyway, the pipes led into the gigantic burners.

Our risky work earned us three pence an hour height money, plus a distinct feeling of superiority over the lesser mortals on the site. Other contractors that were working alongside us installing huge pieces of ducting had two men fall to their deaths – units being lifted by a crane jammed for a moment and then swung clear to sweep them off a girder. This happened when we were having lunch in the site canteen. I avoided looking at the bodies. The site was closed for a day, and work continued next day without any visible signs of increased safety.

Giving

Some give because it's natural, some give to atone
Some give a hand-out to be the big showman,
To give should be to comfort, to a friend or an unknown
And always unconditional; always without demands.

You feel good when you help some guy
That man that needed a helping hand
But remember they have feelings – don't act like God on high
Give like it's a pleasure. Give and then you scram.

Chapter 3: Ned Turns Up

The foreman was Tommy from Slough, a lean, ever-smiling chap aged about forty. He was also a decent skin. He had been living with a few others in a house belonging to Tommy McGovern, a high-octane fellow from Tipperary. Tommy McGovern, aged about thirty, was a cranky, smallish, good-looking fellow with brown curly hair. He was the ganger of our team. He would create rows and arguments with other contractors, up to the point of assault and mostly over nothing, though he didn't argue or fight with us. This Tommy was now in the process in bringing his new wife over from Ireland to begin their married lives. That was the reason why our foreman, Tommy from Slough, and the others had to vacate the house.

Tommy secured this small apartment in Moss Side, a once salubrious area of Manchester. He invited me to share this room which had a fireplace and two single beds. I accepted Tommy's offer, though only after covertly ascertaining from the lads that he wasn't bent, though on that subject I was totally naïve. So, it was goodbye to Livesey Street and Mrs. Armstrong. This new apartment, or to be truthful – room, was equipped with a gas cooker and a sink. A bathroom existed outside on the landing. It was what is now described as a bedsit. I used to bring home a cement bag of coal I nicked from the site railway. How we didn't burn the place to the ground is due to the Almighty.

Our Polish landlord – a very heavily moustached, understanding, tolerant gentleman whom we only saw on Fridays – was at that time in the throes of his first nervous breakdown. A former member of the Polish Air Force, he'd saved every penny to secure a down payment on this fine, four-storey house, just as the West Indians had also found Moss Side.

Though housing was incredibly scarce, once this noisy, uninhibited race became your neighbour, your property's value fell to zilch. Covertly, I used to study them through the curtained window.

From around five p.m. they'd begin to assemble on the pavement, greeting one another as if they had just returned from outer space. Twenty, thirty, forty would gather, others bawling from windows halfway down the street. Often this would continue until two in the morning. The pavement ritual was irritating, even intimidating. Passage was difficult. To avoid the throng, one must walk in the street. It was their way, and harmless enough, though as property prices fell, more came and a ghetto was created. Locally, Mancunians were resentful of the 'invasion' – this behaviour was just not English. Though some opined it was when Paddy moved from zero up one notch in the social scale.

The site where we worked was served with a rail spur leading to large railway sidings. It facilitated the coal wagons which would fuel the station. (This was from where I nicked the coal!) At that time, there was little rail traffic except for a steam engine meandering up and down, apparently breaking in new crews. Tommy, crossing the track with a piece of angle iron on his shoulder, was struck by the engine and immediately hospitalised in a pretty bad way. A few weeks later when Tommy left hospital, he returned to Slough to recover. This left me on my own, though paying rent only for myself. The landlord was very understanding, but after six weeks he demanded full money. A week or two later I came home from work, and on that evening, was informed by the landlord that a visitor had been enquiring about me and would call back later.

A knock on the door revealed Ned Madden, a neighbour from home. Ned was a brother of Whackser, whom I had worked with in the Dublin dairy. Prematurely grey and with a severe cast in his eye, he nevertheless had a demeanour which oozed decency and consideration. It also disguised his exceptional audacity. He told me he was on his way back to Selby in Yorkshire where he said he had a great job, and what's more, that he'd soon have a better one in a sugar beet factory.

"So, what are you doing here?" I asked.

"Your mother asked me to drop in to see if you were dead or alive," he grinned. At that time, before, and ever afterwards I regularly wrote home, a few pounds accompanying the letter.

That night we went to Bellevue, a great entertainment park where Jack McManus, the English wrestling champion, was putting on a show. Ned's visit, which lasted three days, resulted in me promising to join him in Selby in a week or two. Over the next while, the more I thought about it the less I liked the idea in that I had a good job a job which I liked. But I had given my word and surprised my boss Jack by giving a week's notice.

I left Manchester for Selby, expecting Ned to meet me at the station. It was nine o'clock at night when I arrived to find there was no Ned, though I did remember him mentioning Buller Street. There being no taxi at the deserted station of this little town, I began walking. It must have been eleven that same night, when I knocked on the door of No. 24 Buller Street. Mrs. McLoughlan, as she later introduced herself, invited me in. She was a huge, stout, smiling woman of about sixty. Though I mentioned Ned, she still had no vacancy. But her grandson Nigel was on night duty in a canning factory, thereby leaving his bed vacant each night. If that suited for a couple of days, it was available. It suited, and after a splendid supper she showed me the bedroom.

It was a small and comfortable room though decorated with lurid wallpaper – the word boudoir came to mind. Heavy, colourful drapes adorned the window. Hanging my one and only suit in the wardrobe, a certain garment caught my eye… a terylene or poplin robe. It was hard to miss, being bright yellow like the wallpaper. I felt a bit uneasy but nevertheless I slept well. Ned and another lodger slept in the converted attic, both at this moment, in the landlady's bad books.

Hail fellow well met, Ned, who I didn't meet until next morning, said he'd forgotten about me, though he wished he hadn't. For at the greyhound track in Leeds where he'd spent the evening, he'd never backed a winner. "And the reason for the landlady's bad books?" I asked. Apparently Ned and John, both from Dublin, were in the attic smoking when one of them threw his fag end out through the skylight, it landed on a passing lady's hat. She reported it – hence the police. Their speculative eyes watched me, wondering if I would be sleeping in their bed the following week. They were eventually persuaded to visit the victim's house and apologise, it resulted in her dropping the complaint.

I found the landlady an excellent cook; the food was wholesome and plentiful. Her speciality was Yorkshire Pudding. Meat served was generally horse or a tinned variety of some animal or other – she could not be blamed for that. Pudding followed dinner. Then, homemade scones and tea completed the meal. Even at the monstrous sum of three pounds ten per week, it was worth it.

Nigel, about eighteen, was slight and pale, a petulant individual whom the landlady idolised. And brother, did he take advantage! Nigel threw tantrums at the slightest excuse, at times throwing tantrums for *no* excuse. He even complained about Ned with me present! Was this a warning? He hardly spoke to me at all. When my week was up, John of the attic, deciding I wasn't endangering his bed, went home to Dublin for a few days. So, I moved to the attic. And when John returned Nigel was beginning his night shift. Again, I was saved. When I believed I was on my last day, Nigel relented and agreed on sharing his room.

The first night, I slept like a log. Second night I wake up to find my willie in Nigel's hand. This was trauma, big time. Should I scream for help? Strangle him and claim assault? Troubled by those thoughts I turned and delivered an elbow into his snot. A yelp was followed by silence. Next morning, he had a black eye. On querying, his gran said he'd walked into a door. The experience taught me to distrust the sharing of beds, and ever afterwards when circumstances were such that I had to share, I always slept under the sheet on the mattress.

Selby was a nice little town, bisected by the tidal River Ouse. There was a shipbuilding enterprise engaged in the building of deep-sea trawlers. My time there must have been before the development of universal welding, for how the locals put up with the noise of the riveters is extraordinary. The racket of three or four of those automatic tools working together could easily be heard two miles away.

The town also held a market every Wednesday. It had a paper mills with a recycling plant, giving employment to hundreds. The town had a vegetable cannery. The sugar beet factory was also employment friendly, even during the off season — it demanded a large maintenance staff. Of course, through Ned's wonderful wisdom, I ended being employed in the Maltings which had only a staff of three, and operated a six-hour, four-day week, and the pay lousy. The premises was a long, two-storey building with a gas-fired kiln at one end.

In the making of this malt, the previously soaked barley grain would be spread evenly on the upper wooden floors and left for three days, with it being raked regularly as the grain budded. That's where I came in. For a pittance, I would spend a few hours each day at this boring lark, before shovelling the lot into the kiln for it to be roasted and then bagged for the breweries. I resigned after three weeks.

Before my sojourn in the Maltings, Ned had procured a different job and was now employed in the paper mills at a good wage. I, on arriving home from the Maltings that first evening, accused Ned of misleading me, and I called him a rude name. This set him laughing and sniggering for half an hour. Apparently, he found my outrage the funniest thing ever. He was such an easy-going joker I forgave him. Our landlady's husband, Peter, introduced me to a man who was in charge of the maintenance in the paper mills, who, when I asked him, gave me a job at ten pounds for a five-day week, also with the promise of "looking after me."

The beet factory opened shortly afterwards, and Ned jacked his good, steady job in the paper mills to work in it. His girlfriend and future wife Dolly, a lovely friendly girl, came over from Dublin and she also got a job in the factory.

"What's the factory like?" I asked Ned.

A reverential look crept over his face as he intoned, "Fabulous."

Shortly after, and much to the disgust of the decent man who gave me my job, I packed in my boring but well-paid job and joined Ned and John, his roommate, in the sugar beet factory. I also left my good digs to live in the camp.

The road is long, a road that leads but to the grave

For those with nothing but a prayer

Still, from town to town we act out the same old charade

Wasted futile lives—lost souls from God knows where.

Chapter 4: Happy Campers

Ned's pal, the fair-haired John, was aged about twenty-two. He was an intimidating fellow, big and sturdy. He had been a student in a seminary when he fell in love, and was now saving to get married. Saving was a polite word for being miserable. His approach being glib, smiling and conspiratorial, was designed to dismantle your defence, before going straight into your ear-hole with, "Era razor blade?" or, "Where's your soap?" or, "Any smokes on ye?" or, "Giv'us a loan of your towel." And he'd get quite upset when you refused. The other lads copped him on too, and would play malicious jokes on him like filling his rubber boots with water, nailing his coat to the wall, or perhaps hiding one of his shoes. Yes, it was funny, but he began to blame me.

Anyway, at this juncture he and Ned had developed a side-line. Instead of being punters, they now operated as bookies at several greyhound tracks in the vicinity. In the beginning their enterprise was small-time, though Ned swore the money to be made was unbelievable. This statement, based on Ned's previous exclamations, I took with a grain of salt.

From the outside, the camp living quarters appeared as oversized Nissan huts, though inside the dorms were centrally heated and spotless clean with twenty beds in each. The walls were painted green, and the floors polished daily. Each bed provided with its own locker. The sheets changed weekly. Showers, baths, and hot water were in abundance.

The canteen was the pits. The problem was poorly cooked food. Amateur cooks resulted in us on the way to our first stomach ulcer. The sugar beet campaign lasted for four to five months, so a professional cook was never going to chuck his or her job to do shift work on the short-term. The food was badly cooked. I mean, jam tarts half doughy, veg overcooked! Breakfast was powdered scrambled egg and watery tea. When I queried this pale mess, I thought they were joking when they said it was egg.

Yet there was still a bunch of wheedling, scrounging Cocks competing for recognition. They were forever searching for a service or stroke that might deem themselves special, like clearing off tables or sweeping the floor while the man who was paid to do it was dozing in a chair. All their conniving was a gesture of solidarity with the cook on duty. Then one evening it all ended when the Alsatian they called the manageress put the skids under them.

I enjoyed the camp environment with its diversity of people. There were Scottish, Geordies, plus Welsh and English. A number of decent young English lads were just out of the army having completed their National Service, finding their feet and a few quid before deciding what to do with the rest of their lives. And there were the wild, uninhibited young fellows from the north, south, and west of Ireland. Apparently, it was an annual pilgrimage for the Irish, a money spinning interlude from their small farms and coastal fishing.

Other itinerants came and went or were ejected, usually for kicking up a racket after their first week's pay. A supervisor told me the camp was a temporary refuge for the down and outs. They would last no more than a fortnight before getting the heave. Actually, there was one fellow, a gentle lad aged about twenty and always dressed in some shade of green. He was known to everybody as Robin, though he was Charles on his pay slip. The grapevine said he'd been rejected for National Service. I wondered about the name Robin until one day I saw him practicing with a small bow and one arrow. It was a Lucky Bag outfit; the arrow flew no more than twenty feet. I had a feeling Robin was bent. Anyway, he disappeared after a month – the lads said he went back to a forest in Sherwood.

A couple of quare hawks moved into our billet – a large, handsome, fair-haired fellow from Wexford and his mate from Derry, he a handsome, black-haired, brooding, unsmiling fellow. This pair, in their late twenties, had attitude which included superiority. If they responded at all to our hello or goodnight, it was with grunts. At night in the billet they never conversed with the other lads, retaining their resentful, disdainful, covert attitude to all and sundry.

A month later and on payday, this taciturn pair left for town as many others did. They returned a few hours later in evening suits. Yes, evening dress! Paddies in dress suits! Not only that, they each had an exquisite lady on their arm, they too in evening gowns. They appeared and acted like film stars. They escorted their young ladies around the factory as if they owned it, occasionally nodding or motioning toward us as if we were zoological specimens. Having sated the ladies' curiosity, they embarked in the waiting taxi. This caused consternation. Their behaviour was intensely discussed without a logical conclusion.

At three o'clock, three hours after curfew, we were awakened by a great furore. There was shouting and crashing noises. The sound of running footsteps, howls of pain, ferocious oaths and bloodthirsty threats. The mystery men had returned and were in a bad mood. Under the influence of strong liquor, they broke down the front door, trashed the night security staff, and then invited all-comers. With great difficulty, the police eventually removed them and that was the last we saw of them. Rumour had it they were deserters from the Irish Army who had then joined the British one. Apparently it didn't qualify either, and they deserted it. Their sojourn in jail seemed to have made things worse.

By this time Ned and John were in the best of form. Actually, their behaviour was superior – self-satisfied, like that of successful businessmen. Their venture as bookies had become a grand little earner. Indeed, so flush were they that they couldn't be bothered working overtime. Ned told me they were taking the odd chance at the tracks. They were gambling themselves, using, of course, their imagined superior knowledge and dodgy inside information on the runners. Then, as time progressed, one night in Pontefract their luck ran out. Having taken a chance on the first race and winning, they tried the same stroke on the next race.

It happened that the other bookies were giving the shortest of odds on the favourite. The lads decided to give fours, which encouraged nearly all punters at the meeting to bet with them. The favourite won, resulting in Ned and John having to flee for their lives, owing so much money that they were both on the boat for Dublin the following night. Years later when recalling the incident as a guest at Ned's wedding to Dolly, we laughed at the good of it.

There were some grand lads in the factory, like the young Gaeilge speaking O'Malley brothers from Connemara who told me great stories of their simple lives. Living not far from the sea, they along with their neighbours would assemble every autumn. In a joint exercise they'd bring their curraghs to the beach to fish for herring and mackerel before drying or smoking them. Each night for about a week, they would sleep under their upturned curraghs after having a good snort of póitín. This was their routine until they had sufficient fish to see them through the winter. They also told me that when they were children, and on very cold mornings before setting off for school, their mother would give each a couple of spoons of póitín. She said it was to keep the "hate inim."

The decent Costello brothers from Galway came each year, as well as a decent gang from Donegal. Those lads worked a lot of overtime. Barges brought beet by the hundreds of tons to the factory complex by means of a canal which was connected to the River Ouse. The lads in the barge hold used beet forks to move the beet from the corners to where the crane could grab them. It was handy work.

Of course, there was a bit of rancour going on. A big, hulking, morose fellow from Galway was the Stevedore, at least he thought he was. An easy-going local man was in charge of the offloading, and when he wanted men to work overtime he would ask this big fellow who he knew and trusted for many years to arrange X number of men.

Now, the big fellow had relatives also working in the factory, relatives who also came every year. He never selected these relatives because of some long-standing family dispute. It eventually exploded one night when, after a session in the pubs and on the walk home along the canal, the two groups ran into one another. The mixture of curses in Gaeilge and Bearla was educational, and such enmity I never witnessed before or since.

Chapter 5: Fresh Woods

In Scunthorpe, Lincolnshire, pound notes were used as toilet paper, or so I was told. On that supposition and it being near the end of the beet campaign, I packed my case and left Selby, bound for Frodingham Road, Scunthorpe, where I had been told digs would be found. What a joint! Appleby and Frodingham steel works attracted thousands of hopeful transients, most who seemed to reside in these digs on the wide avenue type Frodingham Road. In No. 138 the beds never grew cold, with about eight skins to each room, the clientele of all colours and creeds.

There were queues for the toilet. There were queues for breakfast and for dinner. Indeed, only for half the lodgers were in bed having been on night duty, a queue would have formed outside the front door.

The dining table facilitated sixteen, and sliced pan the panacea. At breakfast, several of these pans would be strategically positioned so starving lodgers would pounce and stuff themselves. Then, when your powdered egg and watery tea appeared, you were already nearly full and quickly departed. Actually, you felt so happy to have had anything to eat you forgot your frustrations. Dinner followed the same pattern. 'Herself', a small, thin red-headed woman of about forty with a blank expressionless face which discouraged communication, would appear with a bucket of mustard-coloured liquid that she called soup. I never tasted anything like it before or since, though it was hot and plentiful. Bloated stomachs rarely accepted all of dinner, which invariably was mashed potato and a tasteless sausage. Procedures ran so smoothly I'd swear this lady invented mass production.

This was category one. Though there were drawbacks! She never slept Thursday or Friday nights. She would be too busy watching the front and back doors for heads doing a runner. Professionals were difficult to catch. An experienced skin intent on a moonlit flit wore double clothing out the evening before. He would disrobe the surplus in a public lavatory and then, for a bob, stow his parcel in left luggage at the bus or railway station. His remaining clobber was easily concealed upon him or distributed among pals going out in the morning. That would be the last she saw of them. The skull who tried to sneak out would nearly always be caught, his belongings held for ransom until he coughed up.

Being there for only two weeks I did not have time to study Cock, though the crowd was so dense I'd probably never find him. Anyway, I was now employed by George Wimpey. My job on the building site was shovelling clay into a lorry.

At half past eight a lorry would reverse into a mountain of clay and rubble that was the result of the site clearance. The driver would shout, "All right, Pat?" and open his *Daily Mirror* and sit in the cab for the hour and half it took me to load. It was then break-time. The lorry would depart and return within an hour. I would reload it and it was lunchtime. This was the routine day-in, day-out for a month; four truck loads per day. The driver was a nice, friendly fellow who at times brought me to the council dump where he tipped the load.

The only point of interest on the site was the method of building. The houses were for coal miners, I was told. The walls were of a composite of something called breeze and used like concrete though not nearly as heavy. The gang would erect the completed shuttering panels for the front, back, and both gable ends of the semi-detached houses. Assisted by a crane, they would manhandle them into position and lock them. A house of panels built on day one. Next morning the breeze came and the cavities were filled. That was day two. While having to wait several days until the composite set, the team, again with the aid of a crane, would lift and gunter into position the already constructed roof of another duplex. Then they moved on to releasing the panelled frame of another built duplex, perhaps cleaning and oiling those panels (which ensured the composite didn't stick to them). The part-finished houses were devoid of anything that could be called decorative. Nakedly grey, I'm sure they were very cold places to live in, though they were already home to thirty or forty families.

The carpentry which included interior framework to support the upper floors, window frames, hanging of doors and flooring along with kitchen cupboards was completed by an Irish subby. It was here I discovered the country lads were far cleverer than the likes of myself. The foreman was a carpenter, his staff were townies and some of his relations, they did the carpentry with the only visible tools which were a spirit level, a hammer and a saw. The foreman registered them as carpenters though I was told none had served their time. After a couple of months of this guidance and exposure they would be accepted on any site as at least shuttering carpenters. I do not know how they arranged their City and Guilds certificate or if one was needed, but the end result was far better pay and more interesting work than just labouring.

I found the house construction a great team effort. Composed of about a dozen team members, all English, they earned three lovely big white fivers per week as opposed to my two. It was good pay for good workers. Before I left this site, I queried the name Wimpey. My driver told me with a straight face, 'We-Intend-Making-Profit-Every-Year.'

By this time, I had found clean digs outside Scunthorpe town, though no parlour for Paddy, and memorable only for the remoteness of the family.

Think deep. Read well the bones before you leap

Ponder the ides before you take Kismet on

For one mistake is fatal with no time to weep

When you burn your bridges-- when you cross your Rubicon.

Chapter 6: Clever Me

Sheffield beckoned. "The crack is mighty," swore the experts. Jobs? "Twenta' pound a week! And bags of overtime," they told me. The question, "Why are you here in Scunthorpe working for nine?" was met with garbled mutterings of being on remand, woman trouble, and court orders.

Havelock Street, Sheffield, was two rows of 19th-century, three-storey houses over basement. These were solidly built, and with granite quoins around doors and windows. I found digs in No. 32, and remained there for about four weeks. The digs didn't even support a Cock, the worst of signs. They were forgettable but for one feature, an archway. Originally it was for your horse and carriage, giving access from the street into a large cobbled courtyard. This yard incorporated the rear of half a dozen houses, and instead of stabling for horses there were a row of outside flush toilets. These toilets were back to back with the next street's toilets. I always felt naked walking across that cobbled yard with my intentions so obvious. Also, even though one brought reading matter, using the toilet was never the pleasurable function I'd previously enjoyed, for the grunts and farts from adjacent stables were too audible and disconcerting.

I moved to No. 63 which was Renee McDonald's. It was on the opposite side of our street. She operated a good food and no-frills joint. For three pounds per week, it was a bargain. It had a bathroom upstairs and down. The rooms were clean with three single beds in each room, each having a chair to hang your clothes on. The clientele, though honest, clean and friendly, were not too sophisticated. They were mostly related by marriage and all from County Clare, many of them employed by a descaling company specialising in cleaning the inside of large diameter piping systems. The subject of sex was the usual table conversation, where Renee herself was often personally questioned on her nocturnal activities. Renee's husband, a tiny Scot and a much older man, was an affable, decent skin who had by this time been consigned to a cupboard which he called his 'own room'.

Cock was Conroy, an ever-smiling, dark-haired, handsome fellow of about twenty-seven or eight – clean, suited and presentable at all times, oozing charm and good will to all men. His sexual exploits were legendary, with him having affairs with one or two young ladies who frequented the digs. At supper at ten o'clock each night – yes, we had supper... the second digs I experienced where one could avail of supper, there were always a selection of girls present. Some were handsome, some comely, and one homely. But all were friendly.

Of the two handsome lads, Conroy was a real bohemian and favourite by a mile with all the females. Then there was the black-haired Theo from Longford, a nice, well-spoken fellow though inclined to be self-absorbed – he did go on a bit about his professional parents and their big farm of land. Theo too was a Don Juan, and ever making himself available. Michelle was one of the girls, a beauty who was always tastefully dressed. She was a gentle girl of about nineteen with light brown, short, curly hair and grey weepy eyes – an absolute stunner. This Michelle, employed as a secretary, began to go out with Theo, leaving the field to Conroy.

Invariably, the debate at supper, with me a silent but appreciative voyeur, would be on which one would be Conroy's lucky girl. After a week I found it tiresome, repetitive, and embarrassing, with the half-drunk idiots vocalising their pornographic dreams. Nevertheless, Conroy was an exceptional Cock – he didn't seek the honour, it was imposed, his persona being such he was idolised.

Linda, the homely one aged around twenty, was not beautiful. She had lank hair and was not well dressed. She had evasive, vulnerable eyes that betrayed every passing emotion. It was she who helped Renee set the supper table, ferry the bread and jam from the kitchen, and wash up afterwards. I asked her out with her agreeing immediately. I brought her to the pictures a couple of times and had a cuddle in the hallway afterwards where she, unlike me, was totally relaxed. On mature reflection I think she was on for afters. Afters which never happened.

At that time, in 1954 I was working on a building site for a company called Booths. The pay was good and included the lodging allowance of three pounds ten shillings per week. The only drawback was the site foreman. He was an ex-army officer, a tense, unsmiling, frosty-faced man of about fifty. He did not suggest or ask an employee to do such and such, he ordered, and in a very challenging manner. In hindsight I'm pretty sure he was traumatised with some personal problem, for he never stopped moving, forever walking about the site with his head down as if contesting his personal demons.

On a Friday evening shortly after the period of dating Linda, I got off the bus with a couple of workmates in Havelock Square Station and proceeded to the Elephant Pub. It was half past nine when I arrived at the digs for supper. Opening the door, an eerie silence greeted me. "What's goin' on?" I asked Renee. She told me Linda had being living with an African lad who ended up abusing her, and she got a barring order against him. This very Friday evening he'd turned up at Renee's door in a drunken state declaring he loved her and wanted her back. Linda told him to f**k off and that she was keeping custody of their two kids. With that he upscuttled her with a punch. The police had been alerted and carted off the howling attacker. Linda had now gone to her mother's with the children. "I have the address if you want to see her?" Renee said. It took me all of a half second to decline. Jeepers! Two kids!? Anyway, my focus was now on developing dislike of my employer.

One particular day, in the absence of instructions, we were stacking concrete blocks which had been delivered by a tip up truck that had left them scattered and untidy.

"Who told you to do that?" he bawled, shaking with anger.

"Nobody, sir," I say. "We just went along and done it."

As he stared at me, obviously not seeing, his features changed as if awakening from a sleep, "Carry on," he murmured, and blundered off. By that time, I was fed up with most of my day spent watching out for this foreman. When I'd see him coming I'd duck out the back door of the unfinished house and hide in another until I'd see him on the next lap of his predictable route.

On every site there were subcontractors, groups who took on a portion of the whole. Deals were made with management to plaster the houses, or to do all the interior carpentry, or perhaps the electrics. Concrete gangs laid down the roads. Then there was the smaller fry, like the one I joined. Having gotten fed up with the foreman's distant manner and no duties to perform, we were left hiding around the place. And worse, left with a feeling I was wasting my time, I jacked that well-paid, easy job.

This sub-contractor – a fat, flat-capped, unshaved, untidy fellow – was dressed, every time I saw him, in the same worn, soiled clothes, along with his concrete-stained rubber boots. He had contracted to lay the pathways in from the road to and around a number of houses. Several lads advised me to have nothing to do with this fellow. Nevertheless I, as usual sensitive to sensibility, ignored good advice and with the other four labourers installing the path shuttering, began working on my own, digging the foundations for the next paths. The first Friday I fell for the glib reassuring excuses, "He'll be here on Monday. Don't be worrying! Your money is sound!" Then, when Monday came he didn't turn up. Nor on Tuesday. The ganger man doesn't appear either because I'm told he's at "the other site."

In response to my agitated whimpering, several told me with significance, "The hoors were all from Brighouse," wherever that was. It left me not sorry for myself but feeling a right eejit, particularly when I had worked hard to impress them.

My landlady Renee had now become abrupt, for she too was living on the promise of me getting paid. Going back into town that second Thursday, the bus passed a large pub on the outskirts of the city where in the car-park I saw the thick, ignorant boss exchanging money with the ganger man and his cronies. I had to wait for the next stop before I could get off the bus and rush back to meet that gang of crooks driving out. When seeing me he smiled and accelerated, and that was the last I saw of any of them.

I spent a depressing hour walking back to the digs, wondering what I was going to do for money and what to tell Renee. The only thing I had to sell was a Remington electric razor which had cost me twelve pounds, bought when I was on a day trip to Leeds. A client in the digs who had earlier envied it, would now only part with a fiver. This I gave to Renee, which she snapped ungratefully, leaving me owing her four pounds. She then gave me notice that I was for the road next morning.

This ultimatum was the result of the new faces at the table that evening. She needed my bed. A crew from Manchester had moved in, one of them with a Dublin accent.

"Taking anyone on?" I asked.

"They're hiring local labour out on the site," he said.

Next morning, I set off walking to the site which wasn't too far, though first telling Renee I'd be back for my suitcase later. The site was a huge steelworks which was in the chaos of restructuring. The crowd I was looking for were putting in a new siding for the railway and the consequent wagons of ore.

Here, I proceeded to lie about my long friendship with my man in the digs. After listening a while he employed me. I now proceeded to work hard, twice as hard as the rest of the motley crew of new starters. When lunch time came I had none, though when the whistle went for restart, I did not spare myself, much to the annoyance of my fellows. Luckily it was summer time, and that evening on retrieving my suitcase I headed for the railway station and for a shilling stowed my belongings. I had a wash in the toilets before returning to the square to lie in ambush near the Elephant Pub – a notorious joint and a must for the curious new arrivals.

Yes, the new lodgers turned up and I put the hammer on Paddy Mooney from Bray for a fiver. Well, one could not blame him, so armed with the pound note he gave me I treated myself to a double fish and chips, and at three and six, it did me nicely.

It was the weekend, and the bus station was busy and noisy. Nevertheless, with my belly full and a gabardine mac over my arm I sat down by a bush in the little sunken park. It was time for reflection, or introspection, a procedure I hadn't considered in ages, my actions up to now having always being impromptu. My cogitation rapidly concluded, yes, I was an eejit. A thundering eejit! I further concluded that my hard work to impress had been abused. I felt so stupid. But what could I do? Remarkably, I wasn't a bit sorry for the two weeks' hard work, though I would have enjoyed it more had I got something for it. Our mother had drummed into us that hard, honest toil was to be enjoyed, emphasising, "Aren't you paying homage to God for the gift of life?" So, on that philosophic and optimistic note I moved closer to the bush out of the dew, exhausted, and I actually slept a few hours.

During that second day, Paddy Mooney told me that management were making up a new permanent gang, and that I was a model. And I was. Later that day a big, fair-headed, American born and Mayo reared Pat Welch asked me, "How ye fixed?" to which I replied, "How's your father?" in his western idiom. "Get the train to Derby tomorrow or Monda'," he said with a grin. "Make your way to the gas works and enquire about Grant Lyons engineering, and you'll be right."

"I'll need a tenner of a sub," I say, watching the grin fade and his jaw drop. A dilemma! His instinct was telling him that to give me a tenner might mean the possibility of seeing me again was nil. So, as he perused me his wallet appeared and he handed me a fiver, grunting, "It'll be stopped out of your wages." Did I race back to Havelock Street to fix Renee up with the few quid I owed? No, but I did make a mental note that never, ever again would I be caught in that trap. That night I was a guest of the Salvation Army hostel.

When you are in a hole your role is to get above the parapet

Though soon as you try there's always some guy pulling you back down

Then, fated to scratch around you cuss that guy in choice epithets

While deep down you know there's never going to be that million pounds.

Chapter 7: Dobbins

For the second and third time I saw signs in front of houses stipulating, 'Vacancies. No Irish.' Two houses in Derby's Mill Hill Lane were guilty. It was unfriendly and it tended to humiliate, probably contrived to, though I admit on occasions there would be genuine reason. Many times, I'd seen a drunken Paddy late at night, still attired in concrete-stained clothing and footwear, caterwauling his way toward his digs. It is unsightly and embarrassing for other Irish, and unpleasant to the public. Also, it demeans the landlord's residence.

Unlike the Asians, Africans, and West Indians who were pouring into the country at that time, quite a lot of male Irish migrants were ambitionless. Beyond the euphoria of their escaping the drudgery of farm work and parental control they were aimless, and now with plenty of money would happily fall into the habits and mindset of their already established village or townie friends – that the crack and the 'rake of beer' was the thing.

To that minority, the neglect of health and appearance was accepted as normal, though rarely were they unruly. Nevertheless, it was unfortunately the spectacle most commented upon by the public. That would be the trend until they a met a girl who would bully them into line. The remainder were more to be pitied than despised because basically, they were decent hardworking skins. Was I one of them? Never! One factor our critics overlooked was that most of these lads were exceptionally honest and reliable. They earned big money and spent every halfpenny in the town. In fact, unlike other migrants, we were ideal.

By this time a category one landlord of a town could identify potential trouble fairly easily. If one misbehaved or had done a moonlit flit, it was on the grapevine immediately. That landlord rang around a warning, the culprit identified by personal description or his ration cards, though in 1954 the ration cards had become defunct.

Prejudice, too, was not confined to other people or race. Irish hired Irish on the building sites, especially the lumpers. Indeed, if you were not a townie or from a certain district or county in Ireland, you got no job. While you starved, they would continue shorthanded until a brother or cousin was summoned. On some sites Polish gangs dominated the steel work – particularly in the power stations, a lot of them at that time with hardly a word of English.

I found digs in Millhill Lane, in spite of the anti-Irish warning notices. It is a long cul-de-sac street, more like an avenue which curved like a boomerang. The houses were semi-detached and although once homes for the well off, quite a few of them now offered lodgings, though the sight of the odd, old, pre-war motor parked revealed signs of those still clinging to the past. The house I selected was a category one. Here, the management relied on their instinct and the colour of your money. Feeling uneasy, I only stayed a fortnight because of the excessive traffic, the place being more like a Salvation Army hostel.

At that time (1954), Derby was booming with huge manufacturing projects taking off. There was Rolls Royce, British Celanese, British Railway Carriage and Wagons, also a huge smelter. These companies offered employment attracting hordes of migrants to the area. Rolls Royce eventually rejected the Irish, the reason being they would put newcomers through their training format, and then Paddy quits.

In my place of employment there was a fellow also looking for improved digs, so we joined in a mutual enterprise. He was a tall, dark, handsome fellow, originally from County Carlow. When introduced, I discerned a glint of devilment in the fellow's eye. Somebody whispered he gets narky when he has the sup on him. Another muttered that "there was a wife and children back in Sheffield," and that marital problems had Dobbins on the loose. The ever-grinning Mick Dobbins, as I got to know and to like, travelled light with only a bundle as luggage – an ominous sign.

The digs we found were a category one house, a fine brick one, and very well maintained. The landlord, a stout, middle-aged fellow, showed us the room while excitedly blabbing about the girls from travelling troupe who had just vacated the place, and how he was a daddy to them. The room with its four beds, two of which were vacant, left little space to manoeuvre. That evening we met our roommates, one a neat and tidy, middle-aged man who introduced himself as Sam, and who was employed in a bank. The other was a sunburnt, grey-headed man of about sixty-five; he had lost his wife and just returned from Australia. During the affable formalities he produced this brand-new pair of brown shoes which he had for sale. Dobbins grabbed and examined them, tried them on, and found they fitted perfectly. A price of three quid was agreed which Dobbins pledged to pay when he got his wages.

Come Friday, Dobbins, the shoes, and a week's rent went missing. I then found myself being surveyed and treated with deep suspicion. I saw Dobbins at work next day and was he perturbed? No, he was not. He guffawed until he nearly burst as I described and had to repeat several times, the reactions of a devastated shoe seller and the irate landlord.

I found new digs in 102 Millhill Lane, having decided not to invite that troublemaker Dobbins. It was another category one. The widowed, fiftyish landlady was well dressed and gamey. She showed me the room with its three beds, while a young blond, fresh-faced fellow hovered in the background. Sprawled on one of the beds was me bould Dobbins with a fag between his fingers, grinning like a Cheshire cat. We made our introductions pretending we were strangers, just for the landlady's sake.

This house, comfort-wise, was top-class – fully carpeted and recently repainted and wallpapered to a high standard. There were also copious warning notices plastered around the place of don't do this, that or the other. It felt more like a remand home than a place of rest.

The food was boring; she seemed to have an affinity with spam. Six days a week it was spam for dinner and spam sandwiches for lunch. I detested spam. Dobbins apparently didn't like it either, for as we rushed for the bus one morning he, tearing open the package swore, "F**king spam again!" and flung it through somebody's hedge.

That evening there was an inquisition. The lunch, now in flitters, was displayed on the table. "Whose?" icily demanded the landlady.

"Warn't me anyway," Dobbins cringed.

The young, blond Ukrainian Cock stuck in his tuppence worth, "Only you two bring lunch. Who?" he crossly accused. Dobbins looked at me and I sung dumb. We were immediately put on a week's notice. Our biggest offence, she told us, was giving the house a bad name.

The lodging clientele were respectable English, mostly white collar, very polite and friendly toward us. Not so to the landlady, though, for they were very unhappy with the diktats posted everywhere regulating their every function, and silently threatening dire consequences for non-compliance.

Later that night and a couple of hours after curfew, a well-oiled Dobbins returned to find the door locked. Several times he noisily banged for admittance. Cock was displeased, and turned up pyjamaed and dressing gowned, then foolishly voiced his disquiet. For his impudence he received a clout in the gob. Our notice was reduced to first light. Why that incident was worth mentioning is the satisfaction the regulars enjoyed at Cock's comeuppance. Every one of them expressed their thanks, wishing a perplexed Dobbins all the best.

I eventually found digs which were about adequate, with meatless meals of tomatoes and onions when the landlady remembered – she was over fond of the local pub. At least I had a bed to myself with the sheets laundered regularly.

What a wasteful life I led, chasing rainbows one town after another with little to show for it. There were thousands like me, all searching for El Dorado. I wasn't saving a penny, and it wasn't terribly exciting either. New territory meant the anxiety of finding digs and a new job, though some skins spent a lifetime on that futile roundabout, ending up friendless and penniless in some home or institution. Of course, I wasn't the only one going from place to place. In post-war Britain, the rebuilding of cities, the switching of factories from producing war material to consumer goods, and the hundreds of thousands of soldiers being demobbed created a mass movement of labour.

Another type who moved from place to place was called the 'Long Distance Man'. These were notorious men, generally Irish who travelled alone, their belongings, if any, in a parcel. Long-distance fellows lingered no more than a month in any one place. And while there they would enjoy cult status. Songs and rhymes chronicled their exploits, mostly for their prowess at the pub counter or on the site, sometimes for fighting. Indeed, these fellows courted the plaudits. Generally, they were prodigious workers and as soon as one appeared he was hired at top dollar, for in Paddy's world they gave the site status.

The Routing House or Salvation Army hostel was the abode of these travellers, where they were of little trouble. They'd be back to that same abode in maybe six months' time on their fairly regular orbit in avoiding similar transients. The long-distance men did not compete with one another, though the notoriety they sought and strived for was what earned them their early graves.

Chapter 8: Wally's Mob

From Mayo, Wally was a fair-haired, low-sized fellow with a stiff leg and a penchant for flashy rings, tie pins, watches and women. And oh yes, a fedora worn on the back of his head to expose his blond quiff. He would be our foreman for about six months, supervising the eight of us, eight deemed the ideal number by the company. Wally was quite genial most of the time. His elder brother Frank, a grand, quiet fellow, was a gang member who incidentally got all the handy jobs.

From where Wally had picked up his plate-laying skills I never asked, but he was an expert. The terminology and function of double crossings, quadruple crossings, points, check rails, and signalling were efficiently and rapidly explained to us. Though it was if and when he had to repeat it that one saw the other side of him. Using the theodolite, studying and following the drawings, and returning the filled work sheets were also his responsibility. Maybe once in three months someone from head office would come and visit the site for a couple of hours, illustrating the confidence and trust they placed on their outliers.

In the 1950s the work was strenuous, with six of us lugging the twenty-foot rails sometimes several hundred yards. We levelled the site with golf ball-sized stone and positioned the creosote-soaked sleepers, drilling them with manual augers before fixing chairs on them to facilitate the rail. The check rails were fashioned by us on-site. They were used to reinforce the rails approaching a crossing, and where the train wheels would be under stress as its direction veered. Often, we would be toiling near gangs of British Rail staff who were easy-going lads, lads who work-wise we would leave for dead. It was fulfilling work I enjoyed immensely. Of course, nowadays there is no such thing as a twenty-foot rail. The rail is now laid from a giant spool, the steel pre-stretched and mounted on a machine and the rail laid automatically. This new method has also eliminated the clackety-clack of the train running over the joints.

Of my workmates, two were Mooneys – Paddy and Paschal from Bray, and John Kelly who was also from Bray. Another was a huge, quiet fellow called Jim O'Connell from Wicklow, near enough to Bray and for a while three Greenes, father and two sons from Greystones. Jim O'Connell came with a reputation as a roughneck, though I never saw him as anything but quiet, decent, and civilised. There was Gerry Brown from Westport, an absolute brilliant good-humoured lad. And one John Broderick from a Limerick farming community, a huge man always well togged out, civil and good-humoured. There was Len, a decent, young, fair-haired chap from Newcastle, not long out of the army. For tuppence an hour extra Len drove our truck.

Dobbins had deliberated with us for a couple of months and eventually decided to return to his wife and children in Sheffield. He was a likable rogue, and I hope things worked out well for him.

There were several other contractors working on the site, mostly at construction. When working down near the gasometers one morning, we discovered a new mob had moved in. Their contract was digging this three-foot-deep trench. What awakened our interest in them was the foreman going berserk. He spent his time bawling and roaring, trying to get a bit of effort out of his mob. If he turned his back for an instant they all sat down. As we gaped with amusement at the performance I recognised one of them, then another. One was Charlie McCauley, the other Jack Madden, old friends and neighbours from back home.

"We're just doing the same as the others," they claimed, when I commented on their lack of effort.

I asked Charlie where he was working before this caper. "In a remand home for women," he laughs, "but I had to leave because I was looking terrible bad."

Anyway, one of our gang could easily have excavated what had taken ten of them. This caper lasted a week until the site engineer dismissed the lot of them, including the unfortunate foreman. A good foreman would always have a pacesetter in front, which meant the others must do their stuff or get out of the trench.

That following Sunday on my way to mass and walking through the town square, I heard a familiar voice shouting, "Anyone want to buy a dog?" It was Charlie with the landlord's Labrador on the end of a rope. Charlie, a-devil-may-care individual who had been to sea for a number of years, told me he was biding his time until he got another berth. I saw Jack a few days later, he too looked great and unworried, and with a beautiful girl on his arm. Why shouldn't he?! While to this day I occasionally meet Charlie, I never saw Jack again.

Having been in Derby for about six months, and the contract nearly complete, Wally called a meeting. We're for Avonmouth in Somerset on Monday, he said. He further explained the contract was a huge railway siding in the dock area, and would mean three or four years' work. We were delighted as new territory meant new experiences. In 1955 we arrived on a bus, driving over Brunel's suspension bridge into that beautiful valley where the River Severn flows.

My first digs were in a housing estate which caused me a little embarrassment. When arriving back from work the first evening, I went to the back door which was on the latch. I entered, hung up my lunch bag, washed my milk bottle and mug, then relaxed on a kitchen chair with a newspaper I found. After about ten minutes I became uneasy. Something was not right. I began to scrutinise my surroundings. I leaped to my feet, grabbed my bag, and was out the door like a rocket. Yes, I had been in the wrong house. I found the correct one a half mile up the road.

I was the only lodger in this house, sharing my room with my landlady's asthmatic ten-year-old son. Her husband, a long-distance lorry driver, was away at the time, a man I later found to be an absolute gentleman. He too was ex-army and suffered from nerves; consequently at times there was tension in the house, though I'm bound to say they always treated me with decency and respect. Whenever he was home for a couple of days, marital disputes erupted – just cross words. After a squabble they were most civilised and always apologetic. That was why when after a month and leaving for new digs, rather than tell them the truth I told them I was returning to Ireland.

Avonmouth, West of Bristol, was a small town with a deep-sea port, a sea port that in 1954 was booming with the importation of beef, lamb, fruit and grain. The edibles mostly came from New Zealand and Australia. Timber and minerals from Africa. Fruit in the form of bananas came from the West Indies. Oil from God knows where. The main export seemed to be motor cars, thousands upon thousands of Fords – a brand which I never saw on English roads. To a casual eye they seemed be of poor quality, though in hindsight maybe it was because they were sprayed with wax to keep them from rusting on their journey.

Our engineering company was now engaged in renovating the existing tracks and extending the sidings for the increasing dock's railway traffic. There were already two other company gangs employed on the job, and for a month this led to much re-bonding and resumption of friendships. Naturally, it was in the boozer, until after a month when we got fed up of looking at one another over pint glasses.

We were only on the site a couple of days when we witnessed a plane crash about a half mile further up the track from us. An Air Force Vampire jet on a training exercise suddenly stalled, restarted, then began to fall, the pilot struggling to level off and miss the oil silos when he could have ejected. It hit the ground head-on, exploding on our railway. One or two of our lads inanely giggled, the rest of us were shocked. When inspecting it a few days later all that remained was a four-foot-deep hole in the ground. Of course, Wally, commenting on the pilot's bravery, reminded us that the discipline the pilot displayed was the same our company required from us. Any breeches of the no smoking or security rules might end up in their nullifying of our company's contract.

Our activities on the dock brought us cheek by jowl with the docker and sailing fraternity. We, wilfully breaking the rules, found ourselves making little deals with the aforesaid folk. A couple of quid would get you a carton of Senior Service cigarettes or a pair of top-class boots or shoes from the Aussie or New Zealand seamen.

The dockers at this time were a law unto themselves. They were rooking the cargoes of sides of lamb, tea by the sackful and whatever had a market with the dealers who flocked to the town. It was organised pillaging. The security was intense though confined mostly to manning the few exits.

Solo or multiple policing activities on the wharves had become too risky, like stuff falling out of the sky injuring policemen, policeman accidentally being knocked into the harbour, etc. Security was confined to fire safety, ensuring there was no smoking anywhere except in a few concrete shelters. The penalty was instant dismissal and heavy mandatory fine, and in mutual interest, this law was strictly observed.

The exit security from the dock area was strict – excessive today and maybe tomorrow, at least once a week there would be an intense rummage. There were narks, there were undercover police, and there were coppers on the take. Security would know when a big thieving operation was on, and the dockers would know when there was intense security raid.

Did the dockers run and hide when a random rummage took place? Not on your life! They'd charge the gates, yelling like a horde of head hunters while protecting the ones with the loot. The police, mostly veterans, would put up a great show of falling over and doing a share of yelling themselves, though carefully avoiding hurting or getting hurt, except maybe the odd gobshite looking for promotion, or a probationer a week or two out of training college. There would be one or two arrests, a couple charged and then fined for making an affray, though they wouldn't miss a day's pay or be a penny out of pocket, and were very seldom sacked. Their union membership ensured that outcome.

There was a huge canteen on the docks that opened at six o'clock in the morning and closed at around ten at night where lunch could be purchased for a couple of bob. We were dining one evening having worked a couple of hours overtime, when this noisy ship's crew came in. They were the crew of the *Irish Pine*, a scruffy, rough-looking bunch of all ages – not troublesome, though they seemed to be well under the influence of drink. They were all sizes and shapes and dressed like tramps, though seemingly very amiable and content with one another's company.

We got to talking and it seems they were out of Costa Rica with a cargo of bananas. Their ship, when we saw it next day we saw it, was a pocket-sized, beautifully built timber ship, more like a sailing vessel. For whatever reason it carried quite an amount of rigging. The crew created no trouble other than to rook both of the ship's chandlers in the town of clothing. They were interned for a day or two until Irish Shipping bailed them. It was a grand little monotony breaker which got their names in the local paper. It was an incident which we enjoyed.

For the good days and the bad days I give thanks
For I am but a ship upon an ocean wave
And often I am sickened by a stormy circumstance
But after every storm "The Lord be praised".

Chapter 9: A Menagerie

My new digs were much nearer our work place. My new landlady was unusual in that she was twenty-three years old, always well dressed and with shoulder-length dark brown hair, and an ever-amused sparkle in her eye. She really was handsome, and was also kind and considerate. Gwen, as she was called, was 'on the game' – not every night, just when the mood struck her. She had someone she loved, a young Polish chap called Frank.

Her Frank, a nice, friendly fellow, was a crewman on a channel ferry. On a regular run he would be gone for a fortnight, then back to the love nest. In Frank's absence, Willie, a Northern Ireland chap, generously stepped in to relieve the situation, of course that without consulting Frank.

Willie, with whom I worked, was about nineteen and a top-class lad. It was him who fixed me up with the room in the digs I now shared with Len. Gwen didn't need a Cock Lodger nor did Willie hang around having fulfilled his duty, for she was trusting, and she herself respected.

We were supplied with a change of sheets every week. When you cooked you kept the kitchen and stove spotlessly clean, as well as your room. There were two Meath men on the ground floor – brothers-in-law and great skins. They too were employed by our company. All in all, they were good digs in that magnificent summer of 1955.

A peculiar feature about lodgers was even though we lived, worked and maybe socialised, your background was seldom discussed. Not that the subject was taboo – it was just unimportant. Members of this fluid community were taken at face value. There was the odd exception like Theo from Longford, a foreman of another gang. He was a personable enough chap who I knew from my Sheffield days. He went on about his parents being professionals of some sort, and he being better educated than the rest of us. Even the fact that Theo had 'the shout' did not impress. It didn't earn him higher status in the digs and the consequent extra helpings. Another peculiarity I noticed was the lack of mail delivered. This led me to assume that other than the married lads the remainder were not writing home. I doubt if they phoned either for most were working class like myself, where a phone was the least of your Irish household needs.

The vast majority of all the Irish, English, Welsh, and Scottish I met were decent skins with no isolationists. They were clean and quiet in the digs, generous when you needed something, and could be fully trusted. Some could be a bit noisy on weekends when they had the sup on them.

Another phenomenon, though you visited the baths only once a week, I cannot recall being turned off by the smell of others which makes me wonder if our senses were not fully developed at the time.

During that twelve months Wally, our foreman, had gone to Australia, though not as a ten-pound migrant. Apparently, he had responded to an advertisement, had been interviewed and landed by all accounts 'a great job'. The upshot was, we had a succession of supervisors. Most were ok, though we gave no trouble. We knew our jobs and worked hard.

One foreman had a weakness for gathering a little group around him in the pub of a night, then reward the one or two sycophants with easy or status-earning functions on-site. One of these jobs was, on very hot days, walking the line and loosening the fish plates holding the rails end to end. These existing older rails buckled in the extreme conditions. Though summer in 1956 was very hot the high-class steel rails we laid never needed this attention, for expansion was always taken into account. Nevertheless, a couple of crawlers worked the line on consecutive days.

This was the worst kind of supervision! Cliques are the initiators of exclusion; a clique is death to the harmony of the gang. Several rows erupted. Friends fell out. Word must have gotten to management because the foreman was replaced with a man from County Cavan called Mick Brady. Mick was a Praetor whose digs were God knows where, a leader who did not socialise with his cohort. He was the ideal foreman and an expert at his job. He was in his fifties, wore a collar and tie, a hat, and a donkey jacket. He retained a constant, sensible, non-intimidating tone which got the best out of us and restored the team ethic.

Fortune favours the brave is written in the stars
And although I'm not afraid, I labour to endure
Because fortune has not favoured me—no champagne or caviar
Just the same routine, always pork and beans and still dirt poor.

Chapter 10: Another Dawn

That Christmas I left Avonmouth for Ireland with no intention of going back. Actually, I cannot recall why or what for I made the decision – the pay was good and there was nothing wrong with the job, no row. Nor was I ever involved in the earlier disputes. Anyway, my brother Lorcan wrote with news of a job back home, a job with good wages. So with three or four hundred pounds in my wallet, I parted company with a great bunch of workmates. Mates all but one, I never saw or heard of again. The exception was Pat Welch, a previous foreman who years later I saw and nodded to in a London pub. Anyway, this was my first visit home in four years.

When I was at home, the Grant Lyons Company who I had worked for sent on my insurance cards, addressed to my mother. There was an accompanying letter from the foreman, Mick. I was astounded with the utterly brilliant reference he gave me, as were my mother and father. When my mother died, the letter was not among her personal effects, as were one or two other letters of appreciation which she had received.

In Dublin, I met up with Ned Madden, a great survivor, now evolved as a builder. He also had a few greyhounds. Nevertheless, he said he was doing nicely, though for survival reasons I didn't press him for a job or for advice on what I might do with myself.

I stayed at home for a month during which I went to Unidare on Jamestown Road, Finglas, to be interviewed about the promised job. There I found about five hundred other hopefuls on the same mission. "We'll be writing to you," grimaced the guy in the office, while staring out at the gathering mob outside his window. Sixty years later I'm still waiting for my letter of appointment.

Returning to Derby in February 1956, I found employment as a rigger with Babcocks and Wilcox, a huge engineering company. Actually, the enterprise was a power station near Castle Donnington, some miles from Derby. I lodged in the camp hostel, more than content with the usual cleanliness and order which invariably existed. Also, the canteen was excellent.

This was the year of the Hungarian uprising. Babcock's, in their generosity, donated a billet to accommodate some of them. They were all young males, unscarred, handsome and self-aware. Their presence brought hordes of girls from Nottingham, Derby and the hinterland, some driving motor cars, many overnighting (as their breakfasting in the canteen revealed). I hoped for a morsel, the charity of mere curiosity? A smile in one's direction? But sadly, no – just the same scornful glance and a muttered, "On yer bike, Paddy."

These Hungarians had no shortage of spending money. Taxis shunted them to Nottingham and Derby on shopping expeditions during the day, to the clubs at night, and then home to the late-night/morning parties. Sleep for the working fraternity became difficult. After a month of it, a deputation met management and on the threat of a strike, the party was over and the refugees were refugeed someplace else.

As camps go, Castle Donnington was excellent. The discipline excellent week-in, week-out. I saw only one squabble in the six months, and that trouble was between family members.

Fierce Pontoon and poker schools operated on Friday nights along with 'Two Up', another terrific way of separating you from your wage packet. In one hour it would leave the losers broke and having to survive on tick. Some while on a winning streak and wanting to leave, wouldn't, scared of a couple of clatters by a still-functioning loser, or being named as a grabber. At least in the camp they would be sober, and onlookers ensured the game was fair. Gambling is a desperate vice; even when one wins satisfaction is momentary, and all you want is the next deal. Alcohol may give you headaches and loss of dignity, but gambling induces despair.

My workmates were top-class. There were three fellows from Cork who had worked for the Ford Motor Company until being made redundant, also a couple from the West of Ireland. Our boss was eccentric. He was English – a tiny fellow with a huge flat cap and never without his overcoat (which he wore opened). With one hand in his trouser pocket and the other holding his pipe in his gob, George was his name – always polite and decent. But only for these Cork fellows, he would not retain his job for five minutes. We operated as riggers, working at great heights constructing work platforms for the engineers and welders. We had nothing to work from except the outer steel framework of the building. The cantilevering creativity was brilliant in producing the safe working conditions for others, at great risk to ourselves.

We operated without safety harness or catchment net, indeed without five minutes' training. As far as I was concerned my assurance of skill was accepted. Though when like Tarzan I would be swinging from the scaffolding, they did shake their heads disapprovingly. That is why I so admired my workmates – they put you right. George imagined the innovation was all his own, but it was those Cork fellows who were the geniuses, influencing me to be innovative, to be efficient, to be careful. Nevertheless, true to form I only stayed for six months until the call of fresh woods and pastures green beckoned, again.

In every town or city one visited, digs would be found by advertisements. Hand-written notices alongside read, 'Commode for sale. Hardly used. Thirty bob secures.' Or, 'Mattress. Slightly stained. Yours for a pound.' These, among a multitude, would be plastered on shop windows in the working-class areas. That was how I found digs in London's Bethnal Green road. It was once a grand, detached house, now looking a bit neglected, as were the others in the row. It had the usual three floors, but with a bathroom or toilet on each. It also had a tired and pleasant atmosphere, in fact I seldom saw or heard the respectable, genteel old woman who was the landlady, or her other clients. It was a category two. Beds were never tended, though sheets were supplied whether you wanted them or not. No meals. No mucking out. The elderly lady was in need of the money, and was too old to earn it. So, we were largely ignored, and except for a large dog always noisily licking and scratching itself, it was nearly perfect.

I shared a room with a gas, young, red-haired Dublin chap called Terry. The room itself was once a capacious parlour or drawing room with French windows through which a large, neglected garden was visible. The moulded ceilings were ten feet high. It also had a massive, ornate fireplace, another sign of former grandeur.

Terry, aged twenty, was an electrician – a chap with an absolutely infectious humour, and a personality that would disarm the devil. Having served his time in Dublin with the ESB, once qualified he was let go, as was then the norm. He was now employed by British Rail as an electrical maintenance man – a well-paid, easy job.

I too had found employment. It was in Martineau's, an Aldgate sugar refinery just off the Whitechapel Road. The pay was not bad and became very good when a shortage of staff left us working twelve-hour shifts, seven days a week. Consequently, I saw little of Terry one week, and too much of him the next. He was one of those fellows who in normal circumstances one would be absolutely delighted to meet – good-humoured, witty, trustworthy. I was always attracted to such characters, but at midnight, him with his pal or sometimes pals, inebriated, eating fish and chips and cracking the jokes? No.

My shift began at six o'clock, which meant arising at five, and also retiring early. But Terry and his pals wouldn't pack it in until two in the morning. Regretfully, I had to leave and ended up in a room over a Maltese café. Though the landlord was a pleasant enough fellow, the place was a kip and used as a pick-up station for girls on the game. Anyway, I remained living over that café until a Russian workmate fixed me up with a two-room council apartment in Sussex Street, Whitechapel. This was in the Petticoat Lane area.

Of course, digs had now become non-u, unfashionable. The rage, the in-thing, was the bedsit – come and go when you like, eat and sleep, likewise, bring home the girlfriend if you could find one agreeable. There was the initial expense of setting up, such as bedding and cooking utensils, cutlery and the like. Nevertheless, I was never more content while living there on my own.

At work and about three weeks after I had been employed, I was approached by a boiler-suited man of about sixty. I had noticed him earlier – it was the friendly way he was greeted no matter what floor he was on. This grey-haired, burly figure was Syd, the plant maintenance man. Syd was also the TWU shop steward, a fellow I got to know quite well. Syd had been in the merchant navy during the war, serving as a fitter. He told me his ship had never been torpedoed though his convoy had been attacked several times. One incident he was more than happy to give me an account of happened on the 17th of December 1939. When leaving Buenos Aires to join the convoy and still on the river plate, they saw the *Graf Spee* was being scuttled. The battleship was well down in the water as they passed, so all hands got a chance to cheer. Syd fetched his camera and photographed the event.

A few weeks later, having docked in London, the same photo insured plenty of free pints in the East End pubs. His son-in-law borrowed the photo without asking and, within a couple of days, Syd's photo was in most of the papers. Syd was very angry, and angered whenever reminded of it. His son-in-law swore he got no reward for it and that his newfound wealth was earned by gambling, money that bought a bigger flat and new furniture.

As for Syd and my job – when I signed on as a union member he promised me that as long as I had the strength to clock in I'd never be sacked. Three weeks later when I was on a night shift, poor Syd himself was sacked and nobody supported him. Months later when I became familiar with all the staff, I enquired why. I was told there had been an ongoing campaign by management to rid themselves of 'the communist pest'.

There were a couple of Wicklow lads also employed. They were from Rathnew. One was John Healy, a low-sized, burly, curly-haired, ever-smiling lad and his freckled cousin, the tall and skinny, red-haired John Freeney. Another was the dark-featured, ever-pleasant Bob Quinn, Quinner.

We were very well-paid due to overtime, but for most of the Asian staff, wages were poor. They were employed in boring, secondary tasks which included packing the bags of sugar into cartons as they came off a conveyor, or changing the large canvas cloths used for filtering the liquid sugar as it emptied from the boilers, then piling them into a steam cleaner. It was hot, sticky work. I assumed they were on the same pay rate as the casuals and rarely did I see an Asian leave, even though there was a huge turnover of casual staff.

I quickly realised I had been lucky to get a job which demanded concentration. Heretofore, all the jobs I'd experienced expected efficiency, and now I was a believer. Whenever possible, I'd develop an improved and sometimes safer method of achieving the purpose. Here in the refinery there was a function called 'the liquor runner'. The operative, during the many processes of refining, would have to race from floor to floor to open and close the many cocks, bypasses, and valves. The pipes were dangerously hot with liquid sugar, some with molasses, steam or water. In this ancient refinery, as the sugar boilers reached the end of the process a host of different flows must be manually diverted or shut down. Dominick, a Maltese with the sorrowful face of Jesus, also the father of six children, taught me. The job would usually take a month to perfect, because mistakes were costly.

Memorising the different valves was the biggest problem, for nearly all the pipework was of the same diameter, and all the same ancient, blackened copper. The second night, out of desperation and fear of making a mistake, I brought in four small tins of paint. With the help of Dominick, I coloured the valves down through the four floors of the factory, ensuring that I was on the right lines. There was nobody more pleased than Dominick, because he himself was forgetful and renowned for his spills. After three more shifts I was ready.

The factory overseer, a dreadful sycophant, on seeing what I had done brought the manager around to view the improvement, implying it was his own idea. This overseer was a tall, skinny fellow wearing glasses, he wore a white dustcoat over a brass-buttoned, blue blazer. The blazer gave the impression he was a sailing, or a rowing, or cricket club member. He was universally disliked. One of the foremen told me that come September, he'd replace the brass buttons with ordinary ones.

The refinery imported bagged cane sugar from South America, Australia, and the West Indies, which they refined to produce white castor and other specialised varieties. Also from South America came bags of tailings. This was sweepings, sugar swept up from wherever market the sugar was sold. As soon as these bags of sweepings were emptied at the pug mill in our factory, as well as the sugar literally hundreds of cigar ends, empty, exotic packets of cigars and cigarettes were accompanied by a wonderful tobacco aroma. This inferior sugar went into the making of treacle.

Our senior staff was mostly English, with a few Scots and Irish and a couple of Welsh. The head chemist was a very polite and youngish Dublin chap. There was Frank, known as the Yank. He was a droll, grey-haired fellow who operated the hoist which unloaded the incoming lorry loads of bagged brown sugar, and loaded the outgoing trucks with the finished article. During a lull, Frank used to shamble around the factory searching for someone willing to chat. He told me, in his American accent, that he'd been years in the States, although the grapevine said two. He also told me that out of loyalty to his country he and his wife returned to do their bit, which left Frank a fire watcher during the war years. It was Frank who introduced me to the writings of the American author Erskine Caldwell, with Frank replacing each novel as soon as I read them – novels which included *Tobacco Road* which I found to be very entertaining.

Wally, my landlord, was Russian. There were also, along with Dominick, a number of Maltese – nice, ordinary fellows, though one or two fierce card-playing gamblers. There was another fellow called Robert, a local fellow affected with scoliosis. He was employed in gathering the empty sugar sacks and folding them into bales. One of the foremen, Albert, told me that during the war and the consequent sugar rationing, when clocking out this fellow used to have two humps.

Don't get me wrong; I can get along,

It's just that sometimes I need to get away

For in these hives where man connives, I feel I don't belong

And must move on to pastures new.

Chapter 11: Last Round Up

A new starter was trained which resulted in me becoming the 'Spare Man'. This was because I now had the ability to perform several important functions in the sugar processing. This position left me with nothing to do most of the time, and with the feeling of being a terribly important fellow. Actually, I saw myself on par with Bob Chambers, an elderly man who for years held this dignified position on his own. I now began to take a disapproving view of staff who increased their sick note deliveries, reducing me to having to work. Anyway, having no particular station to man or to louse in, I would lose myself rambling around the factory.

A pleasant spot to spend an hour was in the basement where the coal-fired furnace was situated. It was here I met Nufy, a Newfoundland ship's stoker. He was aged about forty, huge, and newly married to an English girl. From the body language, things were not working out exactly as planned. Nevertheless, he was great company. He used to spin yarns about his travels, especially about South American ports, and particularly about his own village in a backward part of Newfoundland. It was so isolated, he told me, that when a fellow rode a bicycle into his village, Mrs. O'Brien standing at her door blessed herself and wondered aloud, "Was the poor fellow born that way?" The other stoker was Kiwi, also a very agreeable fellow. At the time he was ashore studying for his bosun's ticket.

Up on another floor I met Paddy, a jaded, skinny, sharp-faced lad who had originated from the flats in Dublin's Parkgate Street. After a bit of small talk about accommodation, I mentioned I had a TV in my flat, though I had no radio to which Paddy conspiratorially winked and muttered, "Fix ye up after work!"

Brick Lane is a warren. It was where Paddy and his two mates existed, only a five-minute stroll from the refinery. This was an ancient, undeveloped part of East End London. It had old warped brick buildings, some with arched entries into tiny courtyards, once used for stabling, or perhaps as now, with two or three more old dwellings. It was a run-down area, though with many thought-provoking remnants of a long-gone age. I was by now familiar with that area, passing through it twice daily coming and going to work. The ground floors of quite a number of houses had been transformed into huckster shops, cafés, hardware, bakeries, tailors, halal butchers, bridal parlours, barbers.

Brick lane had become an ideal starting point for the newly arriving Asians, who for next to nothing could get on the property ladder as these places were going for a song. They bought, paid the rates and waited to be rehoused. Then one could sell one's condemned gaff to the developer who at that time hovered like a raptor, they too filling anything that could remotely house people, also waiting for their redevelopment payday.

It was among those joints that worn stone stairs invited me into a kind of communal building, originally designed a couple of hundred years earlier to house the forsaken destitute and now still facilitating the same. Indeed, I wouldn't have blinked had I met Fagin or maybe Bill Sykes, or perhaps caught a glimpse of Jack the Ripper for the environs encouraged such apparitions.

Paddy and his mates were sharing this one room or flat, as they called it. There appeared to be only one bed, to which I didn't refer, instead keeping my eyes fixed on a lovely radio resting on wall brackets. The asking price was thirty bob to which, without further inspection, I agreed. "D'ye want the brackets?" Paddy enquired. Before I could say yes, aye, or no, he grabbed hold of one and ripped it from the wall, bringing a dozen bricks and plaster with it, revealing the startled, dark-faced occupants of the next flat. As the lads guffawed a piece of cardboard was stuck over the hole; I suggested we report it immediately to the landlord. This provoked further howls of merriment. "We're squattin'," they laughed.

"Who does the flat belong to?" I asked.

"F**k knows," Paddy sniggered.

"And the radio?" I enquired.

"Swear te Jasus, Redser, it's ours."

To reassure me they carried it back to my flat. On the following Friday they jacked, and that was the last I saw of them. So, if any denizen of Brick Lane whose radio went missing around 1958, it's probably still in 32 Davis Mansions, Sussex Street, E2.

I loved that area of London where my flat was so central. Indeed, when looking out the back window I could see the Tower of London not a half mile away. And as I revealed earlier, my Russian workmate was the donor, and it was to him I paid the thirty shillings' rent he had asked, the place being worth ten pounds a week.

I used to pal around with the Wicklow lads having discovered there was a colony of them, and all from Rathnew. John Healy, from the refinery, was doing a line with a girl who he eventually married, her parents being Irish. This girl whose name I forget, used to pal with a crowd of other girls whose names I also forget. They weren't great company though always done up to the nines. I seldom saw one engage in a one-to-one conversation, but babble like a flock of turkeys whenever challenged to communicate. They assumed sophisticated demeanours, beehive hairdos, and affected little woven baskets instead of handbags. In the lounge bar they sipped Mousac from cocktail glasses. None of them had opinions or anything worthwhile to say, except Roslyn.

Roslyn had a personality like Terry's. Everything about her was outrageous – her hair, her clothes, and she had an uninhibited holler of a laugh that could be heard a mile away. At nineteen and Jewish, she was a wonderful character. Her personality was the glue that attracted, and was used by the others. Roslyn was always receptive. She had this wonderful, engaging charisma that magnetised a crowd. John Healy told me she carried a razor blade in her bag in case she might be attacked. I laughed at the idea, and never saw it or believed it.

Throughout my life I had met hundreds of personalities like Rosly, Terry and John Healy, not forgetting Dobbins, and I loved every one of them. Wonderful, warm, infectious, beautiful characters. People that demanded nothing from you. Indeed, even seeing them in the distance lifted the gloom, absolving your imagined problems with the feel-good sensation.

Wally, my workmate, was about forty-five, no more than five-foot-four in height, an immensely strong barrel of a man with an enormous air force moustache. When an absentee demanded my presence at the spinners, during a twelve-hour shift standing next to him, he'd hardly speak a word, but that was Wally. His poor grasp of

English prevented me from prying into his past. He was friendly though nurtured a disdainful opinion of other DPs (displaced persons, which were in their hundreds of thousands all over Britain), and was not averse to rooking them in the card-playing dens along Commercial Road of a weekend.

It was in one of those clubs he met his girlfriend, a red-haired lady aged about fifty, who had acquired a brand-new council flat which she now shared with Wally. Wally had then rented his place to a Polish fellow, also a DP. This fellow apparently caused trouble, and Wally ejected him and installed another. This fellow was worse – he got drunk, created rackets, lost the key and then burst down the door. He too was ejected, which left me the lucky number three. Wally's girl would come around (forewarned) and check out the place and check with the block caretaker who I never met, but who always gave me top marks. It was a lovely place to live. My neighbours were Greek, and I stayed there for five years.

Some of the conditions we experienced wouldn't pass muster now, and rightly so. God, the thought of bedding with another man makes my flesh creep.

I was robbed once. Not me specifically – there were four rooms and four tenants, so we were all done. That included the gas meter. I lost nothing that couldn't be replaced, so no complaints.

My experience illustrates the common decency of those thrown together by fate or circumstance. People just looked out for one another. Over ten years my adventures in England, Wales, and later Scotland were positive. They were years I do not regret, for I was treated well wherever I worked, and if an odd lodging house didn't suit, I was never without the option of finding a better one. Well, except once…

Blank impassive faces, in the street and on the train,
Lost in introspection, preoccupied in dreams.
Nobody looks you in the eye – there is no smile exchanged,
You feel their frustration. You sense their silent screams.

PART 3

Chapter 1: In the Interim

The end of a journey as a new one begins
Another test; a new enterprise,
I'm now finished with bivouacs, and drinking out of tins
And look forward to the high life that Paddy Green described.

The Dublin I returned to in 1962 was rife with unemployment. But due to the good offices of a certain Mick Markey from the north county townland of St. Margaret's, he found me a labouring job with Collen Brothers Builders, and THAT without me even asking him. The place of employment was The Dock Mills, off Townsend Street. I also replied to an Aer Lingus advertisement recruiting for ground staff.

Another astounding event was when I spent my savings on a used Morris Minor car. After the deposit, the repayments were six pounds a month over an eighteen-month period. To prevent a sequestering of the car, the task of obtaining that monthly six quid nearly had me in the poor house. I also had developed a fondness for the few jorums, which was largely due to bad company I was keeping, and it was only the grace of God that saved me on several occasions from banjoing me and the car. At the time I put these episodes down to other drunk drivers. For hadn't I received driving tuition? It was two ten-minute sessions with my impatient brother, Lorcan.

Eventually, I was interviewed in Corballis House, Collinstown, by a Paddy Green for the position as an aircraft baggage and freight handler. Paddy, from Swords, North County Dublin, was an absolute gentleman who, after a wait of a month or two, offered me a job as a temporary aircraft baggage and freight loader.

Around 1950, Aer Lingus possessed two large, four-engine aircraft called Constellations, or 'Connies' with the Aer Linte logo. Presumably they were bought for transatlantic flights, and for some reason or other remained remotely parked for about six months at least two miles from the terminals. When I commenced employment in 1962, they had disappeared.

DC-4. These two-engine aircraft first saw service in World War Two, and afterwards were vital in the Berlin airlift. Aer Lingus had four of them as part of their fleet. In passenger mode they had a cockpit crew of two and one air hostess, she to service the thirty-two passengers. The seating of this aircraft could be quickly stripped and the aircraft used as a freighter. Every evening we would load one, and at times two, with punnets of mushrooms for the Liverpool market. It was a laborious, time-consuming exercise. Incidentally, during the 1948 pogroms in India, this type of Dakota was recorded carrying 136 passengers, illustrating the brilliant lift performance of the sturdy Dak.

Then there were four Fokker Friendships, a Dutch-made, short-haul aircraft. They were a gift to load and unload, being close to the ground, with the main baggage compartment forward of the passenger section. A joke doing the rounds at the time went like this… A gentleman strolling around the airport casually asked, "Where do you keep the Fokker?" A loader suggested he lived above in the park…

There were Vickers Viscounts, also propeller driven – a marvellous workhorse. From our point of view the holds were difficult to work in. This was due to the aircraft's high profile; the freight hold opening was small, and four feet off the ground. This meant only the young and fit could jump up and haul themselves inside. Most had to be given a leg up. Once inside, you had to work on your knees because of the low ceiling height. The BEA Viscount holds were very loader unfriendly, with sharp, grooved floors which hurt and wore the knees out of your trousers in no time. Later, Aer Lingus bought a number of used Viscounts from Belgian Airways. While they had an excellent maintenance record, these aircraft were worn out and caused frequent engineering delays. They were eventually withdrawn from service, deactivated, and sold as scrap.

Of course, loading your aircraft is not the same as loading your van or truck. First, the movement of vehicles around the aircraft must be coordinated and predictable. A load plan must be strictly observed. The fuel, the passengers, the distribution of baggage and freight load must all be considered to ensure safety, as far as humanly possible. Freight was packed and secured, with heavy items tied down to ensure no lateral or vertical movement – shifting loads while the aircraft is in flight could lead to disaster. The load plan is validated several times before engine start-up. A ramp agent or Red Cap ensured the safe dispatch of each and every aircraft.

In 1962, Aer Lingus had two Boeing 707s and two 720s which they used mainly for the transatlantic routes Dublin to Shannon and New York. The smaller 720 often had to be put down in Gander, Newfoundland, for refuelling before continuing on to New York due to head or crosswinds. Of course, there is one other aircraft – the company's first De Havilland-84 Dragon which was suspended from an aircraft hangar's superstructure the last time I saw it.

My first season with the company lasted from April to September. My wage was eight pounds three shillings per week. The magic words 'shift supplement' were not yet coined. Compared to what I was earning in GB, this wage was paltry. But the consideration of returning to GB never crossed my mind. That first season the temporary staff numbered around sixty with about forty permanent staff. There were only two foremen, Paddy Green, a peppery little man, and Tom Purcell, a bespectacled, pale-faced man of about forty who died within a couple of years. This left Paddy Greene to perform miracles of micromanagement.

The training was 'on job', i.e. get into that aircraft hold and pack it. One was asked to produce a driving licence but it became clear that some of my comrades couldn't be trusted with driving an ass and cart, though I admit I was no Sterling Moss, myself. At that time your licence had no identification other than your name. Actually, one fellow hadn't a clue of how to drive though he was a top-class worker.

"Who gave you the licence?" I asked.

"It's me father's," he laughed, "an' he can't drive either."

Still, we got by, mostly due to the kindness and tolerance of the permanent staff, though some of them were also unable to drive.

My friend, like quite a few of the newcomers, learned the rudiments of driving while on night duty. Evidence of their nocturnal activities was visible by the amount of vehicle damage, to which there were never any witnesses. Also, there were reports of dangerously driven vehicles careering around the apron, vehicles which did not stop when requested.

We operated in three-man crews, with one crew to all aircraft except the larger transatlantic aircraft which required two crews. You were delegated a specific task and with aircraft turnaround of forty minutes, there was no time to waste.

I enjoyed the challenge of operating to tight schedules. I liked operating the equipment and I never found the work beneath my dignity. From day one I saw myself as serving on a ship, a frame of mind I retained until the day I retired. I think it was the actual physicality of the work I enjoyed most. Then, I always was an idiot.

Back then, the equipment at our disposal was in very short supply and was pretty basic. One small, aluminium, three-wheeled truck was christened 'the ice cream yoke'. Another lorry with a peculiar short, black body had an enormous steering wheel, so large it ensured your fingers got trapped between it and the window, so much so that one had to drive with the cab window open. Of course, this ensured that in rainy weather one got a wet ass. The monstrosity was called 'the coal lorry'. We didn't complain, but you had to be sharp to grab whatever equipment was available or else you'd have to physically tow small truckloads of baggage to the aircraft, or tow a couple of empties to offload it.

During the busy periods we had to use large, ancient, canvas-covered, four-wheeled trailers, similar to the prairie schooners seen in cowboy movies. With regards to aircraft safety, these wagons were lethal in windy weather, or when caught in the wake of a taxiing aircraft. Whoever at the time was employed to supplement the equipment needs certainly hadn't safety or a user's perspective in mind.

Chapter 2: The Culture of Make Do

Me getting ready for the late shift, c.1970.

Of all the staff recruited that first year only one was retained, a lad who had started a month after me. I objected through the union but their evasiveness gave me no confidence, though they promised to make enquiries. They returned with a fairy tale, that our two names had gone into a hat, and I had lost.

In early December of 1962 I was re-employed, this time in Cathal Brugha Street. Our task was to segregate the destinations of Christmas turkeys (dead ones), which our customers were sending to friends and relations in Britain. I suspected quite a lot of our customers were in poorer circumstances than ourselves, so thankfully they insisted on slipping a couple of bob or half a dollar into your often-reluctant hand. A fellow who used to clean the place told us a story, an event that happened a few years previously. Management decided on a cost-cutting exercise. Apparently, there was severe consternation among the staff as to how many of them were going to get the push, and the only casualty was the messenger boy.

Three days before Christmas we were ordered back to the chaos of Dublin Airport where we resumed as loaders up until the end of January.

For the first few seasons the company made most of us redundant. That was when (without asking) my friend Mick Markey would intervene with his builder foreman and I'd be fixed up with a job for a few months. Matt Weldon, the local publican, also offered me employment, for he was always involved in maintenance and expansion of his premises.

The following April, I was among the first batch invited to return. I collected a second-hand boiler suit, a beret, and a pair of Hawthorn boots from the clothing stores. The boots were the most comfortable footwear I ever wore. It was then straight to work. The amount of equipment hadn't changed, the same six heavy-duty tractors, two conveyors, the ice cream yoke, the coal lorry, and two other smaller Leyland flatbeds. There was a variety of aircraft steps, two which were motorised and the remainder manual or towable. Two ancient forklifts and one newish model completed the equipment pool. The conveyor was vital for loading high-profile aircraft, plus the nose holds of the Daks.

Quite a lot of the new staff was from North County Dublin. This situation upset skins from the city, accusing Paddy Green of favouritism. They suggested he was looking after his own bailiwick at the expense of others, which he probably did and good luck to them. I do know for a fact that Paddy was bombarded with parents petitioning on their family's behalf. Sure, what harm was that?

Over the next few years the outfit became more organised, though still no training. When poor Tom Purcell died, a number of foremen were established. One was Tommy Duffy from Whitehall who became Paddy Greene's assistant. Another was ex-army sergeant John Brady, better known as Tucks – the Tucks nickname earned from his days in the army while inducting recruits. Apparently, while presenting a new bunch in the army canteen, from behind them he'd roar, "Giv'm tucks o'spuds!" while signalling two with his fingers.

Paddy Farrelly was another ex-army, and now promoted foreman. His nickname was Fly, earning his title when he'd validated permission for some loader to go home early which caused the furore of a late aircraft departure. When management tried to identify the signature, it was 'Mr. Fly' they deciphered. Another great character and worker was Christy Madden.

Nearly all the older permanent staff were ex-army or air corps. All had features in common – personal tidiness and honesty, though quite a few were not amenable to hard work. The promoted foremen were mostly ex-army with three or four of them having held sergeant's rank. The promotions were based on seniority, which kept the union reps quiet. Reps who were beginning to flex their muscles. Reps who in those days were contained in the work area by Paddy Greene.

In 1964 I was deemed a permanent employee. This was very satisfying in an era when only civil servants and professionals in semi-state companies were worthy of such security. Yes, I felt privileged, and the feel-good sensation was fortified a couple of years later by the adoption of a company pension scheme. It was also the time I was bitten by a building bug, though I didn't know much about actual construction.

Running parallel with my job in Aer Lingus, this newfound purpose in life was really fulfilling. It began at home with a local government building instructor. The venture was to build a kitchen and bathroom extension onto our cottage. Working to a plan, I dug the foundations. The advisor came to inspect. I mixed the concrete and filled the foundations by hand. The advisor came to inspect. I laid the concrete blocks up to damp course. The advisor came to inspect. I began to lay the first course of cavity blocks and luckily, the advisor who was in the area dropped in to inspect my work and told me I had laid them upside down! After that bloomer I never had a problem.

Later, and during my off-duty hours, I tore up all the stone floors and laid wooden ones. I also installed oil-fired central heating. The first oil fill cost £100. When the next fill was due it cost £300. So, I dismantled the oil burner and bought a solid-fuelled Stanley range for £300 which operated beautifully until I sold the house in 1994, by that time having built on a granny flat and roofed the slated house with tiles.

The Boot after the extension during the big snow of 1984.

A friend and workmate, Mick Caul, originally from Drynam near Swords, gave me a greyhound pup. I put several pairs of my Hawthorn boots to the test exercising it, the dividend being it won quite a few races, prompting me to get another couple. A big mistake, for to be in with a chance one must feed them better than yourself. They were also subject to injuries and ailments which were from an arse to an elbow. I would advise keeping a greyhound as a pet, but not as a money-making venture. In fact, the owners of racing greyhounds worldwide are recognised by the holes in their socks.

Another great friend was Hugh Williams. We had joined Aer Lingus about the same time. Hugh was from Malahide where he had a small farm. Hugh was also an avid fisherman and huntsman. In the summer we often fished out of Malahide in Hugh's boat, a few times having wonderful catches of codling. A few times during the shooting season we vainly hunted pheasants, I by this time having acquired a shotgun. These were troubled times in Ireland, and on possessing a gun you could be targeted for it, so discretion prompted me to desist. I had enjoyed being out and about, in particular in cattle and sheep grazing areas. So, to legitimise my presence in the wilds I decided to acquire a ferret. Gabriel Kelly, another friend and workmate, said he knew a man that could supply one.

Gabriel brought me to a north county village where this man lived on the outskirts. It was a small four-room, whitewashed cottage. The door was open and with a rap on it a voice bid us to enter. Due to the tiny window it was gloomy at first, but there sitting at the table peeling spuds was Bob. I liked him at once for he had an air of innocence about him.

He was flat-capped, small, stout and aged about sixty-five. He wore a dark, old-fashioned suit with a waistcoat which could have done with a trip to the cleaners, that along with his once-white shirt. These incidentals I observed as Gabriel made known our business. By this time the spuds were peeled and Bob shuffled across the flagged floor and tipped them into a simmering pot on the gas cooker.

To the right of the cooker and hanging from a nail was the frying pan from which oozed years of dripping, now hardened like candle grease and congealed to the wall. "The ferrets are in Tipperary," said Bob, "an' for a two-pound deposit I'll get wan' sent up by rail." By this juncture the spuds were beginning to boil, and Bob with pot lid in one hand, a packet of salt in the other, shook a little into the pot. "When the ferret arrives, I'll tell Gabriel an' he'll tell you," Bob continued while unhooking the pan from the wall. Then, gripping it with both hands he gave the grease-covered wall an almighty scrape and placed the pan on a second gas ring.

While giving us a rundown on his satisfied customers and the efficiency of their ferrets, a pork chop was unwrapped and placed on the pan. With it nicely sizzling, he turned to us and inquired, "Would ye' be interested in a coupla' live rabbits?" He pointed to a bag by the door with its neck tied. "The hoors got out last night an' me an' the brother had to put up a net to ketch'm," he complained while testing the spuds with a knife and proceeding to drain them. "A greyhound fella said he wanted them but he never turned up," he observed over his shoulder. The chop was turned, the spuds were mashed and tipped on a plate, and as we took our leave Bob, with pan in hand dumped its contents over his lunch. The ferret? He became a grand little pet who we christened Bobs.

There were five of us living at home at that time. Lorcan was now married and living in Drumcondra, and earning a living as a salesman. Frank, also married, was living in Swords, employed as a transport driver. This left Margaret, who was a confectioner and Jack, an apprentice barman. Our father, having been pensioned from farming, had found employment as a mushroom grower with an Englishman called Len.

Imperturbable Len, about sixty, had a cadaverous look about him. He was stooped and affable, and extremely polite. Len was a visionary with the extraordinary gift of creating sure-fire ways of making money. This mushroom venture following a failed chicken rearing enterprise, which followed a failed turkey rearing/glasshouse and tomato and cucumber growing business. Only God knew what had preceded it. This new enterprise was created on the premises of Mr. Weldon, the local publican who owned the store-house which was now deemed the mushroom house. As part of the deal, Mr. Weldon was a serious investor in the project. The enterprise was successful for a spell, with Len's van bringing the produce to market. Our father was engaged in all the blue-collar work.

One day my father, having swept some refuse from the growing and packaging department, heaped it up outside and ignited it. An inferno developed, the day being windy and the fire too close to the building. That was the end of the mushrooms and the mushroom house, and the end of his job. When stoical Len was summoned to the scene, he just rubbed his chin, muttered, "Oh dear," and without another word got into his van and disappeared. Our father, with a liking for the few jorums and to ensure the supply thereof, found another job, this time employed as a lorry helper.

Our resourceful mother had by this time thrown herself head over heels into breeding Yorkshire Terriers, and between my greyhound slavering for a kill and these yelping hoors always under my feet, I suggested that she take up croqueting or the making of lamp-shades, even stamp collecting. Any civilised occupation more becoming of a lady.

That's when my father, generally in the dog house and in an attempt to re-establish himself in her good books, mentioned pigs. He suggested we resume the pig fattening enterprise we'd had in the previous cottage, and suggested a pig-cot at the bottom of our large garden. Before the concrete had set, my mother had two Bonhams in it. In the terrier world she had made good connections and her breed fetched good prices, so she persisted with them for a few more years.

My mother (Bridget Redmond) in The Boot, Cloghran, holding her pride and joy – one of her many litters of terrier pups.

Bingo was another hobby our mother enjoyed – six nights a week and twice on a Sunday, catching the CIE bus outside our house. If for any reason she wasn't outside waiting, the driver, Mick Howard, would stop and blow the horn. Indeed, on many occasions he left his bus and knocked on the door to see if she was alright. May God be with him. RIP.

I liked dancing, not that I was good at it, but included it on Saturday nights in Clery's with my girlfriend Eithne. I had also grown fond of the odd play, also Friday evenings St. Francis Xavier Hall where for my ten bob the Radio Eireann Light Orchestra performed. Indeed, in relation to the theatre, to the present day I have kept the optimum seat numbers of The Gate, The Abbey, The Eblana and The Peacock, numbers I would quote when booking.

Later I bought a sixteen-foot sailing boat and eventually moored it in Malahide, just opposite and below the hotel. It was useless for fishing because of the boom; no matter which way I secured it, it was always in the way. I recall one Saturday morning sailing out to Ireland's eye and becoming aware of water around my ankles, and I discovered we had sprung a plank. The leak wasn't bad and I did have a bucket to bail, and with a favourable wind I picked up my mooring about an hour later. Over the following week it wallowed three times, but because of the buoyancy tanks fore and aft it would not completely sink. I towed it home and repaired it.

A month later I towed it back to Malahide to find a thirty-footer on my mooring. This boat was now established on my position with a new buoy and mooring chain. After a spate of rude language, I towed my boat home and eventually joined the Rogerstown Sailing Club. Sailing might sound romantic, but rarely is. You are always wet, always concerned with weather changes, and the maintenance of wooden boats is never-ending.

At the airport, Sean Fitzpatrick was the station manager. In public he was a well-dressed, balding, rotund, debonair man who was seldom seen abroad without a carnation in his lapel. I never spoke to him other than bid him time of day to which he'd politely smile. Rumour had it he could be a tartar if you pressed your point. Most agreed he was a decent man. His watch had overseen a huge intake of staff, and a terrific increase in aircraft schedules meeting the public demand for more air transport. Later, to our surprise he appeared as canteen manager. A demeaning relegation? Those in the know whispered that Mr. Fitzpatrick had been accused by senior management of operating a departmental empire, and consequently was demoted. From our point of view, he commanded respect. In ground ops he had delegated responsible supervisors to vital positions, and did not interfere. As an aside, the most horrible act one human can inflict on another is to humiliate him. Mr. Fitz retired a couple of years later. Our Paddy Green was a loyal supporter. I recall one day when Paddy was being harangued by a couple of union reps on the need for more porters. Harry Keogh, a rep, was beside himself in frustration claiming half the tipping passengers were 'escaping' because of the want of a porter. He then accused Paddy of being a company man. Paddy leaped to his feet, shouting, "If Sean Fitzpatrick asked me to run up that f***in' wall, I'd run up it."

Paddy Green was a loyal supporter of Sean Fitzpatrick, as I am sure many others were, because he was a good and thoughtful manager and earned their respect. Sean was replaced by a Mr. Beard, another polite man, who now and then came from above to be among us. He was also reported to be a decent sort, though the grapevine said he subjected himself to the sycophants.

A new passenger terminal with several piers was built, and later, huge aircraft hangars. Some of this construction reduced the beautiful original terminal to nonentity. Indeed, the planning then and as it still appears, was makeshift.

This new terminal created new aircraft loading routines. Previously, checked passenger baggage was automatically conveyed outdoors on to a large carousel or roundabout, as it was called. It was where allocated staff worked in arctic conditions, sorting the baggage flight numbers and dispatching the loaded trucks. Quite a few staff avoided this duty by swapping shifts, others claiming all kinds of illness. Nevertheless, there were a few reliables who never complained, such as Larry Quinn, Jackie Coulahan and Paddy Cahill – absolute gentlemen. Then there was Denis 'Spider' O' Rourke, Mick O'Hara, Martin Redmond, Tom and Jim Smith, and Bertie Hillard. All bright and cheerful employees. Well, most of the time.

The new terminal facilitated indoor baggage sorting, and the consequent better working conditions. This fact ignited a whole raft of applications from staff, staff that had earlier done everything in their power to avoid it. They now claimed priority because of some physical ailment or other. Mr. Fly observed that the baggage hall had become a chamber of horrors. These changes coincided with and perhaps infected the same plague on the older loading staff, the cause of which was as follows…

A ritual existed whereby the older staff rotated from being a porter one day and an aircraft loader the next. The position of being a porter was an extremely lucrative occupation, and the Valhalla of all concerned. Of course, as the new employees, we hadn't a snowball's chance of getting on the gravy train, therefore we enjoyed the antics of our elderly comrades in their efforts to win by any means this dignified position. First, they refused to drive on the grounds of not having been trained (though some of them had motor cars). Secondly, they refused to work, claiming disabilities.

This activity was only half-supported by the union reps, they being relative newcomers, though they themselves itching to be established at the airport front door as porters. The manager, Mr. Beard, surrendered and created on a seniority basis a permanent staff to assist the passengers. The ineligible ones took it with dignity, that is except Bertie, ex-army and a regular on the roundabout. He swore, "There wasn't enough coal in hell to burn them."

One particular day, having finished my duty and about to enter my battered and now hand-painted Morris Minor, I saw a wallet on the ground. There was about forty pounds in it. I walked back to the arrivals building and left it in Lost Property. About a month later I received a letter accompanied with a postal order for thirty bob. The letter explained how delighted he was to know there was at least one honest man in Dublin. How my mother laughed, exclaiming, "The eejit must have lost a half dozen of them." In 1990, the year she died, that letter along with another of a similar nature (which she received in 1956) was among the few treasures she hoarded.

Facial expressions tell you everything – that smile, a laugh, a frown
It reveals when you are happy – contented as a king
When in love, grinning like a clown,
Expressions are just like a statement—the state of your mind,
Pessimistic or optimistic we all read the sign.

Chapter 3: Follow My Leader

It was in the middle sixties that three of us decided to take advantage of the staff subsidised travel, and take a holiday in the Canaries. Our leader was the indomitable Gerry Feeney from Whitehall, and the third stooge was my friend and neighbour, Billy Murray. Our day of departure was a Friday, and we presented ourselves at the check-in counter to be informed the aircraft was full. Gerry, ever intelligent and alert, astutely grabbed our tickets and beelined to the booking desk. He returned after negotiations with tickets to Frankfurt via Manchester and Brussels. From Frankfurt, the day after arriving, we would fly by Lufthansa to Las Palmas.

As we were boarding the Viscount I noticed a bearded fellow wearing a raincoat, a raincoat favoured by the horse racing fraternity. What drew my attention was this fellow's air of confidence – that of a seasoned traveller. Our arrival at Manchester passed without us having to leave the aircraft, and within a half hour we were airborne again.

On arriving in Brussels, the aircraft parked quite a distance from the arrivals terminal. Through the window we could see a receptionist meeting the disembarking passengers. When she had about a dozen she briskly headed toward the buildings with a thin and widening line of peds trailing behind.

When we disembarked there were about fifty despairing elderly passengers milling around at the foot of the steps, the procession having disappeared. I then noticed the raincoated fellow. He had disembarked behind us, and he set off walking in a very positive manner. "Com'on," said I, "this lad knows where he's going." We immediately got in behind him, with the throng puffing and blowing behind us. Into the building he led us, then down a corridor about a mile long, the agitated mob behind us walking on our heels in fear of being lost or abandoned.

Then we entered another long corridor and halfway along it his nibs abruptly stops and pushes open a door. We all crowded in behind him. It was a toilet! A small, multi-gender toilet which our man used before fighting his way through the crowd and away with him, with us in hot pursuit. A couple of minutes later he led us into the arrivals hall.

Billy bought *Lady Chatterley's Lover* at one of the stalls while Gerry and I had a beer and a good laugh. After an hour's delay we boarded our plane again – this time without the raincoated fellow, to land in Frankfurt without further incident. In Frankfurt, all the hotels were booked out due to a leather festival. So, after a skinful of beer we overnighted in a very comfortable tenement-type building. The next day we caught our flight to Las Palmas for a sunny February holiday.

Up to this time the ground ops staff roster had been compiled by two clerical staff, namely Joe Ward and his secretary. Tony O'Toole, an operative and a decent man from County Mayo, was delegated to the duty. When Tony retired, Tommy Duffy replaced him before the incorruptible Patrick Hartnett was appointed. It was an onerous and thankless job, with staff members appealing for all kinds of alterations to suit their lifestyle. I suppose most were genuine, though the same faces were to be seen loitering outside his office with regularity.

Overtime was a curse that many embraced. They couldn't get enough of it, and strokes were pulled to create it. A couple of rogues devised a brilliant tactic. As soon as the Gaelic football calendar was published, one or two would request in advance this and that Sunday off, on the grounds of wanting to see Dublin playing. Come a couple of days before the Sunday game, they'd put their names down for overtime, preferably the early shift in the hope of working two shifts at double time. They were banking, of course, on a measure of staff absenting themselves on that particular Sunday, which they did. Did they put the overtime cash to good use? Only God knows. It certainly wasn't gambled or spent in the pubs. How they spent it, if they ever did, is a mystery, though one or two drove cars that reflected millionaire status.

Ex-President Eisenhower was the first president to visit. It was a private visit with very little security. Mr. Eisenhower arrived in a helicopter from Britain where he had been playing golf. I was a crew member sent down to look after his baggage, and for our efforts we received the wonderful sum of seven pounds each. Sometime later the same year, President Kennedy arrived on a day that had a holiday feeling about it. Again, I was a crew member dispatched to look after his luggage, but unfortunately there was no seven quid, not even seven bob.

It was in the seventies when France opened her doors for the importation of lamb. This was a great boost for the farmers, for the export figures, and the hauliers. It was good for our staff, also. I recall the extra flights beginning early in the year and creating lots of overtime with chartered aircraft having to wait until men were available to load them. This was that time of year when all temporary staff had been laid off, and an act of Parliament would be needed to re-employ some.

Some export agents began to boost our enthusiasm by offering a fiver apiece, cash in hand, if we would load them. I recall one such agent – a large, wavy-haired, naïve fellow of about thirty cajoling the lads with the promise of a fiver each on completion. When the aircraft was loaded with the usual three hundred or so carcases, he tells the lads he has no ready cash but if they wait a while he'll rush home and get it. The six lads retire to the canteen to wait, and after an hour the expletives began with most agreeing that the hoor had codded them. Others speculated he was in some pub at their expense. Jimmy Gaynor, a brilliant, good-humoured lad, stated, "I know where he is! I bet he's at home now laughing and telling his mott, 'Wait till I tell ye a good one... there's a bunch of f***in' eejits out at Dublin Airport waiting for me to bring them back a fiver each.'" Eventually, the agent appeared and paid up in full.

Chapter 4: The Age of Conflict

The seventies saw the replacement of Viscounts with the marvellous Boeing 737, its palletised flooring enabling the seating to be stripped in minutes and reloaded with seven huge pallets of freight. The roller-matting floor was a feature created during the Berlin airlift.

Unions and union reps had always existed, and rightly so, but in the late seventies an eruption of work stoppages in both engineering and in ground ops reflected deep frustration. The engineering stoppages were led not by red flag wallahs but by highly intelligent, overqualified personnel who would fiercely contest with company negotiators. In ground ops there were several unofficial strikes which created havoc for passengers. Eventually, the engineering union, AGEMO, negotiated several excellent monetary and conditional improvements for their members. The unions representing the operatives obtained pro rata agreements. This then angered the tradesmen who again went on strike in dissent, goaded, no doubt, by the antics of some of said operatives leaping about in delight and hollering, "Youse shake the tree an' we'll pick t'apples!"

In ground ops, Joe Whorriskey was now station manager, a big, gruff, remote, calculating man from the north. He brilliantly chaired the morning delay meetings. With a few caustic comments he'd get to the kernel of every incident and aircraft delay. Delayed departures created major problems. Scheduled aircraft would have had a slot waiting for them in London, Paris, and most other large international airports. If an aircraft was delayed departing it would very likely be kept circling at these airports for ages awaiting another slot. This resulted in that same aircraft being delayed for its later commitments. And that is why the ten o'clock morning meeting left those accused of lacking or making poor managerial decisions at the time, gulping and passing the buck, often times when an honest account of the event would have been accepted by the manager.

I believe that during this period the majority of staff at our level thought much about the union reps, but reluctantly obeyed the diktat to strike. Anyway, the stoppages – with one exception – were unofficial, lasting no more than two or three days. To make up the financial loss, there would be overtime available for those who wanted it.

At holiday peak times there were many, many occasions when there were severe shortages of staff. On one Sunday morning for instance, Tucks was struggling to handle multiple aircraft movements with insufficient crews. He handed the worksheet to a junior staff member, letting it be known that he was going off to procure more men, and promising to be back in an hour before leaping on his bike. The same bike that was seen shortly afterwards leaning against the wall of Kealy's Pub a mile from the airport. The upshot was, neither extra staff nor Tucks appeared. The next morning, he entered Joe Whorriskey's office, stood before his desk, gave no explanation except to stand erect and salute uttering one word – "Guilty."

On another occasion, a Saturday evening, a crisis arose due to the shortage of staff. The senior traffic officer (the clerical supremo) stated in a very positive manner that he'd 'get men', and off he popped. After a couple of hours, a collection of inebriated fellows arrived without the traffic officer. He apparently went sick for a week and we heard no more about it.

Many factors created staff shortages, such as bad weather which delayed arrivals and departures. Aircraft grounded and delayed in Dublin or overseas by fog, snow, or crosswinds, led to loading staff – the vast majority willing and hardworking – being overwhelmed when they got the all-clear. I recall one such afternoon when, allocated with a crew to turn around a Viscount, halfway through the operation I noticed another Viscount landing and then taxiing onto a stand and being ignored. I sent one of our crew for aircraft steps to facilitate the passengers while continuing our own duty. Having completed it we then offloaded the still-ignored aircraft. When we returned to base we were questioned as to our whereabouts. As I explained the clerk said thanks and handed me another hour's duty, informing me that we had forfeited our break.

Nowadays baggage and freight are containerised indoors, before being transported to the aircraft and mechanically loaded. Up until the year 2000 most domestic and continental flights were physically loaded. It was bloody strenuous work.

The middle seventies saw the introduction of a Hump, a DC-6, and shortly afterwards, another one. They were much bigger than the DC-4. This DC-6 had gone through huge modification with the forward nose area massively enlarged and fitted with a casement door which could manually and quickly be pumped open. This aircraft operated as a multi-purpose transporter, such as a horse freighter with two horses per pallet. It could operate as a full passenger or a full freighter, or as a partial passenger and a couple of pallets of freight.

When Aer Lingus acquired them, they were used to facilitate passengers and their cars. This novel idea was very popular for a time. The aircraft operated mostly to and from Perpignan in the South-East of France. The pilots dreaded them, they were slow and subject to engineering fragilities. I clearly remember one particular frosty night having loaded one and waiting for it to move so we could have our break. The plane revved and revved, moving twenty yards or so only to stop. After another twenty minutes it would move another bit. During these manoeuvres, Billy Walshe, a Red Cap and, like us, ready for a cup of tea, stared out of the window and observed, "I swear that f****r is afraid of the dark."

I recall one of the Humps overshooting the runway because of brake failure, and ending halfway across the Naul Road. I was instructed to get the Hilo, a piece of equipment of about forty feet long and weighing several tons. It was used, and is still used, to load and offload pallets, cars, and horses. Anyway, with a Garda escort I towed this Hilo down the Swords road, then across the back roads. When we arrived at the aircraft there was no room to manoeuvre the Hilo into a reversing position, so I had to reverse a half mile, turn and reverse it back to the aircraft. I then positioned it into the offloading position. When stabilised, using its own power, an operator raised the loading platform to the required height and within twenty minutes we unloaded six cars, freight and baggage, and were gone. The efficiency was very satisfying.

Marino Branch
Brainse Marino
Tel: 8336297

Paddy 'Friend' McGrath, Mick Brennan and me in Slattery's, Dublin.

Gerry Feeny, Willy Murray and myself in London en route to The Canaries in 1966.

Me with Eddie Martin in Washington on an Aer Lingus work trip to the USA, early 1973.

Larry, Eddie, Andy and me in New York on the NY leg of our Aer Lingus work trip, 1973.

Chapter 5: A Cruise

Yes, it was another idea of Gerry Feeney's, though at a thousand quid each, it was pricey. It was a fourteen-day cruise to Madeira, the Canary Islands and La Corunna. The cruise was organised by the Franciscans. Apparently, it had been an annual event for a number of years. Assembly point for our trip was in late July, in a warehouse in Alexandria Basin. I was one of the first to arrive. Most of the early arrivals were elderly, coming either by taxi or ferried by relations, they and their luggage hastily abandoned thereby adding to the growing pile of suitcases on the damp floor of this ramshackle shed.

There was no receptionist, so on this dampish July afternoon we wandered around. From what we could see of the ship through the cracks in the shed's galvanised wall, it was painted white and had a blue streak at the waterline. It had two main decks and two tiny upper decks; I guessed the ship's length was about three hundred feet. It was called the *Armenia*, and that name struck a bell! Hadn't Mr. Khrushchev arrived in Egypt in 1964 aboard the motor ship *Armenia*? Apparently, it was to open the Aswan dam, the dam which Russia had financed.

When about fifty of us had gathered, the shed sliding door was pushed open and like a herd of cattle we rushed to board. The efficient ticket collector was female and Irish. The others were Russian or from its satellites.

Our cabin was on the first deck, and about ten feet by eight with a bunk on either side. A small compartment at the end of each bunk served as a wardrobe. A large square porthole gave ample light and viewing, and a toilet-cum-shower room completed our quarters. This was to be our refuge for the next fourteen days.

Happily established, we studied the boarding activities. Taxis were doing a roaring business, and private bus loads were arriving and disgorging families and larger groups, all pushing and scrambling to grab their luggage as if the ship was going to leave without them. The children were either gaping in wonder or excitedly shouting and gesticulating. Adults queued with expressions of self-conscious pleasure, perhaps with expectations of adventure – exploits that would bore all and sundry for years to come.

At five that evening there were still seven or eight anxious-looking males and females with their suitcases on the quay. A deal was being made with the tour organiser. Money changed hands and gleefully they stumbled up the gangway.

At six and on a near full tide, a tug arrived and bullied us out into the road. The cruise had begun. Even though it was blustery and with a little drizzle, the decks were lined with smiling voyagers all admiring the grim industrial arse of Dublin. The Esso oil bunkers, the deserted wharves, the still barely covered stinking mudbanks of the Bay. Soon as we cleared the shelter and turned south, a tangible roll was apparent. Fifteen minutes later the decks were almost deserted. From this time onward only one person was continuously contented for the whole length of the cruise – the adaptable Gerry.

The cruise itinerary recommended a dress code; formal for dinner, informal for lunch. This first evening only five or six couples turned up for dinner, and all dressed casually, but they didn't linger. Indeed, before dinner was even served they had bolted, green-faced.

The dining room was large, nicely decorated with plastic flowers, and with tables casually arranged even though they were bolted to the floor. The staff? They were smiling and efficient, and nicely turned out. First course was vegetable soup of a peculiar brown hue. Main course consisted of monster, tasteless spuds boiled in their skins, and whole carrots, ditto. Meat was a roast, I think. But it could also have been boiled. Or even baked or fried. Indeed, there was plenty of it, though to this day having questioned many I still cannot determine what animal it was.

If there were awards for blandness, this cook was a winner by a mile. "It's their first night," we shrugged. Anyway, there was free bottled vodka to wash it down. Though our hearts were willing, queasy stomachs refused a second glass. We retired to our quarters for Rennies or Bisodal, and hopefully, a good night's sleep. The ship's gait through the night ensured few turned up for breakfast, which incidentally was ok. Plenty of fruit drinks, a good selection of cereals, eggs in whatever form you wanted, though bacon wasn't on the menu.

You gleam as my beacon in a sea of insignificance
A shining light to set my compass by,
Or that North Star in the morning in a fading firmament
So beautiful and heartening to the eye.

Chapter 6: Getting to Know You

We'd slept well and looked forward to socialising. A sortie out on deck revealed another blustery day and a lumpy sea. At regular intervals the ship's deck would be saturated with spray. We joined other fugitives on the lee side, huddled under the hanging lifeboats. This was more or less our first contact with fellow travellers.

During the day a picture developed. There were groups from Cork, Northern Ireland, Dundalk, Tipperary and Dublin. The majority were sociable, though there was a rather diffident bunch from the midlands. It's as if they were suspicious of us. They kept to themselves, responding abruptly to our friendly overtures, though in uncompromising tones, one or two made negative comments on the weather, the food, or whatever.

At eleven that morning we were summoned to the boat deck for an emergency drill. The instructor had poor English but nevertheless was comprehensible, and the safety rules were more or less like that of an aeroplane, i.e. pull this or push that, etc.

I mentioned to Gerry that I couldn't recall whether in an emergency, we were supposed to get in the lifeboat on deck, or climb down a rope ladder. "Wouldn't matter a shite," Gerry said, "be drowned anyway trying to understand that fella!"

I decided to explore the ship – which took all of about five minutes, though discretion prevented me from venturing below the orlop where the majority were packed.

The dining and function rooms were below the main deck, on the waterline. There was a bar in each that was closed until six in the evening. There was another small bar with a television forward of the dining room, also closed until six in the evening. The brochure lauded a library, so on this squally day a browse through the shelves would pass a pleasant hour. A diagram of the ship directed me to a hatch.

After persistent knocking it was wrenched open, revealing a female face writhing in aggression. "Wha' you wan?" it hollered.

"Books," I stuttered in surprise. She rooted savagely in a drawer under the hatch, slapped a sheet of paper down in front of me, and nearly severed my hand slamming the hatch shut as I picked it up. So much for the library. Anyway, who wants to read about 'Soviet Trade with Outer Mongolia' or 'Agricultural Successes in Uzbekistan'? Henceforth, I directed only those I disliked to the library.

Dress was formal for tonight's dinner. Neither Gerry nor I had evening dress or a tux. A tie would have to do. Gerry said it was all a load of bull, and I agreed, though later it was embarrassing. Three couples turned up superbly attired, with several others in tuxedos. A few more, like ourselves, were in collar and tie. The rest could be generously described as *casual*. The dinner? Exactly the same as the night before! Few finished the meal, and only the fish dined well.

A band played in the function room, but there were few attendees due to sea sickness. Experts said that the ship was built for the inland Black Sea, hence no stabilisers, and instability. I spent the evening in the smaller bar covertly watching a selection of widows celebrating the voyage. Brother, could they make brandy and gin disappear!

Though the sky was clear and it was getting warmer as we headed south, we still needed our coats. A horizon devoid of land greeted us, Ireland having disappeared during the night. I counted eighteen fishing trawlers, with more appearing as we sailed. The ice was breaking among the passengers, the common dominator being the ship and the food. Mealtimes were anticipated not for the culinary efforts of the cook, but the superlatives describing his failure.

Dolphins raced alongside, leaping high out of the water, seemingly to exude joy and absolute pleasure in their existence. They kept at it for about an hour before disappearing only to return again later. Well, I think it was the same bunch. At around eleven o'clock an aeroplane appeared and swooped low over our ship. It was an RAF Nimrod, and we were getting the once over. It climbed and circled, then swooped again so close that people ducked and children screamed in alarm.

On a calm sea it was becoming very hot, so calm they decided to uncover the swimming pool. When revealed it was about twenty feet by twenty, and about six to eight feet deep. Most, bar us, were now clad in swimwear. Pat, a burly, twenty-four-year-old school teacher from Cork, good-humouredly challenged everyone to a dip. When Pat jumped in there were already two young lads and a couple of middle-aged codgers serenely floating in the pool.

The youngsters climbed out, apparently not liking the glint in Pat's eye. Pat began to flounder, creating a wave. The codgers at first thought it funny until the waves began to send them sky-high for a couple of seconds before their arses struck the bottom after a couple more. One cunningly tried hanging onto the rim of the pool to climb out as the wave descended. He nearly made it until the wave caught him on the way up and sent him howling into the air again. Crude as it was, I never laughed as much. The victims took it in good spirit, but were never again seen in the pool. Whenever Pat appeared the pool quickly emptied.

I passed a pair of the Midlanders one day. A blocky, red-faced lad wearing a peaked cap and a red pullover breasted me, "Wha'cha think o' the grub?" he challenged.

"Not too bad," I replied, "just a matter of getting us…"

"Twas shit," he swore, cutting me off and spitting over the side. "Pure shit! Ain't that right Tom?" he said to his companion.

"Twas surely," Tom gravely replied, both abruptly turning their backs. I was dismissed.

The entertainment manager was the good-natured Al Banim, beginning each morning at ten with physical exercises (after nine o'clock mass), with bingo after lunch for those interested.

A dance band played each night in the function from nine until two. It was all rock 'n' roll, and well attended. A section of that room accommodated the bridge players. They were mostly genteel people from Northern Ireland and of course, Bob. Bob? Yes, Bob. A grey-haired, distinguished-looking gent originally from Dublin. Years earlier he'd migrated to the US, joined the army, and was severely wounded in Korea. After demob he was employed as a ticketer in the New York transport system. Now retired and using two sticks, he was back in Dublin living with his sister.

Late at night as the band played, Bob, a real nice guy, left himself available as a sage to the bewildered and the troubled who found his ear accessible and his advice sound.

Other individuals were noticeable at this the witching hour, the two 'quare wans' for instance. In their early twenties, they were shapely and dressed to kill. They maintained an aloof aura during these early days. They sipped high-balls at the bar and danced only with each other.

Another quare hawk was a client called The Docker. He was about five-foot-seven, stocky, aged about thirty-eight or forty, with a pock-marked, beery face, and hair dyed black and craftily manoeuvred over his bald spot into a Tony Curtis. He was always dressed in fawns and reds, with a penchant for jewellery, such as glittering medallions, rings, and bangles. He had the eyes of a predator and seldom left the bar. Also, like Dracula, he appeared only at night. The grapevine suggested a wife and family ashore. These three were some of the group who joined the ship at the last minute.

Another head worth mentioning was a skull who wandered about the deck at night with an accordion. He was about fifty and stooped, quiet and respectful. He was monopolised from day one by the Midlanders, cajoled into playing the old come-all ye's. You know the crap; 'Rose of Tralee', 'Road by the River', 'Patsy Fagin'... Jesus!

A decision was reached to break up the monopoly. Pat and his beautiful girlfriend Marie, a Tipperary nurse, Gerry and I intruded when the concert started and insisted on democracy. Our choices must be considered. From then on Pat, a brilliant singer terrific at rendering Gilbert and Sullivan operettas, invited the accordion player to accompany him, but he was unable. The Midlanders had a nose for a while, but gradually accepted the improvement.

And of course, there were the widows – eight or ten of them who seemed to have gravitated toward one another like flotsam, all enjoying the fruits of their dead husbands' financial efforts. Their watering hole was the forward bar where they spent most of the late evening, nattering and slugging small ones.

There was an unfortunate family of four from Northern Ireland, devastated by the loss of a husband and father – a judge, murdered by the IRA. His eldest, a fifteen-year-old daughter, was the wonderful mainstay of this tragic family.

A notice appeared on the bulletin board informing all and sundry that in Madeira an Irish cook was waiting to board ship to supervise the galley. All went happily to bed looking forward to landfall and normal grub.

On day four we awoke to find ourselves sailing on a flat, calm sea off the coast of Madeira. Rising out of the ocean were its high, sharp mountains, the result of volcanic activity, so the brochure told me. We docked at Funchal at noon. Madeira is a beautiful island, extremely colourful, and in 1983 not yet vandalised by concrete. Small, cottage-type houses individually exhibited their owners' taste in hanging baskets and in the subtle colours of the house's walls. I liked that – people, although poor, were proud of their little patch.

Funchal is a town of cobbled streets and a small square. Brilliant, full-sized concrete replicas of Columbus' three ships are on view, for apparently Madeira was his last stop before the Indies. A bus tour brought us up to the top of the mountain which dominates the harbour. Our ship seemed as a toy far below.

There was a market with hand-made lace table cloths, handkerchiefs, religious vestments, highly recommended by the experts. There was no menswear on show except for slippers made from shark skin. The usual tourist junk was also available, including Funchal in a water-filled globe in which snowflakes appeared when shaken, even though it had never snowed on Funchal.

Next stop was a village called Monte. The attraction here was a long, steep, cobbled street with sharp bends. Large wicker baskets designed to hold four or five adults, were positioned at the top of this steep street leading down into the village. Two local men per basket yoked themselves, and away they galloped. It was for a pittance, and I didn't enjoy it. To me, it seemed too much like slavery.

As we climbed up through the hills the scenery changed from intense banana plantations to pine forest, possibly because the mountains are too steep for terracing. It was Sunday, and outside the neat little houses of the villages groups of men dressed in white cotton shirts and trousers, and wearing straw hats, sat around talking. The women sitting outside their doors appeared to be knitting or embroidering, or just chewing the rag with their neighbours. They took not the slightest notice of the gaping Paddies as we trundled past.

The winery was set into the side of the mountain with a split-level balcony suspended over the valley far below. The views were tremendous. The sales and tasting apartment were indoors. This was where we were greeted warmly by the smiling manager and staff.

Hundreds of tiny glasses of the labelled wines had already been laid out on a long counter like regiments of soldiers. Shyness where drink is concerned not being one of our national traits, we immediately got stuck in, beginning with sophisticated quaffing which quickly degenerated to gulping and swigging, as the glasses were refilled and refilled. Some gobshite offered a few bars of 'My Way' as the smiling, friendly faces behind the counter were changing to glares of consternation as empty glasses were proffered again and again. Gerry, a non-drinker, said we were making a show of ourselves as we spontaneously broke into 'Molly Malone'. Smiling management faces returned when we gave our orders for take-aways.

The journey back to the ship was enjoyable, at least the bits I remember. In the confraternal warmth created by good vintage, we looked forward to the prospect of a good Irish dinner later.

Long faces and sour looks were the order of the following day. Groups of angry, gesticulating passengers were to be seen here and there in fierce discussion. Last night's dinner had been exactly the same boring fare as the days before! Furthermore, Red Pullover had entered the galley to check on the Irish cook. Before being ejected, he'd ascertained there was no Irish cook. A junta was formed; their brief was to approach the cook and demand change in the quality, variety, and presentation of the meals. Up to this point some passengers had resigned themselves to tanking up at lunch, and avoiding dinner. Tonight was different, the dining room was crammed, all to bear witness to the cook's comeuppance.

Side-plates were laid, heaped, as usual, with the inevitable cucumbers which would return to the kitchen untouched. The strange brown soup, likewise. Heads turned toward the plotters. They, in turn, stared pointedly at their spokesperson. After a number of silent head movements, hints, and nudges, she shakily got to her feet and teetered toward the galley followed by a couple of what were supposed to be supporters, but which turned out to be spineless voyeurs.

Several versions exist of what happened in the galley, the most believable of which was that the cook didn't understand English. To her credit, the spokesperson laid into him hot and heavy, pointing to the unpeeled spuds and huge whole carrots. The cook, a huge benign man dressed in white apron and chef's hat, stared down at her with concerned interest. Suddenly, he came to life and began shouting orders right and left. We saw the swing doors of the galley burst open, and waiters dashed out bearing trays of second helpings. I never witnessed such naked fear and panic before. Believe me, it's not a pretty sight. How there wasn't half a dozen killed vacating that dining room God only knows. Our arrival off Tenerife prevented a mutiny.

Is paradise something we may touch

Or is it just a state of mind?

I would love to join the crowd there –

I bet there's a crush.

And somebody nice to find – somebody warm and kind.

To love, I am resigned.

Chapter 7: Watch Your Pockets

Arriving by ship is a brilliant way to visit. From far off you see as the ancient mariners saw, that is, before you sail into Tenerife's huge natural harbour, a harbour that bunkers over fifteen thousand ships per annum. There was great excitement onboard – the grapevine promised loads of duty-free bargains. Everyone wanted off the tub if only for a day, some to get away from the oppressive moaners, the rest of us to get something normal to eat. Gerry and I joined the bus tour. Even the widows joined, dressed to the nines, their shades roosting on their perms. After four or five days on the razzle they had decided enough was enough.

We had to fight our way through a throng of hawkers to board the bus. This island is much different than Madeira, with its developed concrete apartments as far as the eye could see. Where Madeira was natural and colourful, Tenerife is commercial. Outside the city and up into the hills, every square inch is used for banana and tomato growing. I found the countryside uninteresting, but then I'm not a farmer. With no winery in sight, it was a damp squib.

The hawkers were still active when we returned, and my scotch was replenished. Back on board one old-ish fellow was flashing an Omega watch. "Forty pound an' me own," he bragged.

"A fake!" we told him. Normally affable, he didn't speak to us for two days, and only then he admitted the watch had stopped and wouldn't go again.

I saw the two quare ones chatting up two of the crew – the sailors showed little interest. The ship's main deck was now so hot even sandals were uncomfortable. Previously we couldn't get enough sun, but now we skulked in the shade.

The mood on board was sombre. Most wore resigned expressions. Only revenge would satisfy this group. Red Pullover swore, "We'd been codded up to our eyes an' the hoors should be med' pay." Our arrival at La Palma put paid to immediate action. Santa Cruz, the port town and capital, seemed untouched by time – narrow cobbled streets, colonial-type balconied houses, flowers of all descriptions were thriving in the tropical environment.

Strange, though it being near midday there were very few people about as we took the obligatory tour inland and up into the mountains. Grapes are the major crop here, and a very labour-intensive process it is. A metre depth of sand must be cleared so the vines can be planted. As the vines grow, sand is gradually shovelled back until the metre is restored. Apparently, the sand retains whatever moisture is gained by sea mists that drift in at night, thereby giving life to the vines.

We visited the national park where the largest volcanic crater in the world exists; seventeen miles in circumference, it last erupted in 1949. The tour bus passed loads of wineries, but the driver never stopped. That evening we set sail on a two-day journey to La Corunna.

For the second time there were articles missing from my returned laundry. Nothing expensive, a towel, maybe a shirt. Still, if things progressed I'd have little left when we hit Dublin. I decided to approach the cabin stewardess. This was difficult, for when I waited she didn't turn up. Gerry, a late riser, told me that when I left she immediately appeared and went through cabin duties like a dose of salts. I decided to use cunning to trap her.

I left the cabin at the usual time, noisily climbed the stairs, and slammed the door to the dining room but remained outside it. On my knees on the stairs, I watched our cabin door. Sure enough, she appeared within a minute. "Where's me shirt?" I demanded in an aggrieved tone. "The one from laundry!"

Her mouth half-opened and her jaws moved as if articulating, but no sound came. "Poor ould hoor is dumb," Gerry reproached, "lave'r alone for Jasus' sake." He made me feel so guilty I gave her a fiver and told her to forget it.

It was amazing the number of skins who kept asking, "Where are we going next?" I'm positive if they were told it was the Falkland Islands, they wouldn't have known the difference. One knowledgeable lad, a self-important gobshite employed by Dublin Corporation announced, whenever he got an audience, that La Corunna was just around the corner from Gibraltar. Actually, he said, you can *see* La Corunna from Gibraltar. In reality, they're about a thousand miles, including Portugal, apart.

> *How minuscule I feel when I dwell on thee*
> *We who are as bees within a hive.*
> *And our actions so predictable yet*
> *You always know it is me in where a*
> *Multitude of recidivists abide.*

Chapter 8: La Corunna

At night the band still played the same tunes, with rock 'n' rollers mechanically going through the movements. Dreamers and spoofers lobotomised one another at the bar. The widows were back on determined drinking. Bob still held court each evening, hearing confessions and dispensing wisdom. The two quare ones, their sophisticated accents replaced with mine and Gerry's working-class Dublin ones, had joined a disappointed bunch of male and female topers each night on deck, engaging in serious drinking sessions.

We were lazing on the deck the day before making landfall at La Corunna when the subject of food arose again. A rumour had spread that the tour organiser was aboard and was secretly residing in the deluxe suite under the captain's bridge. This was real news, though we'd never seen cabin attendants approach, indeed any movement at all near it. Red pullover swore his info was reliable, and furthermore, that "the hoor had a blonde with him." The docker agreed, he said he knew her and that she was a Leeson Street brasser. Under some pretext, a couple of skins sneaked up and tried the door. It was locked but through the porthole they saw nothing but spare ship gear. Red Pullover said they must be hiding him somewhere else. So much for paranoia.

Not a drum was heard, not a funeral note

As his corpse to the rampart we hurried.

La Corunna is ancient city with stirring history, including Wellington's Peninsular War. Though a couple of years before Wellington, Sir John Moore was killed retreating from Joseph Napoleon's army and is buried here. The Phoenicians and Romans were here. Drake burned the place in 1859. The Tower of Hercules is a lighthouse. The Spanish claim it is the oldest in the world. On seeing it, it looks 19th century. It's a very pleasant city, a credit to their corporation.

Now in August, flowering flora in ordered beds were placed wherever possible. The city centre is beautifully preserved. The cleanliness of this city of about a million is impressive. The climate in this region of north-western Spain is wet and warm, a commercial city with fishing and farming the main industries.

Our ship, still flying the hammer and sickle, was not universally greeted. We were getting more of the two fingers than welcoming smiles. Some passengers, on making their way back to the ship, were deliberately sent astray, and they weren't even gargled. Others were refused service in the shops.

I'm not sure if this part of Spain is on the tourist trail, but there were enjoyable differences and to us, unique. I became aware of little customs which I had not noticed elsewhere. Like in the afternoons, some cafés and restaurants cleared the tables to facilitate the hordes of children coming from school, mostly under the care of their grandmothers. They noisily conversed, played cards and I think, dominos. They appeared to purchase little, if anything.

Having done the tour which included the Church of St. Francis, we saw the house where Peron's second wife lived. Then, left to our own devices, we topped up with fish and chips before we boarded for the two-day trip to Dublin.

Cabin fever, stir crazy, or whatever it is called, is a terrible affliction. There is nowhere to hide, nowhere to run to escape the continuous moaning. Here we were within hours of journey's end, and they were still at it. Adaptability or make do seemed to be beyond them. A new rumour was of a competition to be held. First prize was another glorious week on the Armenia, second prize was two weeks…

The ship hove to in Cardigan Bay that sunny afternoon. The word was we were waiting for the tide to enter Dublin. Lolling about on deck we listened to the radio as Dublin and Cork replayed the football semi-final which Dublin went on to win. Only other thing of note was the captain invited anyone interested to visit his bridge. It was surprisingly small though fully computerised, and had a satellite positioning installed. Captain himself was a giant, in his late fifties and dressed in khaki trousers and tunic. He was friendly and tolerant, particularly when being asked the same questions time and time again.

We were now looking forward to getting off the ship as prisoners waiting for release. In fairness, the staff had always been clean, efficient and polite, except for the head-case in the library. The food was boring, but by the standards of the Soviets it was probably OK. The real problem was ourselves. It was the containment – we couldn't get away from one another. After only three days aboard and out of boredom, I would gladly have worked my passage. There were others, I am sure, of the same frame of mind. Gerry was the only passenger who really enjoyed himself, who had no complaints whatsoever. As we disembarking I heard a voice calling, "Bye-bye" – it was the bloody cabin attendant, the one who couldn't speak, leaning over the handrail smiling and waving.

Everybody dreams, dreaming dreams of chivalry and love

For dreams are part of what we are.

And all aspire to following a star

Until life's realities grind us into drudgery.

Chapter 9: Lilliput

Back to the reality of Dublin Airport, a rumour-filled landscape of promotions, strikes, lump sums and overtime. That alone wasn't enough for some who were prophesying "big changes on the way."

From my own perspective, and as I mentioned earlier, I enjoyed the work… and good companions made it extra enjoyable. I liked it particularly when we had a good crew leader. John Higgins from Cabra was an example of the best. A small, balding, energetic fellow who, without raising his voice, would get a rhythm going that was like music. He was always kind and informative to new staff. He was a supervisor who remembered your name, always getting the maximum response. People loved working with this fellow. There were others such as Tommy Stafford and Jim Turner, brilliant leaders who never moaned, and who never shirked the most unpopular duties. Always dedicated, Jim and Tommy could not be influenced to join any clique, movement, or set. There was also Joe McGuire, Willie Parker, Mick Driscoll, Mick Regan, Andy Larkin and Tommy Ryan, an ex-soldier and absolute gentleman. These were the fellows that we used as examples of the best of the very best, when later we were indoctrinating new staff.

The only thing I detested was night shift duty. The nights, seven in a row, especially during the winter months when Dublin Airport was as cold as the arctic plateau. Often, we would load a freighter, and then to be told the Mag had dropped and the aircraft was now unserviceable as it took hours to recharge it. We'd have to offload tons of freight, get a new aircraft and load plan, and reload under pressure to maintain the schedule. Still, these were the challenges, the conditions of employment.

It was not a merely mundane labouring job, it was a flexible role providing purpose and fulfilment which was missing in other lives. We were now operating better and novel equipment, and regularly handling the bigger aircraft. To me, efficiency was its own reward.

This was the period when our sister Margaret and her husband Michael bought a house in Santry on the outskirts of Dublin city, having been refused permission to build a house on a site in our large garden. We missed them terribly, especially their children. Soon afterwards I built on an extension to their new home, thereby enlarging their dining room and kitchen. This event set in motion a demand for my services, resulting in about fourteen different building jobs over the next ten years – enterprises I never made a halfpenny from. Indeed, some left me out of pocket.

With my airport activities demanding more of my presence, my building projects were constantly delayed. This resulted in farewell to the feel-good factor of some of my clients. I didn't blame the odd housewife giving me sour looks while trying to cope with her kids, with the lunatic that was me under her feet for a few hours each evening. Anyway, most of them still talk to me.

Our brother Jack, as I mentioned earlier, was now a barman. His uniform was a daily white shirt and white apron. He had served his time and was now employed in Berigan's pub down on John Rogerson quay. Mrs. Berigan, a bustling, low-sized, strong-willed widow, had mostly dock workers as her clientele. These gentlemen would fill her bar for their ten o'clock morning break and at lunchtime, and without a bother would scoff five or six pints each before returning to work.

The odd night Jack would arrive home with shirt and apron not just soiled but saturated. He would be noncommittal when asked to explain, fobbing off the enquirer with "a barrel burst." The truth emerged much later. Apparently the docker who had reached a certain point on his credit allowance would be asked to fork out. If unable, Mrs. Berigan would order Jack to "give that fella' n'more drink." The result was that when your nibs was refused, he'd grab the nearest pint glass and fling the contents over the barman – Jack. Mrs. Berigan, anticipating the backlash, making herself scarce. This drink-throwing reaction was only an occasional occurrence. Usually the client would give his opinion of the widow in a vocabulary that made paint peel.

Jack eventually went to work in Patrick Street for a Mr. Brennan of Brennan's Bar. Having been there a while, Mr. Brennan bought The Stoneboat in Drimnagh, to which Jack also moved. He loved the clientele in this place, which included the Behan family and Christy Brown. Indeed, he used to joke about drinking poor Christy's pint for him, i.e. he'd hold the glass up to Christy's mouth. The foreman in the pub was a Jim Hynes. Hynes then bought a pub in Church Street beside the Cattle Mart, which still bears his Hynes name, inviting Jack along. It was there he stayed until July of the year he made the decision to quit.

During my shift, I ran into Paddy Green and asked him if there were any staff vacancies. "What's the use of asking me now!" Paddy roared back, "we're chock-a-block!"

That following Saturday morning at home, I heard the gate opening and somebody roaring. "Where is he?"

"Where's who?" I asked Paddy.

"Yer brother," he howled. "He's to start in cargo on Monda' mornin' at nine o'clock." That said, Paddy dashed off. Jack began work in cargo on that Monday and so remained until he retired. Now, why wouldn't I like and respect Paddy Green?

Back at the airport, I applied for another job because of it being day work. It entailed refuelling and checking all the ground equipment associated with loading, catering, and cleaning. It also included washing the catering trucks and buses.

There was a staff of four in this equipment unit, with Joe O'Reilly from Swords our honcho. The other staff members were Joe Crinnion, also from Swords, and my friend Hughie Williams, a brilliant, principled lad from Malahide who acted as driving instructor for the department. The job was a responsible one. Equipment used in close proximity to aircraft must have undamaged buffers in the contact area. The vehicles lights, brakes, tyres and hydraulic systems must be in top-class working order. Though the maintenance unit serviced them regularly, we had to pick up and remove any unit we found unreliable and deem it unserviceable, that after checking with our supervisor, Joe. So, the fleet was checked daily for it had happened many times that a user, rightly or wrongly, blamed the equipment he was using when involved in an incident.

Before leaving this period of 1973, I cannot but remember a few incidents experienced in the washing of the equipment. This was in a quadrangle between the aircraft hangars called the wash bay, an AMA bailiwick, and where they washed the aircraft and aircraft parts. It was also where ground ops staff were made to feel unwelcome. This was where the redoubtable Johnny Judge was their union rep. We used their facilities to wash our equipment… to the irritation of a few of the aforementioned AMAs.

When there was no aircraft in the wash bay, we'd drive our truck into it and begin our work, first hosing out the interior, and then soaping and washing the exterior. During the hour it took to wash whatever, a collection of sour-faced AMAs would assemble outside one of the aircraft hangar doors. As soon as I or one of our team completed washing a truck, we would sweep up the mess. Then, the serious, bearded little Johnny Judge would be summoned. Backed by his glowering cohort, he would boldly approach and sternly declare, "Who told ye to do dat! D'ye know yer' doin' a man ou've a job be sweeping up here?" he asserts.

"Sorry," we'd offer in return.

The next day, usually in the afternoon, we'd return to do a stint, and if we were being watched we'd leave the sweepings on the ground. One hour later our honcho Joe would tell us there was a complaint from the hangars that we left waste on the ground.

These battles continued on other fronts, with that same AMA hangar staff thieving our tractors and forklifts to facilitate their hangar activities, leaving a shortage where it belonged. The fact that we breached their bailiwick daily and retrieved our equipment without asking was what made them real sore. Johnny? He was a decent skin, and a most effective rep with astounding self-awareness and gigantic audacity to go with it.

Most of the operatives had been temporary loaders, and had been lucky enough to be offered permanent jobs as AMAs. A footnote to that is that an Englishman, who I believe was part of a survey team, asked one of the aircraft engineers what an AMA was. The caustic reply was, "Always miles away when you need one." In actual fact, AMA means aircraft mechanical assistant.

During winter, the aircraft cockpit and cabin staff were encouraged to take unpaid leave to relieve a staff surplus. Many took it because their privileged travel ticket gave them a certain priority, a perk which wasn't available to rankers, but now it was made available to others. I applied and was granted leave, and booked my passage to Leonardo de Vinci Airport in Rome where I would attempt to get a seat on one of Alitalia's flights to Kingsford Smith Airport in Sydney, Australia.

On arriving in Rome, I immediately went to the check-in desk and had my name put down as stand-by on a flight leaving in a couple of hours. Earlier, somebody had told me if I secreted thirty quid in the leaves of my passport they'd have me sitting in the pilot's lap. That is, until the first stop on these multi-stop journeys, then you're dumped off. I was not having any of that.

It was when I was just hanging around a voice enquired, "What the hell are you doing here, Dan?" It was Billy Walshe, a very amiable and likable fellow from ground ops Dublin, who was now functioning as Rome's Aer Lingus station manager. After I explained my situation, he insisted on me staying at his apartment if I didn't get on the flight. I didn't get on, nor did I ring the number he gave me – I made up my mind not to impose myself on his generosity. At the airport at eight o'clock that evening, Billy approached me with one word – "Com'on." I imposed for three days before my name was called. Thanks again, Billy, wherever you are.

Chapter 10: Grenville

In October 1973, my plane landed at Sydney's Kingsford Smith Airport after a two-day trip, my last couple of hours aboard being spent filling embarkation cards for a number of young Italian passengers, with two of them having finished serving as cooks in the Israeli Army. It also left me time to view a most dismal sight, mile by square mile of tin-roofed bungalows climbing up and down the rolling landscape.

In May 1787, Captain Philips RN arrived in Botany Bay with eleven ships. The site looked great but with little fresh water and unfertile soil he was not entirely happy with the place. On surveying the coast a few miles further south, they found the entrance to a great, sheltered, natural harbour which he named Port Jackson. That harbour is now known as Sydney, which we are told was named Sydney by some creep after the then Minister of the colonies back in London.

Captain Philips, as First Governor, reported that his 717 convicts, which included 180 women, were well behaved. Expecting supplies and assistance, he was dismayed to see the second fleet of three ships with no supplies, but with another 700 convicts aboard having dumped 250 dead and dying overboard.

At this stage the colony had made their way up the river to find new settlements, Parramatta being one of great importance. A future governor built his residence there, a fine Georgian house that is now surrounded by a lovely park that is open to the public. The house itself is much the same as the best Georgian houses here in Ireland, it too with a quadrangle at the back of it. The quadrangle incorporated byres, stables, carriage house, grain stores, and a well in the middle. Also, lest I forget, it was minus the adjacent haggard with its dung bank, and one of our beautiful Pierce-built haysheds.

I digress. As most of the alien entry inspections had been carried out on board the grounded aircraft by a group of very officious police, passing through the airport was rapid. A bus brought me to Central

Station, and from there I caught a train for the sixteen miles to Parramatta, passing through several small stations, including Granville.

At one o'clock I got off the train in Paramatta, banjaxed. I set off walking with my objective being a hotel. There were plenty of them about the small town, but none offered me a bed. They did offer me hard looks and abrupt NOs before it struck me that the hotels were pubs.

Back at the station on the opposite side of the tracks, I found the only real hotel in the town and booked a couple of nights. I woke around eight that evening, it already being dark, and looked out the window. Across the street I saw an old, three-storey, brick-built house with a sign outside announcing vacancies. There always would be vacancies in the lodgings of Mr. and Mrs. Bevins, a London couple who had been twenty years in Aussie. Eventually, I stayed with them for six months.

Next day, I walked the Sydney road looking for employment. It was a road with quite a few car sale establishments. There were also plenty of factories, though bland-faced receptionists offered nothing but a polite, "No, not at the moment."

A couple of miles further on I saw a sign announcing Granville, that same station we passed on the way out. I tried a few more factories in the vicinity, but with the same negative replies. While resting on a low wall I saw a ReadyMix truck emerge from a dirt road. *This is more in my line,* I thought. So up that road I walked and rounding the corner I saw three middle-aged guys wearing dusty grey shirts and shorts. They were conversing outside a wooden builder's hut. As I approached, all heads with pitiless eyes and expressionless grey faces turned to diagnose me. "I'm looking for employment..." I began. Noticing no softening of features nor sensing charitable vibes, I continued babbling about it being near Christmas, and how I needed a job. I also alluded to my penurious position. Mostly baloney, but anyone who has experienced being idle will understand that employment is resurrection. Employment is security. Employment makes all things possible. First, get your foot in the door, then establish your position by being punctual and hardworking. Now, if I had qualifications above my first aid certificate, great! When one hasn't any, you must prove your value by the sweat of your brow.

"We have a fellow out crook," said the skinny fellow with the extra inscrutable face and mechanical jaws. "He'll be back in a couple of days, so when he returns that's it!" he added. My foot was in the door and evidently, the crook fellow was fired, for I never saw him. Maybe there was no crook fellow, but that would be the skinny fellow's excuse for getting rid of me if I didn't square up.

Bag'n'Bulk was a subsidiary of ReadyMix. It operated from a large corrugated iron shed, adjacent to the concrete plant. The cement was fed from the jointly used silo to our bagging machine. Our job was humping the full bags, then stacking them eight high in readiness for the private and commercial customers. The bags, each weighing twenty kilos, were not heavy, but handling them for eight hours did leave you tired. If the stacked bags were not purchased within a week we had to break down the stacks, turn and restack them. That was a chore that frequently occurred. Why? Well, Wally the gaffer had an ornery streak. Also, if the plant manager nicknamed 'Sack'em' saw us hanging around, he was liable to fire us as being surplus to requirements. So, Wally created work to preserve his staff for the busy times, which were at the end of each month, just after the customers paid their last month's bill.

The other two lads were youths; one, a haggard-looking lad of about sixteen named Pete, and the other named Mick, a muscular, dark-haired, Turkish chap who was eighteen and usually good-humoured. Mick was lazy and of course Mick was not his real name, it being unpronounceable. It created a debate between Wally, the gaffer, and me as to what his real name was. Wally suggested Marty. I suggested Mohamed. That gave Mick a good laugh. Said he didn't care, but if the older Muslims heard me they would be very cross. Point made and accepted. As for Pete? He only lasted a couple of weeks and was fired for absenteeism.

After a day on the job a few small blisters began to appear on my arms and face. A chemist informed me I was allergic to the cement. I considered packing in the job until a fellow in the digs who was employed in a roof tile manufacturer observed that I was earning much more than him. That cured me, and I remained in that job operating a forklift and humping bags of cement for six months until I voluntarily left.

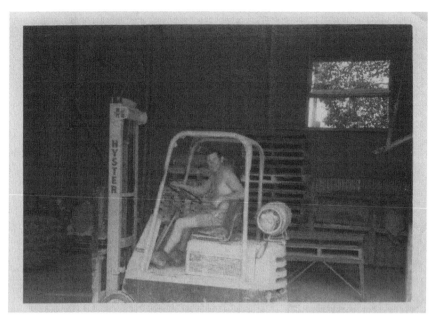

Me in Sydney c. 1993.

The car I bought in Sydney for 79 dollars was a Hillman Estate.

Parramatta Graveyard, Sydney.

Parramatta Graveyard Sydney.

The digs were spartan and the clientele, unsophisticated; it was not a place that encouraged you to lounge about. Actually, there was no place to hang out except your shared room. Paramatta, being on the fringes of Sydney, was the first stop for young Larrikins arriving from the outback. Apparently, it also was a first refuge for marriage break-up victims, judging by the percentage and quick turnover.

When some of the young country fellows got the ale in them, they were a heap of trouble. If after a month they hadn't moderated their behaviour, the landlord chucked them out. There were about twenty male guests along with myself, the number being made up of cranky ex-service men who were also to be ejected for uncivilised behaviour. Within a week of their eviction and after much cadging, they would be restored to their beds, for Tom Bevins didn't savour empty spaces inside his premises, and the devils he knew were more welcome than them he didn't know.

The ex-service men were pensioners and a nuisance when they had drink taken. They were a nuisance in the bathroom too. There was more of their dung around the pot than in it! On pension payment days and under the influence of grog, they argued a lot, graduating to insulting language. On several occasions, it culminated into a free-for-all. And when they were spent, monetarily and otherwise, they'd sink back into scowling reticence. I found it amusing because it was the behaviour of naughty children.

We were supplied with two meals per day for five days per week, breakfast and dinner. The food was plentiful and not too bad. I recall Mrs. Bevins as a large, friendly, bespectacled lady who, on Australia Day, enquired as to who liked pumpkin, a dish she had prepared in celebration. I immediately declined, not relishing the great pile of yellowish vegetables steaming on a platter. A big, crabby, black-haired fellow started to shovel it onto his plate, shouting, "I'll ate it! When I was in Korea and behind enemy lines for three days, I swore I'd ate anything if I survived."

There were three of us sharing the bedroom. One, a usually cranky ex-naval service guy who would return to the digs around midnight, inebriated… that's if he turned up at all; he'd spend hours talking and arguing with absent friends. The other was a dark, countenanced, Latino-looking chap of around forty, his ancestry unknown. He was friendly enough and very adaptable, employed as a carpenter or bricklayer, whichever job was available at the time. He was the only one who had a car, an ancient Holden.

The nights were exceptionally hot and humid, making it difficult to sleep. After a week of sleepless nights, I began bringing my bedroll out onto the veranda of our room. This was a great improvement. The ex-Navy man passed no comment. The other guy sneered and suggested I was like the 'black fella'. Two nights later, the bricklayer rolled up his bedding and slept out on the lawn, and there he stayed until that severe hot spell moved on. Something awoke me a couple of times on the veranda before I discovered it was a long-haired rat. The landlord reassured me they were harmless. Still, I felt more comfortable without his presence.

Paramatta was a small town, though was once very important. As I mentioned earlier, it possessed a large public park where the original governor's house was situated. I didn't notice any other feature of earlier settlements except a caretaker's lodge in the park, though the roads and bridges in and around the area were of earlier times. These old bridges were identical to the huge ponderous one I saw in Dublin before it was demolished. It too had two small pedestrian arches, and one vehicular, and it used to cross the Phibsborough Road into the Broadstone railway terminal, which is now a bus station. Seemingly all early bridges within the empire came off the same drawings.

Of an evening, quite a number of rugby teams trained in the park with severe and nonstop intensity. There were running club activities, and archery. A lot of individuals were also doing their own thing, such as shot putting and field sports.

The town's main streets were paved, and most of the side ones were gravelled. On my meanderings of an evening I discovered an old neglected graveyard on the outskirts of the town. It was a melancholy experience, examining the head stones, most bearing Irish names. Kennedy and Byrne were names that predominated. The death rate of infants of the 19th century was horrific. The headstones of some graves even referred to the cause of death. One in particular drew my attention. 'Here lies our child Samuel, aged 3 years 7 months, who was drowned in a well its cover not replaced by a careless servant.'

I usually frequented a pub on the way back from my walkabouts. The bar was a dark, ill-lit place. Each night I'd sit near the same bunch playing four-handed euchre. One guy will always stick in my mind; a big, coarse, brutish fellow of about sixty, wearing a wide-brimmed hat, shorts and a nondescript shirt. Everything about him was coarse, including the language he used to his partner. They never became violent, nor did they stop playing.

There was a fire station nearby, and at shift-changing time some of the staff would come in for a schooner or two. One night, a bunch entered in a rancorous mood. Apparently, there had been a union meeting where motions passed had not suited the moaners. A loud argument developed between an ornery-looking guy of about forty and a large, friendly-looking fellow who was reluctantly drawn into the discussion during which his opinion was demanded. The ornery fellow insulted the big guy who still refused to be drawn, that's until the ornery fellow called him a coward, and invited him out to the yard if he wanted to do anything about it.

Big guy took a slug from his schooner and followed the gang out to back yard. Within a minute, all returned with the ornery-looking fellow now looking dazed and meek, and being supported each side by his mates. Big guy was in a quite bullish mood until his opponent staggered over to him and apologised. Then, fair play to him, he bought the house a drink (which was for me and the card players, us being the only other customers).

Having been in Paramatta a month or so, and with no pub openings on a Sunday, Mick, my Turkish workmate, brought me to a car auction. The auction was held every Saturday morning. The stock included wrecks masquerading as cars. Nevertheless, a respectable-looking ten-year-old Vauxhall with two months' registration remaining was pushed out, and for thirty quid I bought it. While the body was ok, the engine ran on only three cylinders, making it difficult to start, also resulting in me having to park it on a hill a few hundred yards from the digs. Driving it meant all windows must remain open to prevent asphyxiation from the fumes. This banger got me the twenty miles out to near Penrith on a Sunday, and a few times out to the Blue Mountains. I also swanked it a couple of wet mornings by bringing it to work.

On my sorties out toward Penrith on a Sunday, the poor-quality land was rolling with vast amounts of it uninhabited. In this area grew forests of tall, straight, pine-like gum trees. When the early explorers saw those trees, they thought them priceless for ship building... until they found the trees were hollow. I did notice during my forays into the hinterland there was little of the ribbon construction that we, in Ireland, are familiar with.

At times, the Penrith Road ran parallel with the river which had several access points to it for swimming or water skiing. At a fairly desolate intersection on the way, there was a well-used pub; it was where amateur bands and singers assembled of a Sunday, obviously trying to make a name for themselves. If loud noise was talent, they all made it. I never saw any bother during my visits, and the bar staff were very relaxed. The few jorums used to buck me up no end and the six-pack I brought back improved the mood of my fellow lodgers.

Tom Bevins, my landlord, was a Londoner and an ex-policeman. He was also a dead ringer for Henry Cooper. He had served twenty-five years in the Royal Navy where, for many years, he was the lightweight boxing champion. While his wife managed the digs, Tom operated as a mobile washing machine repairer. They had one daughter who was married to a Northern Ireland chap, a nice fellow, when sober, and not so nice with drink on him. In passing, the Bevins were Catholic converts.

I got on well with Wally the ganger, he of old Irish stock and curious about us. We had a lot in common, one factor being the poverty of our youth which had we both accepted as quite normal. His mother used to do their laundry down by the river, spreading the clothes over the bushes to dry. He, like me, had enjoyed his childhood and never decried it. He told me that another Irish fellow had worked here in the plant a year or so earlier. This lad was from Cork and was ex-Irish Navy, he was popular with all and sundry. Wally mentioned he understood his accent better than mine. That surprised me to no end.

Wally had a son-in-law working in a shed next to ours. He supervised a couple of young lads packing tiny bags of cement for the retail outlets. His name was also Mick, a burly, morose chap of about twenty-two. He and Wally didn't speak. Wally said Mick was unthankful for all the favours Wally had done for him. Mick didn't speak to me either, probably because I was friendly with Wally, though observing this fellow's muscular build and seething demeanour, I didn't encourage intimacy.

Back to the Cork chap. He had been in the Irish Navy, and when out on patrol one night, the watch was asleep when the Corvette drifted and struck a rock. The damage wasn't very serious, but was obvious, so the ship changed course. The captain assembled the crew and had them swear to silence, before then radioing in from their new position, having hit a floating object. Apparently, the report was officially accepted. I asked Wally where he hung out so I could have a chat with him.

Wally invited me out one evening saying he knew where his drinking hole was. Wally was a careless driver, especially after the few jorums. He fecked the car around corners with abandon. Whenever he met a car with Melbourne plates he'd toot the horn and, along with a couple of expletives, give two fingers. The climate being hot and car windows open, the answering expletives were quite audible. Having tried several joints, we never found our friend, but we had a good night out anyway.

Though I had the old car, most mornings I would walk to work. The journey would take me down the bungalowed streets, the gardens enhanced by a blue, flowering shrubbery. In the mornings, this shrubbery radiated the most wonderful scent. In the evening as I returned, there was not as much as a whiff from them. The cicadas, a type of insect, were not early risers, but they made their presence known in the evenings with an annoying racket. All the bungalows stood on stilts, keeping them a foot above ground. On enquiry I was told that this was to prevent them being assailed by wood-eating ants which, when established, ruin the house in a year or two.

The ReadyMix management consisted of a couple of office girls and manager, 'Sack'em', a bald, fat, low-sized, self-important fellow of about sixty. He spent most of the day out on sites, or so we were told. He'd barely nod toward us, indeed, more often he'd totally ignore you. Wally told me he'd built his grand house with graft.

Sack'em's understudy was Morry, or Murry. He was dour and dusty with a lean, leathered, truculent face. It was he who hired me. He, like his boss, liked to impress.

One morning Mick and I were alone in our workplace when Morry drove up in his Ute (utility truck). He asked where Wally was, and we told him he'd be in later. "Load twenty bags of cement on the Ute," he said, "and there's no need to tell Wally because I'll tell him myself." A couple of minutes later, he shot out the gate with his load.

Later, when Wally arrived, Mick, with a big grin, told Wally about the cement. "The Bastard!" swore Wally. "When I asked him for a couple of bags for home maintenance he refused me, and only the other day I reported that there was cement disappearing."

As soon as Morry returned, Wally confronted him. We couldn't hear the conversation but afterwards whenever Morry had reason to come and discuss the work with Wally, Morry was "Ever so 'umble."

The concrete mixer trucks were exactly like the Irish ones, except they were equipped with a much larger water container. The reason was that the trucks transported a dry mix to the site, and only then would water be added. The result of this was that there were no leaks, the trucks were much cleaner, and if a breakdown occurred, a dry mix would not set.

Wally invited me to his home for Christmas dinner. As a gift I bought a bottle of Black Bush whiskey. It was in a presentation package and included two crystal glasses. It wasn't expensive, but they were delighted with it. They responded with a boomerang, leather-covered clothes brush. Dinner was much the same as in Ireland, except there was no beer.

A new lodger arrived on a motorbike, a twenty-year-old called McKay. He was a fuzzy, black-haired chap, and was very amiable and polite. He told me he was a mechanic from a small town out the back. He had, like so many others, made touchdown in Bevins before finding a job. By this time the landlord's Irish son-in-law would knock me up for a chat on his Friday visits. I remarked that I hadn't met any Irish besides himself. He then alerted me to a pub in Sydney where Paddies hung out. Mac, who was present, proposed a trip to which I accepted. The next evening we set off on the bike and, without any bother, we found the pub.

There were about thirty customers in the bar, all slightly woozy. I immediately got talking to a young chap no more than twenty who told me he was from County Carlow. His girlfriend, he said, was from County Mayo, and worked in a bank. As we chatted, I recalled what Liam Boylan had told me back in Dublin. Liam had married a girl from County Kerry, and she had a brother working in Sydney. Indeed, on foraging in my diary I found his address. While handing him the diary,

I enquired from this chap had he ever ran into this fellow.

As he studied the diary, he said nothing for minute or two. Then he stared at me, and in a cool tone asked me from where I had got this fellow's name and address. I explained I got from Liam, a workmate. "This fellow is my boss," said the Carlow chap in a relieved tone. "We are working down the coast on a drainage contract, and we only come back to Sydney on the weekends. This address," he said, "is my address. I moved in when Joe got married."

As I mentioned earlier, I'd rather starve than impose myself on others, and I only wrote down the address out of respect to Liam who gave it to me in good faith. But what a coincidence. I've often wondered what that young Carlow fellow was so worried about. Anyway, Mac quickly found a job in one of the car sale establishments, so I didn't see much of him after that. Indeed, he left our digs to live in an apartment with someone he knew. He was a top-class chap.

Some Sundays I'd get the train into the city and hang around Bondi. It's not much of a beach, though there were plenty of boarders trying to impress on ripples. Jeez, I often saw bigger waves in the bath, though the shark patrol boat cruising back and forth beyond the surfers lent a sense of unpredictability to their adventures. The beach scene required you to have your board, your bird, and a Holden van. If you hadn't got those you were shite.

Kings Cross was a vibrant, downtown area. It was for hotels, pubs, cinemas and shows. There were nude exhibitions where if you wanted to waste five quid, you could watch the girls posing stock still with only their lips moving in grimacing smiles. The most impressive sight in the city was to take the ferry across the bay to Manly. Then, to progress along the shore to the harbour entrance. It's only now you can see the massive Sydney heads jutting out into the huge seas outside the sheltered harbour. There is a central park in Sydney. It has its speakers' corner, though it isn't a patch on Trafalgar's. Nevertheless, if you have a crib and anybody to listen, you're free to out your spleen.

Sydney in 1973 had two stadiums. One was Harold Park which was used as a greyhound track and sulkie racing, or the 'trots' as they call it. I visited the greyhound racing a couple of evenings, joining four or five thousand other punters. Even in 1973 it was far better organised than our tracks. The Aussie likes his gamble, loves to bawl, cheer, and finally, cuss his fancy right through the race. The other stadium was Ranwick, largely confined to horse racing.

Coming near the end of my bondage, I speculated on whether I should settle. Without any heart rendering, I chose to go home. The people were friendly, and the country vast... though not very colourful. It provided great opportunities for skilled personnel. In boring joints (like where I worked) there was little to be joyful about. The wages were not bad, but conditions were poor. Here was Wally in his early sixties, a dedicated, honest worker who drank little, and who didn't smoke. He had reared six children, and had spent six years in the army during the World War. If for any reason he was fired, within a fortnight he'd be in a serious financial position. Looking at Wally's and my own position, I reasoned I was just on a busman's holiday.

For my mother, I spent forty quid on buying a gold brooch with an opal stone. A few years later, when she was stuck for a few bob, the pawnbroker would only offer her a fiver for it. In other words, I was had. On the way home, we landed in Singapore. It was there I bought my father a beautiful Meerschaum pipe. Back on board the aircraft, while examining it I saw printed on the shank *Made in the Republic of Ireland*. If my father ever discovered it, he said nothing about it.

On the morning I left, I drove my jalopy to the airport. I pulled up outside the terminal building, grabbed my bag, and walked away. At two o'clock the plane took off, and so another door closed.

As a footnote to the mornings I walked to work, I used to cross over a huge Victorian era stone bridge which spanned the railway. The elevation encouraged me to stop for a moment to view the river and the gum tree covered wilderness beyond.

Back in Ireland one morning in January 1977, I read on the front page of the *Irish Times*, "In Granville, near Sydney at eight in the morning, an old bridge collapsed, dumping 380 tons of rock on the Nullibar bound train, killing eighty-three passengers."

Routine, custom, practice – they are all one and the same
And where the seeds of man's discontent are sown.
And though I carp and complain, many times call out my name
But the Gods don't heed the cry of a drone.

Chapter 11: The Return of the Chastened

The first thing I noticed when the plane landed back in Dublin that day in April 1974 was utter drabness. The overcast sky hung over a withered landscape. A sea of pale faces didn't help either. The only colour I observed as our aircraft was landing were the hedges dotted with flowering furze. It was as if the land was reluctantly emerging from hibernation.

It took me weeks to readjust but one feature I looked forward to in the seventies and that made life sweet was the success of the Dubs, and Lorcan being one of the management team. With me not being on shift work, I, along with our father and my brother-in-law Mick Howard, followed this wonderful team all over the country. That team, with a few changes of personnel, would raise the spirits of the county for the next ten years. During that time, Lorcan became the most successful Dublin manager of all time. For some reason or other, the then manager was not available and Lorcan was appointed for this one match that we won... so there! For ten years Hanahoe and Heffo's management served without asking or receiving a penny... everything sacrificed on the cross of the Dubs.

At work, two other lads had joined our crew. They were from Cavan, both brilliant lads. One of them was Christy Purcell, and the other, Tony Brady. The established crew was the amiable Harry Dowdall, a fitness expert and an excellent soccer player. Tom O'Keefe was another good soccer player, and a great, reliable, good-humoured lad from Finglas. Our scope and unit title had now broadened to training, standards and equipment. To help us, we attended several courses in staff training, there enlightened by a tolerant chap called Colm Crowley. These operational changes coincided with the promotion of the ubiquitous Jim Ryan. His promotion was as a replacement for the retiring Jimmy O'Keefe. As for his job title? I forget, but as a trouble-shooter Jim revealed himself a poor shot because he never seemed to be out of it.

Me, Kevin 'Heffo' Heffernan and my brother Lorcan Redmond, c.1976.

Jim was a mercurial individual, at times difficult. Nevertheless, he was a decent honourable man. One factor where there can be no dispute – he added a sense of the bizarre to the drama that was ground ops. It seems Jim had either been elected, appointed or perhaps was launched among us to deal with two or three very united union reps. These reps had a hard core of about a dozen members who could on a minute's notice respond to the call for a union meeting, thereby causing a work stoppage.

For years there had been periodic standoffs between local management and the union reps. For the reps, it was a game of asserting themselves. To management, their effrontery was exasperating. It appeared that Jim Ryan was given a free rein to keep this nuisance at bay; his strategy seemed to be appeasement. Remove the reps from the work area, thereby denying them the exercising of their power. So, for five days per week, Jim began to engage with the reps. Subjects discussed at these meetings were never divulged. This tactic was costing a fortune in overtime, for these guys had to be replaced on the work roster. If their absence was predetermined, other staff would be called in on double time.

The disappearance of the reps was not total, for periodically one would appear – generally on a weekend and an overtime shift – also in an undemanding role. This was a Ryan miscalculation, for that rep would spend the shift listening to the whinging of the eternally disenchanted, thereby accumulating ammunition. After many months, the reps disappeared from the work roster and, with Jim Ryan, they would be missing for weeks on end. During these absences they would be seen boarding aircraft bound for the continent or perhaps the USA, returning four or five days later. Though it was puzzling, staff used to smile in admiration at the antics of their reps.

When a disagreement arose between these world shakers, the reps would appear on the work station fully uniformed and ready for work, then immediately call a union meeting. These meetings would be at crucial aircraft turnaround times. There would be no agenda other than a verbal, "Management is trying to pull a fast one over us." During these stoppages I never heard a resolution proposed or adopted. This was the time the highly energetic Jim Ryan would be in a frenzy, for a work stoppage represented utter failure. Management busybodies who had egged Jim on, now frowned and tut-tutted. There was nothing Jim could do but concede to the reps, and return to the status quo. Now, who was managing who?

Up to this point we, in the training and standards unit, had been mere onlookers to the circus that was human resources. But our new brief brought us face to face with it. We had to encourage efficient operating methods relevant to the security and loading of aircraft, and the use and serviceability of equipment. This included a reawakening of awareness and attitude, casualness being the first step to indifference.

These minor changes in staff attitude were meat for the reps. I didn't realise it at the time with us being so busy, that added to our brief was familiarising and advising the Special Branch on security and hijacking. We familiarised them in the use of our equipment and routines. We also obliged the Army Rangers in the same way – hijacking now having become a favourite weapon of the world's disgruntled.

We established a booklet for each grade of staff, indicating that employee's priorities, his responsibilities, his loyalty. It was for the most part an enjoyable task. Of course, we were dealing with friends and workmates we respected, and were respected in return, consequently the word was respected.

The union reps didn't give us overt hassle, their annoyance was not personal. Though I recall an occasion when we were giving a presentation on what we were about, sitting in the front row were the three reps. Probably there to intimidate, and perhaps to impress one or two agitators who whinged about everything. The reps did not criticise what we were doing, but intimated that this and that wasn't our job. I disagreed – as far as I was concerned it was all about the ship.

There was always an undercurrent of annoyance. We were successful, so union reps who thrive on dissention were critical... It was part of the game; they needed wounds to scratch. They needed to retain the status quo. Any improved, efficient methods of operation introduced meant Jim and reps got airline tickets to Timbuktu to see how the Hottentots dealt with similarities. We made the point that printed rules protected our staff. It revealed the demarcation of responsibilities. One or two of the supervisory staff were also unhelpful, all because of our progressive efforts in search of excellence.

Just to give the general view of the comedy that was union versus management. One evening during an operational lull a debate arose among the clerical staff who shared our base. The subject was reincarnation. One fellow swore his Nirvana was to be reincarnated as an Aer Lingus operative shop steward.

Chapter 12: Titch

I continue this narrative with the death of our father who had been ailing for some years with a prostate problem. It was 1983 and on a Saturday morning at eleven, he slipped coming from the bathroom. As I helped him to his feet, he commented matter-of-factly, "I'm a goner." He displayed neither fear nor panic, but a calm acceptance of the inevitable. An ambulance parked us in a crowded Blanchardstown Hospital waiting room, along with two jockeys in their racing gear.

Jack arrived as the nurse found us a cubicle, and between us we held our father over a bed pan; he had lost control of his bowels. No doctor came for ages. Our father began to chain-breathe – I think that was the term the nurse used. I shouted in alarm. A bell rang and a bunch of doctors appeared, and five minutes later he died as he lived, a stoic to the end.

He was buried in Swords cemetery, sharing the grave with our brother Bill. He would have been proud of the full military honours granted, and with the Minister of Defence present.

I had another experience in that year of 1983. Ordinarily it would not have been worth mentioning. It was an introduction to a client which a few years down the line, would have an unhappy outcome.

In conjunction with my airport activities, I was in the habit of visiting my sister's house every evening for a chat, and to see their children. One winter's evening my brother-in-law Michael Howard, a generous, decent fellow, prevailed upon me to help one of their neighbours. This poor fellow was crippled with arthritis, his hands so painful he was receiving nothing less than gold injections. I immediately agreed. Apparently, this neighbour had bought a movable hut which he planned to use as a garage. Our task was to haul it into position and stabilise it. Usually, unfortunates such as this fellow stirred my sympathy and respect. But from the moment I met him I was aware of a premonition, a foreboding I had never ever experienced before.

I am not one to pre-judge, though one tends to appraise the representation before you decide whether it is a horse or a human. This fellow was about five feet tall and portly. Of course, height is not the measure of a man; smallness is not a barrier to greatness. I've known small men who were and still are giants. But with this man I sensed intolerance despite his giggles and merry quips. Anyway, we hauled the hut into position and levelled it, my brother-in-law promising he'd see a builder who might supply concrete for a floor.

A few weeks later my brother-in-law called on me again to concrete the hut floor. Every sense I possessed warned me not to go, but I went and spent a couple of hours shovelling and screeding the floor to a suitable finish. The concrete was supplied for nothing by a local builder Mr. Joe Sline, RIP.

When the job was completed we were then invited inside for a cup of tea where mine host discovered there was a biscuit missing from the packet. His instantaneous rage shocked me. Over a biscuit?

It was not long after that episode when my brother-in-law prevailed again. Apparently, Titch's place of employment was moving to other premises which meant their heavy, bulky equipment also must be moved. The new premises was in the basement of one of the Edwardian age buildings in the same area.

I knew from my own experience years earlier in Bolton Street Tech where print presses were established in the basement and where students were trained in compositing, moving a printing press was not a simple task, as they were bulky and of solid iron. Anyway, by means of my brother-in-law's lorry and crane, we loaded the equipment and drove it to the other premises. Means of entry was through a large trap door in the pavement. The crane could not lower the bulky press, but I had taken the precaution of supplying two heavy timber runners. And so, with the crane controlling momentum we allowed the press to slide the down into the basement and on to rollers (also supplied by me), and push it into the required position. They were a tension-filled couple of hours, but it left himself overjoyed. And why not? Job done and it hadn't cost him a penny. I mention these acts of decency and generosity as a preamble to his later frolics.

"Who are you?" a stranger asks as father's corpse is carried by;
Aware of future and the past; "I am my father's son says I"
Within a chain I am a link; the chain that binds the old and new
Where those long gone are n'er extinct but through my being are renewed.

I climb the hills and walk the streets and never feel that I'm alone
And I ignore those whom I meet for they disturb a monotone,
I hear them as I drowse at night in sheltered glen or mountainside
And regarded as an acolyte; a host to a myriad of my tribe.

Chapter 13: New Broom

By this time Joe Whorriskey our station manager had retired, and the reign of Con Clarke had begun, that after fraught competition. Apparently, Con's objective was not to run the operation as others had. His approach was very intrusive.

I must qualify the following as being a situation as I saw it, perhaps I am wrong, for I was never engaged or familiar with the politics of management, and eventually not even curious, but then I wasn't looking for anything.

Indeed, up to this point I can recall on two occasions being summoned to meetings and never told why my presence was needed or the subject to be discussed. At one extraordinary meeting, the manager asked my opinion on new ground handling equipment and before I could answer the three shop stewards immediately stood up and walked out... the meeting, at that point, was abandoned – a meeting which included at least twenty top section reps. I had a vague feeling of being used, though the conclusion I came to was that the union reps had now claimed authority over the running of ground ops and in the absence of an explanation, the reason for my presence there still mystifies.

That aside, this was the eighties and the country in the grip of austerity, so perhaps the manager was pressurised into cost-cutting. Anyway, he was very unlike the previous managers, such as the urbane Sean Fitz or the sociable Mr. Beard, nor in any way similar to the remote, poker-faced Joe. Highly energetic and physically fit, the captain left the bridge and, like Superman, tore about the ship at full throttle. His hands-on intrusion was probably well intentioned though it left a feeling of mistrust.

From my perspective, he wore his heart on his sleeve. That is not in any way detrimental. Indeed, I have found those so fated to be honest though overly blunt. Anyway, I recall on a couple of his early morning sorties down onto the ramp finding myself the object of his very hostile, accusing glare. It was as if he'd caught me playing with his toys. He ignored one for no apparent reason, and fawned over others, particularly the ones that cosied up. Bizarre as it was I didn't dwell on it, though again it was a divisive trait encouraging sycophants and story carriers.

One would have expected the new captain to present himself to the ship's officers, and the non-commissioned such as I. This would give him an opportunity to disclose his philosophy, reveal his priorities, or the changes of his ship's course. Then, maybe he did and I just wasn't invited to the party.

I clearly recall the manager rushing into the ten o'clock morning meeting with his briefcase and a bundle of papers under his arm, flinging himself into his seat and immediately breaking the news that "left, right and centre, the airlines of the world were losing money," and that they were all sacking staff. Indeed, Pan Am had just sacked two hundred of their line managers. Liam Boylan, a deputy rep and a droll individual observed, "At least they started in the right f*****g place." That got a few sniggers. Nevertheless, when I retired the manager gave me an excellent reference.

Before leaving this subject, the results of another survey were revealed. The navel-gazing view of Aer Lingus at the time was that management were whiz kids. This survey revealed that in Japan a 737 turnaround took thirty-five minutes and involved thirty-six employees. In Dublin, our 737 turnarounds took thirty-five minutes, but it involved 126 employees. Anyway, weak grins, embarrassed smiles and thoughtful expressions were very noticeable after that bombshell. Though in hindsight I imagine factors calculated in the surveys were totally different.

The middle 1980s are remembered for the work stoppages and for the staff early retirement policy. This had been proposed to those aged fifty-five and over. Courses were being offered to help the retirees to adapt to doing nothing and to advise them on how to invest the lump sum inducement. I suspect this was a management means of weeding out staff deemed as surplus to requirements. Quite a few operative staff did take the 'lump' and vanish into the mist and if they were replaced it was under less favourable conditions. These changes gradually altered the attitude of those remaining, most giving one the feeling their allegiance was only to overtime and even larger lump sums whenever they decided to bail out. New staff wavered between obligation to duty and the dissenters. I felt that from top to bottom, a psychologist was needed to motivate staff from self-serving to saving the ship. There were work stoppages in ground ops. Some appeared to be prolonged by management who initially had created the monster of rep empowerment, and were now trying to neutralise it.

For many years an underlying resentment had been seething in the engineering department, manifested in arm-wrestling strikes about very little. The real problem was a bias favouring ground ops clerical staff being promoted into the engineering top table of management, thereby stifling promotional opportunities. For a spell it felt like operating in an earthquake zone because the strikes tended to trigger aftershocks in other sections. Eventually the engineers were no longer Aer Lingus staff, but employees of a Danish engineering company and if there was dissent, it was muted. At least they were not the standard bearers to disrupt other sections.

It was sad to see excellent and loyal staff being pushed onto the scrap heap. Everywhere, greed was the in-thing, whereas before when one saw something needed to be done one went along and did it. Now, there must be a price put on it.

Chapter 14: Titch's Extension

During this period, I was cajoled into extending the kitchen and dining room of Titch's house. When I met him, I was astounded. His new dentures had transformed him into a well-known TV personality, whose affectation he'd adopted.

I built and roofed the extension and a contractor covered it with felt. I then assisted another Frank, this one a bricklayer, whose task was to build them a front porch. I roofed it with concrete and to this day it still looks good. I built a garden wall for them, and finished up by laying paths around the whole building. During most of the outside work I saw little of 'himself', and when finished I only asked for one hundred punts.

John Paul

The direst strait is when a heart is closed

Closed to truth, is blind to reality

And wilfully oppose though clearly see your woes

For the bloody minded will still refuse to see.

Chapter 15: The End of an Era

On a day in March 1989 I clearly recall meeting a fellow supervisor on the tarmac, he with a glint of amusement in his eye, or on reflection, was it triumph? He revealed that a manager wished to speak with me (not Con Clarke). Innocently, I went to his office expecting our unit to be complimented, clear and content in my mind that we had transformed the methods, attitudes, and efficiency of the staff under our direction. I had always been on good terms with this fellow, what with him being very unaffected and affable, but today his sour demeanour and accusative tone shocked me. The meeting turned out to be a thirty-second dressing down – the twenty or thirty words he spoke were dismantling. He accused me of "making changes." That I personally was "overzealous."

"Explain," I asked.

"I don't know," he said, getting to his feet and slamming some papers onto the desk by way of finalising the diatribe, "but there are complaints."

I obviously had been the subject of a local union/management meeting. Obviously, no one supported me – their easiest way out of the dilemma was to kick the dog. In eight years our methodology had never been questioned. No fellow supervisor ever warned me of dissatisfaction, though they would be present during these local union/management face-offs. While walking down the fourteen steps to ground level I realised I had been denigrated, and I decided to quit – for when you have lost the trust and support of your senior officers, you have no business on the ship. I was disappointed, but I was physically fit and well... and ready for a new Everest.

I had never been ambitious, but always wanted to be the best at what I was engaged in... though I was never a bester. I was content to wait my turn until seniority earned me my other rank's stripe. Indeed, the only time I applied for promotion, I got it through the good offices of a friend and fellow worker, Brendan Moran. Not gifted with anything other than energy and interest, nor had I benefited from education – Aer Lingus gave me a chance to expand and see the big picture, and that I valued. Along with the top-class crew I served with, my own interest in the job, and the help of staff training, I enjoyed every minute of it.

This being late March, the following June I would have reached the age of fifty-five, the age at the time when you may retire. I retired, but without the big pay-outs that other staff were offered when the company negotiated to get rid of them. Still, I never envied them, I bear no ill will, nor did I ever complain. Never for a second did I regret retiring, missing only friends and workmates. Another door closed.

Psalm 88

Desperation is, when you have lost your way
And arrived at the end of the road.
Reached that dreaded terminus – a place of disarray
Now exposed, a desert begins to impose.

PART 4

Chapter 1: Taking A Breather

For me the year of 1989 was a satisfactory one during which I added an apartment to our cottage, and was pleased with the result. I was even more pleased when a phone call from Conor, an aircraft engineer and my nephew, informed me that I had won a car in the St. Joseph's Credit Union draw.

During the next couple of years our mother's health declined. Now in her 80s and only partially mobile, her needs gradually became more demanding. Our sister Margaret, a mother of four school-going children and living six miles away, was a wonderful nurse. She would spend four hours in the mornings with her, and then again, every evening. My brothers and their wives were also a resource ever-available, Lorcan in particular who would turn up each evening to massage her arthritic knees and feet. They and I, having done our duty looking after her until her condition needed constant medical attention, booked her into a rest home. I visited her every morning to the chagrin of some of the staff. Mother still recognised me, but dwelled in the distant past. This particular morning, I tried to pierce her drowsiness by asking her, "How long does it take to cook cabbage?" My intention was to have bacon and cabbage for lunch.

She struggled to concentrate and mumbled, "About twenty mins… but it depends." She closed her eyes, worn out, and with Frank present, she died in that rest home that afternoon. That was after a six-month stay.

It's only the reality of death that brings to mind the sacrifices she made in the interests of her family and neighbours. She'd had a tough life, and enjoyed it even more because of it. But as a wonderful, talented, and resourceful woman, she gave her absolute best for her family. She was a godsend to so many others, consistently going without a thing herself to facilitate neighbours. I didn't always get along with her because she was a bully. "For your own good," she'd say, that after nearly taking the head off me with a clout. Funnily enough – though not funny at the time, she was very moderate toward my brothers.

I remember her many, many episodes of kindness to tinkers passing and then camping on the Brackenstown Road during their annual pilgrimage. And to the Mansfields who had once lived in the area, and who had gone to England; once (and unexpectedly), two of their unsettled teenagers returned and stayed in our house for a couple of weeks, before moving down the country to live with relatives.

Then there was the firewood incident. This occurred in the Brackenstown Estate where we lived for about eleven years. The incident was brought about by the employment of a man to monitor the pedestrian gate next to our three houses. This wicket gate gave access through the woods and up to the servants' entrance of the main house of the estate. The poor cottagers from a mile down the road accessed it to gather firewood. When the gatekeeper saw two kids, Johnny Behan and Paddy Rodgers, going into the wood, he locked them in. When they returned with their bundles of firing, it had begun to rain, but because of the padlocked gate they were prisoners.

The gatekeeper stood at his door looking out at the two disconsolate lads sitting on their bundles. He was enjoying their discomfort. Our mother saw them too, and waited a while to see if they would be released. When nothing happened, she charged out with a pitch fork, tossed the bundles over the gate, and brought the lads in through our back door and let them out the front door onto the road. There, they heaved their bundles and headed off in the rain. That was our mother – impulsive, sympathetic and generous. I often wondered if Johnny or Paddy remembered her good deed.

Generosity wasn't always a two-way street. Like when in 1936, a couple of years after arriving in Dublin, she discovered that rural customs differed. Pat Shields, a neighbour and progressive local farmer, had a field of cabbage nearly opposite to where we lived. Apparently, Pat saw her climbing over the gate then leaving with two heads. He knocked at our door that evening and demanded four-pence. My mother explained that in the parish where she came from, it was the custom that your neighbour could help herself to a head of cabbage. Pat persisted, saying, "Paying for it is the custom in this parish!"

She wasn't too upset. She just speculated if the "Feckin ould bags up the road still had a snot on him." I wonder, do they communicate now that she lies beside him in Swords graveyard?

Another incident brings a smile on remembering. We had left Brackenstown in 1946 and were living in a small cottage. At the time, our eldest brother Lorcan was employed by an antique dealer in the city. Occasionally he would bring home a knick-knack which, after an auction, was deemed by the dealers to be of no interest or value. One day he arrived home with a velvet cushion tied to the crossbar of his bike. It lay around the house for ages before our mother commandeered it to support her in bed at night while reading the penny-dreadfuls. Early one night a scream awoke us. We rushed down to her bedroom to find her among a roomful of feathers with her on her hands and knees in bed frantically fleecing and tearing the cushion. She'd discovered a bundle of notes hidden in it. It was early 19th century money, coloured blue and red and of around fifty pounds. I think most of it was in ten-pound notes, and was elaborately designed. I, about fourteen at the time, vividly recall seeing a large, blue note with a man ploughing with a pair of horses. Word got around and she swapped them for their face value. Anyway, she told us that when she had finished reading, and while readjusting the cushion, she had felt the lump inside it. The stitching was so fine that she was reluctant to investigate at first. But our mother, true to form, smelt money, and we were the better for it. If one word were to describe her, it would be indomitable, with a million spontaneous, generous acts of her common decency recorded in the annals of the saved.

I completed an FAS welding course in 1992, and found work experience with an engineering company in the town of Ashbourne. There, one had to work. There, health and safety rules were minimal. But the only thing that annoyed me was a hoor of a radio blaring the most horrible, rubbishy 'hits' all day long, accompanied with the drivel of the presenter.

The three other lads employed were in their teens, and all of them members of the local Gaelic club. Earwigging their chat, it seemed that they were all fond of the sup. There was also a foreman who was another decent fellow. I got a chance to innovate a rig which made hard work easy. The contract was a large P&T one. It demanded thousands of specialised steel inspection covers. One of the staff, Keith, had to lift a heavy iron plate onto his bench, and then lift and turn it twelve times to weld the different angles. He would process about fourteen per day. At home one night, doodling with a pencil, I designed a rig where he would only lift the plate once, making it much easier for him, and increasing his productivity. Next day, in one hour and unknown to the foreman, he made up the rig and was delighted with the result. The foreman, ever watchful, saw the pile of finished units and he too was delighted. He congratulated the young man for his ingenuity and he, to his credit, told the foreman it was my idea. I developed another time-saver at my own bench during that week, but there was no medal or increase in the three quid an hour they were paying me.

I remained there for the six months before packing it in, for another idea had developed. The Donnelly work visas for the US had come and gone, but a Mr. Morrison re-enacted them. I applied for the papers and eventually went to Ballsbridge for my interview. There, I acquired a ten-year visa that allowed me to travel if I had a sponsor, i.e. a company willing to give me employment. A niece in Boston had a Galway chap as a boyfriend, and he secured a letter of appointment from his employer, and passed it on to me with a proviso, "Don't turn up looking for a job!"

After about a month, I installed a couple of my nephews and a niece in my house and departed.

If your bank roll is small it is better than none at all,

Just tighten up your belt a notch or two.

For there'll always be the good times and times that may appal,

But never prey on them worse off than you.

Chapter 2: Six-Dollar Man

In 1993, Gay Byrne announced that in the Midwest of the US, unemployment was only three percent. So, here I was on my way to Denver, Colorado, though there was no welcoming committee for myself and two unneeded friends (a Danish couple of a mother, and her son Peter).

He, a tall, well-spoken chap of about twenty-eight, was employed by airport security in Copenhagen where he had secured two restricted airline tickets. She, I conjectured, was in her sixties. I met them in Saint Louis where we were waiting for a connecting flight to Denver. Our plane lifted off at about midnight on our ninety-minute flight, mirrored by a full moon the confluence of the two mighty rivers, the Mississippi and the Missouri were revealed below.

Later, while waiting at Denver baggage reclaim, I took the opportunity to ring one of the many motels advertised. For obvious reasons, budget was my choice. Meanwhile, Peter was retrieving their luggage and reassuring his non-English speaking mother, while also keeping his eye on me.

He had asked if they could use my motel and share the taxi fare, to which I raised no objections. The motel reception office was a temporary-looking affair with a cautious male receptionist behind the counter, who later told me he was English. I booked a single and was satisfied with the fifteen-dollar tariff. When Peter asked to see my room I became wary, but he assured me it was to see if the bed size could accommodate him and his mother (because the double cost twenty-two dollars). Apparently the single suited, and at three in the morning we celebrated with a belt of scotch from my bottle of duty free, promising to meet again later in the morning.

I arose at seven o'clock anxious to get going. I needed to get established in the city, but breakfast was my first priority. The diner next door was a homely joint with plenty of potted flowers and plants. Mexican voices shouted orders to and from the kitchen. The place was busy with what seemed a good passing trade. The customers were mainly construction workers. The scrambled egg and toast was ok.

I hung around waiting to say goodbye to my friends, but anxiety getting the better of me, I rang for a taxi. On my suggestion, the taxi left me at the outskirts of the city, stopping at a motel called the Super Eight. There, just two hundred yards away, was the famous Mile High Stadium – a slight disappointment with the amount of permanent scaffolding supporting the stands. I booked into the hotel for three days, which I hoped would give me time to get aquatinted with the city.

During those few days when not roaming around, I combed the classifieds for employment opportunities and apartments. A job at eight to ten dollars an hour would suit me grand, as I had no verifiable skills except a first aid certificate, and I wasn't banking on that.

Four to six dollar an hour jobs were available with certain provisos, such as you must have your own transport. Others insisted on a drug test. I accepted the situation. If it was good enough for Denver people, it was good enough for me. My first concern was to get established in an apartment or a room, so armed with a few addresses copied from a newspaper, I set forth.

Apparently, it was against the law for taxis to pick up passengers on the streets, so I walked toward the built-up part of the district until I spotted a cab parked outside a hotel, its driver leaning over the bonnet smoking.

"Are you available?" I asked.

"Sure, sure," a youngish man answered while snuffing his fag. I got in the back. "Where to?" he asked. I gave him one of the addresses, and off we went. A couple of minutes passed before he turned around and commented on my accent.

"I'm Irish, God help me," I quipped.

"I'm Irish too," he exclaimed excitedly. "Well, my grandparents were. O'Sullivan is my name," he told me.

Gary O'Sullivan told me he was a writer from Boston, working down here for a change of scene. We shook hands at the traffic lights. "This address?!" he asked diplomatically. "You mind tellin' me why you're going there?"

"Accommodation," I replied.

"Bad area," he said, shaking his head. "Black," he warned.

Personally, I had no problem with blacks or any colour, but I wasn't going to ignore a warning. "Hold everything," I said, and produced my alternatives. He examined them, shaking his head.

"I'll bring you there, but they're bad areas." Well, I was flummoxed.

"Thanks very much for the warning, and I'm sorry for disturbing you," I began.

"Wait a minute," he said thoughtfully, "there's a vacant apartment in my block. They're clean, but a bit expensive." I was delighted.

"Sounds great," I said, and gave the signal to go.

York Street off Colfax was the address – a square, concrete building four-storeys high and set among a row of old but distinct and well-maintained houses. The manageress was a small, fit, formidable-looking woman of about fifty-five. She had short red hair, her uniform a dustcoat, and eyed me suspiciously as Gary told her what a fine fellow I was, adding with significance, "He's Irish." I winced, remembering my years in England where a statement like that was more likely to get you out the door than in.

After much himmin' and hawin' about my lack of references she relented, declaring, "A hundred dollars deposit and two hundred and seventy a month," adding grimly, "in advance!"

It was a ground-floor bachelor apartment with a large sitting-cum-bedroom furnished with two divans and an armchair. An L-shaped counter enclosed the tiny kitchen. Another door led to the bathroom and storage area. It would be ready for occupancy in two days. I paid the deposit and rent and went outside to Gary. He acted a bit embarrassed, telling me he'd forgotten to turn off the meter. Never mind. The fare back to the motel was seventeen. I gave him twenty and he drove off happy enough. I'd been in his company for over an hour. I appreciated Gary's spontaneous generous gesture.

Chapter 3: Ready for the Big Time

Denver is systematically laid out, as are most cities in the USA; streets ran directly east to west, and avenues and boulevards north to south. The exception here were the two freeways which meandered their way across the city like two snakes defying man's efforts of perfect symmetry. My street, York, was over ten miles long. Colfax, which bisected it, was roughly the same length.

I spent a week trying to acclimatise and get my bearings. I felt tired and thirsty all the time, not realising that it was the elevation and the consequent dehydration. There was no bedding or cooking utensils in the apartment, so I kitted the bed from Woolworth's and the kitchen from garage sales. Most items cost next to nothing, which was what some of them were worth. The press iron, for instance, became red-hot in seconds... this meant plugging it in for a minute before unplugging when smoke began to rise from the garment. I always began at the tail of the shirt or singlet, which ensured I became the owner of the most tailless shirts in Denver.

About eight miles away an employment agency in South Broadway offered employment. This south street ran parallel with Colfax though about a mile apart, so I packed a lunch and at six in the morning, set off walking. When after an hour I found myself panting, I caught a bus. The agency was a hive of activity. The clientele were of multiple races, hues and gender. There were also a couple of old codgers with their own vans ferrying groups to the various jobs. Inside a large, bare-walled room of about sixty by forty, it was like a poor church with rows of wooden benches to accommodate the parishioners.

I filled in a couple of forms and took my place on one of the benches. My watch showed seven fifteen. Most of the punters appeared to be regulars, and most were Spanish speaking. A few were greeted with familiarity by the counter fellow. These clients were sent on their way with a tin hat, a dollar for the bus, and at times, a brush and shovel. The jobs offered were all labouring, including traffic point duty for where road maintenance was involved. I noticed most filled their canteens or plastic containers with water before they left.

Vans ferried some groups as they were being sent to where there was no bus service. At eight I was becoming uneasy, for about four hundred had come and gone. By nine o'clock I was positively anxious, my mind searching for reasons as to why I wasn't hired. But there again, I'd always had trouble selling myself – I was usually the last man to be called.

Ten o'clock came. Me and one other guy were all that was left. My confidence was at zero. The other chap was a large, sour-looking fellow of about forty. He had been called several times but had declined what was offered. *Plan B will have to be implemented*, I told myself… such as, be here at five tomorrow morning.

"Two hands needed out at Mineral," the counter-man called, "four bucks an hour." We were handed a shovel, brush, and a tin hat each, and were queried about our financial position before being given the reluctant dollar for the bus fare. Nobody took the slightest bit of notice of us on the bus, though I confess to having felt a trifle self-conscious at the time. The other fellow turned out to be a decent skin.

We arrived at the construction site at eleven o'clock, the site being in a small valley which contained a reservoir, about twenty miles from Broadway. Two nearly completed clapboard houses stood near the entrance, and others were beginning to take shape. At the entrance, a couple of caravans and a wooden chalet housed the site office and the sales rep. The site superintendent drove up in his white pick-up to detail us. "My name's Paul," he informed us in a civilised manner, thereby winning my confidence straight away. "We're expecting some investors tomorrow, so the whole place needs to be cleaned up!" he said. "If you work well we'll give you extra hours."

He was a courteous man of about forty-five, dressed in jeans and a carefully ironed shirt. He brought me inside the house and showed what needed to be done. I got stuck in, and about an hour later the thirst began. I thought that there'd be taps all around the place, but no, the place was dry. The lake was there of course, but there was a lot of flotsam to be seen. I then investigated the toilets to see if there was a water source but found they were dry and foul smelling… all six of them, placed strategically around the site.

The temperature was about eighty when the superintendent came by again. My friend enquired about water. "She has a water cooler in the chalet," he said. "Just go in and ask."

In the air-conditioned chalet a stout, beringed woman, aged about forty and dressed for a party, lounged in an armchair, reading a magazine. Her distaste at being disturbed was obvious – her undisguised anger bloomed on her heavily made-up sulky face as she half-filled a couple of beakers from the cooler, and slapped them down in front of us. "More," I croaked, in my best Oliver Twist voice. She gave me a poisonous stare as she lifted the phone and began complaining to the superintendent in an icy tone that she was "operating a sales office and not a social service." I took the opportunity to refill my beaker, and departed outside with it.

My workmate was taken away to operate a tractor-driven road sweeper – a hoor of a job, for the unfortunate fellow couldn't be seen for the clouds of dust. I began the second phase of our program, using my shovel to scrape the dried mud from the driveways.

That first day was a nightmare. The thirst and weakness of my limbs became almost unbearable. In the afternoon, a young man drove up to take a gander. In a haze, I heard him ask where I was from. When I told him, he said his father was Irish and he offered me a job. "Six dollars an hour and all the hours you want," he promised. I knew I wouldn't make it the next day, which was Thursday. "I'll start Monday," I croaked, "I have a couple of things to do tomorrow." At five we rode the bus back to Broadway where, from a faucet in the agency, I drank about a gallon of water. It relieved the thirst but not the weakness. The superintendent was as good as his word – he'd booked us in for a full day. Downside was, the skimmers in the agency deducted a dollar an hour for the full day. It worked out at about two punts twenty per hour.

By Monday I had recovered – a salt tablet a day for a couple of days afterwards sorted out the dehydration. This time, I arrived at the job armed with a gallon of water.

All the work at the site was subcontracted. First, the machinery came to scrape large holes in the rock-hard ground, holes which would eventually be the basements of the houses. The sewerage pipes followed. George Parker and his Mexicans concreted the foundations to ground level, and laid iron girders across.

Guatemalan framers took over to supposedly level the girders, but they didn't – they built the wooden house frame on top of them as they were. Roofers came next to felt and shingle the roofs. Mexicans working in pairs fixed the clapboards. All the air-conditioning, insulation, plus electrical was contracted to subbies.

My job description could be described as a PUS (or Picking Up Shit), such as timber off-cuts left by the framers that needed to be put into skips, felt off-cuts, shingles or whatever one gang left, I cleared away before the next gang started. Normally, these lads were supposed to do their own cleaning, but the project was running late and I was willing.

Paul, the superintendent, was from Florida. I rarely saw him. Apparently, he'd grown fond of the air-conditioned trailer – too fond. At eleven o'clock one morning, the travelling site manager arrived. Daryl was a huge, confident fellow of about forty-five (an ex-wrestler, somebody told me). He called Paul outside and fired him. I kept my head down in case Daryl was told I was a friend of Paul's.

Mark was the new superintendent. He'd been working for the firm for over twenty years. He too was a nice guy, the only problem was, he never left the site. Another of my chores was preparing the finished house for the painters. Every speck of dust had to be swept and vacuumed because the interior painting was by spraying only. So, dust removal was vital. These painters would enter the house dressed like frogmen, and three hours later stagger out with exhaustion.

Big Daryl called me one day and proposed a new job as a utility man. My duties would be installing kitchen equipment and general patching before the investor moved in. Eight dollars an hour would be the new rate. Unfortunately for me, he hadn't told Mark.

Management were becoming concerned. The site had cost them a million and because it was in a valley, sewerage had to be pumped up sixty feet to meet the mains, a half mile away. It was a huge investment of money and time.

To make progress, Mark had advertised for more staff and Randy appeared as the eight-dollar man. He was about thirty, well-built, fair-haired, and generally smiling, but he had a wild look about him. When we got to know one another, he told me his background. Born and raised in Nebraska and miles from anywhere, his father, ex-army, was away most of the time working heavy equipment. Randy said he was in trouble from day one. 'Car stealing and hell-raisin" was how he explained it. The judge gave him one last chance – join the armed services or two years inside. Randy joined the navy. There were problems there too but he didn't elaborate. He had married but was now divorced and in big trouble with a girlfriend.

Did I feel sore with him getting my job? My feathers were ruffled for a day or two, but Randy was a good, efficient worker and I liked him. Two other guys started in the guise of framers or carpenters, Gerry, a well-built, dark-haired fellow who was originally from Indiana and Butch from Fort Collins, a town here in Colorado. He was a short, blond, good-looking fellow with a moustache. Both were aged about thirty. Gerry began to address me as 'dude'. 'What time is it, dude?' or, 'See ma' spirit level, dude?' It was their way and I wasn't offended.

One element that makes boring work bearable is the characters one works with. Gerry and Butch provided bizarre entertainment. They had come to an arrangement with Mark, the superintendent, that only Butch was officially employed and at sixteen dollars an hour (which was double the normal). Butch then paid Gerry. Apparently, Gerry was wanted by the police and would be easily traced through his social security card if officially employed. He'd been in jail before for assault.

"What happened?" I asked.

"A dude was beaten' the shit out of me so I ran to my car and got a hatchet and I cut lumps out of him. Got two years over the bastard," he told me, sadly.

"You kill him?" I asked.

"Naw," he spat, "the bastard is still runnin' around."

The on-site standard of work was awful. The unplumbed girders on which the house frames were built were causing havoc for tilers, decorators, finishing carpenters, and the installers of kitchen equipment. How the house framers weren't fired was puzzling, until someone told me about the contract. The contracts involved payola to the agent who dealt with them. For instance, the house builder in his estimate charged thirty-six dollars for each framer (for tax purposes), but subbies like Butch and Gerry only got eight dollars each. This conundrum left it difficult to penalise the subcontractors as Mark told me they were all skimming. Mark's solution was to hire a couple of framers to rectify mistakes before the finishers began, hence Gerry and Butch. "Floor is a few inches off," the parquet flooring installer complained. Mark would call the two boys and the guntering would begin.

Scientific analysis and meticulous preparation was not their forte – hydraulic jacks, crowbars and sledges were the optimum. It was educational to watch as jacks were positioned in the basement under the end of the supporting girder, and pumped until Butch judged it to be level. Tortured groaning of stressed timbers and of door frames buckling filled the air, even after the jacking up was completed. Distorted dividing walls were then battered back into new positions, and buckled plastering boards ripped out and replaced. The most difficult task was trying to cure the upstairs room floors of their horrendous squealing. One day I watched Gerry pumping the jack, and with Butch bent over his spirit level, a white flake drifted to the floor. I looked up to see two inches of daylight through a full-length crack where the roof had split open. They weren't upset. "Just lift it on the other side," Butch ordered, "That'll fix it." This, of course, left the house as unbalanced as before, and definitely not waterproof.

Randy, the eight-dollar man, began to work all hours, some mornings beginning at five. I always left him behind me in the evening. He was most definitely the white-haired boy. About a month went by before a flaw or two appeared. Payday was every fortnight, which began to coincide with Randy being sick on the following Monday, then Monday and Tuesday. He arrived in one morning, his face black and blue. Apparently, his girlfriend had taken off with her former lover, bringing with them most of Randy's belongings, including the TV. Randy had followed and caught up with them, then got a hiding for his pains. He really went downhill after that. "I loved that gal," he'd tell us, sadly.

Aeron was an electrician, about forty, and a very pleasant fellow. He was tall and athletic, and had a moustache. He was neat and efficient at his job. He was a fellow Mark the superintendent paid a lot of attention to. Aeron and a framer began to disappear at lunchtime, not returning until maybe four o'clock, arriving back half cut. Sometimes they didn't return at all. Randy joined this group. After a month of this caper, Mark, the superintendent, warned him.

Randy then went missing for a week and was fired. I never saw him again. He owes me twenty dollars.

Aeron, Mark told me, was a recovering addict. Apparently, his wife was also one, and the law had taken their children from them. That was three years earlier. Lately, their drug liaison officer had given Aeron and his wife the all-clear, and they were now waiting to recover their kids. Mark worried but had no authority over him, so a sad situation was getting worse.

Chapter 4: Jeff

An assistant superintendent called Jeff was employed, a young guy straight out of college. He was about thirty, fair-haired, and had an unchanging, smiley expression. As he later told me, he had been a framer working in Alaska. He had earned big money there, saving it to buy a couple of years in college. He now had his degree and this job – his first as a specialist. He seemed a nice fellow and became quite familiar, confessing he was married to a Japanese girl. He even loaned me his pick-up a couple of times to move equipment from site to site. For some reason, Gerry wasn't impressed with Jeff. "I just don't trust that dude," he'd say.

The mornings were the best time of day. The mountains would appear quite close, looming dusky blue against the western sky. Practically every morning at this early hour, air balloons with gondolas attached would rise from somewhere near the foot of the mountains, probably taking advantage of warm air spirals. The tranquillity reigned for an hour or so until the scream of power tools brought me back to reality. By midday the heat became intense, with temperatures reaching eighty or ninety degrees. Invariably, around two in the afternoon a pleasant breeze arose, often accompanied by black clouds. A downpour could last a couple of hours, and one hour later everywhere would be as dry as tinder again.

I didn't work the weekends due to the bad or non-existent bus service. Saturday morning was for stocking up my larder. I also went nosing around the garage sales. It was a sensitive occasion, looking at what a guy had to sell. I felt sympathy for him, though they never seemed to be embarrassed. They were mostly fellows moving on to pastures new, and without transport they sold or eventually dumped whatever they couldn't shift.

My Saturday afternoons were generally spent downtown, only a thirty-minute walk away. 16th is Denver's main street. A free bus service is operated continually on its mile or so length. Just off its southern end was the railroad station and the nearby Mile High Stadium and the Chicago Inn. It was a boozer of sterling quality in which I spent many a happy hour. It catered mostly for young people and football fans. I counted eight large TVs positioned strategically around the huge bar to facilitate the supporters, though the food attracted all generations. There would be much discussion, debate, and cheering, but never bad language or trouble. I was never short of company for there was always one or two opinionated moochers like me looking to discuss and solve worldwide problems.

York Street, where I lived, was also very convenient to a couple of large city parks. The Botanical Garden was only a five-minute walk away. Around the Botanical's perimeter, little patches of garden of about ten square feet were rented to some of the citizens, where cabbages, onions and carrots were lovingly tended. A waiting list of thousands existed for hopefuls. The Natural History Museum in city park was absolutely brilliant in its presentation of Colorado's flora and fauna, and also of the Native American history; I spent many a pleasant Sunday afternoon admiring the different sections. I was amazed to see gulls swooping for titbits on the park lake, a mile high and a thousand miles from the sea.

Chapter 5: Along Comes Bob

When Randy disappeared, I wasn't promoted, a new eight-dollar man was transferred from another site. Bob was fifty, short, and stout. He used to be a schoolteacher until a nervous breakdown ended his career. He was a greenhorn who had started with the company seventeen years earlier. An instant dislike developed between Bob and Jeff, the assistant superintendent. Jeff reckoned Bob was too slow. But Mark, the superintendent, was an old friend of Bob's, so his position was secure for the moment.

The harmony which existed on-site was now being undermined by Jeff. He pushed and interfered everywhere with negative results. Finishing carpenters resented him looking over their shoulders, and when they finished a house they quit. Meanwhile, poor, agitated Bob wore a hunted expression, the result of Jeff giving him the silent treatment.

With every house came a garage which, up to this time, had no doors. One day the contractor arrived with a truckload of automated doors. The installer was a Canadian, a gentle, low-sized fellow who spoke with a drawl. It only took him an hour to frame and fit one. He was on-site for two days and then was gone. I noticed Bob inspecting the doors, opening and shutting them, standing back with his head tilted, eyeing them. I left him at it as I raced for my bus.

A day or two later I saw Bob with a couple of iron bars working at the garage door of one of the already occupied houses. "Broke?" I asked him.

"Not really," he said, "just a bit out of alignment." I peered a bit closer and asked him how he fixed it. Bob looked smug – he was like a ten-year-old with a tuppenny bag of bullseyes and not prepared to offer you one.

"Ah, com'on," I said, "Jeff might want me to fix a couple for him."

Bob's eyes flickered. He developed a superior expression and offered, "I'd like to, but the faults are different so I can't really say." I was only having him on, and I'd swear he was bending the runners himself before reporting to Mark. It's the old trick of making yourself indispensable.

When Daryl the roving superintendent came by, he'd immediately be collared by a fawning Jeff for a tour of whatever he was involved in. Ominously, Mark too was being isolated. By August, there were twenty very luxurious houses completed down by the lakeside. Most were occupied, except for one or two owned or nearly owned by ornery investors.

One was an accountant called Mitch – a large, black-haired bachelor aged about forty and wearing glasses. An engineer accompanied him on his second visit, and between them they compiled a list of defects a yard long. Thereafter, whenever Mitch came by to see progress on his house, he'd be accompanied by a horde of his nieces and nephews.

Mitch was not happy with the standard of work, and was forever complaining. As soon as he arrived, Daryl the roving superintendent, Mark the site superintendent, Jeff the assistant and the sales person (they came and were fired regularly) all fawned and licked as they followed Mitch and his relations around the house. I lurked in the background to watch the entertainment – in my official capacity as PUS. When Mitch halted to criticise, all halted, the kids open-mouthed, staring admiringly as their uncle lambasted the company team. The procession would start again to another point of interest.

After Mitch and company had gone I'd ask Mark, "Did he sign?"

Mark would grin and say, "We have him on the edge – just needs a little push." I liked Mitch, he always had a friendly word when you met him and eventually he signed.

The landscapers arrived and in two days the site was transformed. Four-dollar men from Broadway raked and levelled, swept and hosed. Seven- or eight-foot-high trees were planted. Pre-designed flower beds were laid. A couple of acres of lawn was unrolled, giving the estate the appearance of maturity. The four-dollar men had plenty of water to drink, and I shared my lunch with a guy who had nothing. Most of them had the dull, lifeless eyes and peculiar whine of substance users.

On one of the many (unpaid) bank holiday weekends, I rented a Toyota and applied for a driving licence. I passed the exam and driving test, and went for a drive. I took the freeway south to Manitou Springs, seventy miles from Denver. The small, one-street town was the beginning or end of one of the original native trails leading through the mountains. It is now overrun by tourists from May to September. It got its name from the natural, white soda water springs that bubble from underground. Along the street there were several fountains where you could help yourself, but you had to bring your own scotch.

There was a lot of natural phenomena, including caves, peculiar rock formations, and native cliff dwellings. It must have been beautiful place before the asphalt and concrete was laid. Nowadays, it's not much more than a public park. A few miles further into the mountains is Pikes Peak which, at seven and a half thousand feet, is the second highest in Colorado.

When Lt Pike discovered it in 1806, he deemed it unclimbable. Today, one can walk up, drive up, or take the cog-wheeled train which pulls itself to the top. There's an annual marathon from Manitou Springs to the peak, and an auto race to the summit has been held every year since 1916.

That night I stayed in a motel in Manitou Springs. It was a bit pricey at twenty-five dollars. Next day at noon, I crossed the fast-flowing Arkansas, stopping to watch a group of young people rafting – a high-risk entertainment. It seemed that with the rapids and the strong current, the rafts were difficult to control. This is the same river that joins the Mississippi in Alabama, eight hundred miles away. The roads through the mountains are impressive – monuments to human engineering skills, gouged from the mountainsides leading to a suitable spot to cross a river or to save a mile.

I crossed the great divide beyond Twin Lakes, and stopped at Aspen (the ski resort). The bare, ski-scarred slopes had a weary appearance, and the log-cabin-simulated buildings that were so romantic in the snow, in May looked brutish and ugly. I overnighted at Glenwood Springs before taking the interstate back toward Denver, one hundred and fifty miles away.

I pulled in at Vail for a bite to eat, another resort and a very picturesque one. It was there I met my first Irish person in six months. I can't recall his name, but said he was from Monkstown in Dublin. He was a bit evasive about what he was doing for a living, though I observed by the way his clothes hung around him he certainly wasn't overeating. I told him about my construction job – avoiding the PUS bit – and all the overtime that was available. His eyes glowed with interest, and then began to fade when I mentioned six dollars an hour. I enjoyed the little trip. It made me speculate on the hardships suffered by families on the wagon trains a hundred years earlier, trekking for three weeks across the two hundred miles through the Rockies. Now in your air-conditioned car, it takes just three hours.

Me in Colorado's Garden Of The Gods National Park.

The Arkansas River, Colorado.

Paiute Houses, Manitou Springs, Colorado.

Denver's Mile High Stadum in the background.

Chapter 6: Chief Deputy

Management was becoming fidgety in the absence of new investors. The superintendents wore worried expressions. Strange faces appeared, fellows bearing briefcases and wearing frowns. Consultants, somebody said. Others swore advisors. The result was, Mark was fired.

Guess who was promoted? Not me. Jeff was now cock of the walk – more than likely now employed for half Mark's salary. Two days later, a devastated eight-dollar Bob was fired, and the six-dollar man began to feel unloved. Ever optimistic, Daryl said the sales slump was cyclical. He said that house property didn't move until the fall. The subcontractors said different, they swore the houses were too expensive.

The twenty or so with large balconies and built along the lake shore sold like hot cakes at three hundred and fifty thousand. The others sold at various prices, depending on size and location, down to one hundred and fifty thousand. The most difficult to move were centrally positioned ones with no views. Indeed, they were the same as featureless units of a state housing scheme.

Productivity slowed to blend with poor customer demands. I was sorry to see the Guatemalan framing gangs disappear. They were a sociable, good-humoured bunch, practically every one an ex-soldier, here in the US as a result of an agreement in the settling of a revolution in their country.

With regard to Jeff's potential victims, it became open-season for the remainder. He began intercepting me at knocking-off time to do some unnecessary chore or other. I had a twenty-minute walk to the bus stop to catch the five thirty. If I missed it, the next was at six with a fare increase of fifty cents. I reminded Jeff of this one morning after he kept me working in the rain. The next time he pounced I refused, pointing out that what he asked was petty and unimportant. A shadow crossed his face which promised me a career change.

September the 2nd was a Sunday; the temperature was a high eighty as I walked back from the park to the apartment on York Street. The forecast was for a temporary change. As usual, next morning I rose at five, and washed, shaved and had breakfast. Outside it was snowing, and already three inches lay on the ground. The elevation and heat had left me without any body fat, and brother, did I feel the cold. Out at the site a strange and wonderful phenomenon had developed – clouds of steam rose from the lake and the still-warm earth, the surreal cottonwoods suspending their snow-laden arms to the ground.

Nobody else turned in, so I paraded around making a racket, conscious that that the company boss had a luxury home on-site and might notice me before I did a runner. Daryl's arrival put paid to that. The snow stopped at eleven and the sun imposed itself on Mineral once again, changing it from a fairyland to a bog.

Whatever the constituents of Colorado clay, it's the gluiest mixture I ever experienced – one step and your foot grows to three times its normal size, two steps and your boot weighs a stone. A small amount of water on it creates dough which dries quickly to a concrete hardness. I'm an expert on this subject. Fellow workers, once indoors, headed straight for the stair step or any sharp angle to scrape off the mess. And guess who cleaned up after them? You bet, the six-dollar man.

Jeff was sore the next day when he discovered I'd turned in and he hadn't. He was sorer when I gave him a week's notice, depriving him of the pleasure of firing me. I don't like the cold, and my days were numbered anyway.

I used to spend about three hours a day riding the bus to and from work. Three rules were strictly enforced – no food, no music, no smoking. The bus was also an education in social intercourse. Conversation could include half the passengers, each giving his or her opinion or remedy to whatever. On Monday to Friday I boarded with several clients at the downtown civic centre, some well-dressed, but the majority seemly down on their luck. We'd pick up more of them on the way, most bound for the employment agency in South Broadway.

One little lady proudly revealed that she was a Ferris wheel junkie. At weekends she'd travel to fairs in Kansas or Nebraska for a new experience. She knew where the biggest, the smallest, and the quickest existed. She also told us she was divorced. Small wonder.

Another lady, about forty-five, said she was an upholsterer. She picked up a few clients from the passengers who invited her to inspect their suites and to give estimates. One morning a lady friend of hers boarded, and as there was no empty seat adjacent, a conversation developed halfway down the bus. "Ya sure look much prettier with your new dentures," the upholsterer remarked. This was not meant to embarrass or humiliate – it was a genuine observation. The false teeth lady took it as such and smiled broadly to an admiring and interested audience. And a debate commenced on the virtues of dentures.

Midwest people are very uninhibited and outspoken. It was on the bus I asked a man how the city of Denver got its name. He told me it was a Kansas politician, a governor no less, John Denver being his name. He supported Colorado in its claim for statehood, he told me, adding, "Ah, he weren't much help."

On payday evenings I took the bus on the Santa Fe, leaving me near the bank where I could lodge my cheque. About twenty poorly dressed ex-servicemen would board the bus outside a welfare office, while hundreds more milled around outside. They'd have a few drinks on them – the conversation generally about the extent of their disability and where they'd caught it. The mood was satisfaction that they'd made it, though for some, the war would never be over. Those with the greater disability – and the consequent larger pension – would offer advice to their comrades on how to convince the assessment officer next time round. (There appeared to be an annual assessment.)

From Korea in the fifties through to Vietnam in the late seventies and again in Iraq, these men and women gave service to their country, and some reluctantly. I believe their loyalty and sacrifice for world order should be admired. Cynics will say that US governments interfered in order to manipulate our world to their capitalistic shape. The question is, what kind of world would we have if the US had not helped defeat Hitler, the Japanese, or the containing of Communism? How many tin-pot dictators have had to think twice before controlling their excesses? We Irish and others, who have contributed very little, are welcomed and well-treated, reflecting the ordinary American citizen's generosity of spirit.

Chapter 7: Goodbye to All That

It was usually seven when I got home in the evenings. After a shower and something to eat, it was eight. I would visit one of the nearby bars, lingering over a couple of bottles of Miller while watching the sports on TV. The Greek-owned bar was my favourite; the bar staff were female and friendly – good lookers too. I met a young couple there one Thursday evening and got talking. She was pretty and about twenty-eight or thirty, friendly and talkative. He was younger, broad and taciturn. They were Boston-Irish, she was manageress of a restaurant, and he was a graduate in Celtic studies, now working as a cook.

The girl and I engaged in a conversation about Tara and Knowth – to the annoyance of his nibs. Heads turned as he loudly declared, "I'm a graduate in Celtic studies. And I've written a book."

"On Celtic studies?" I asked.

"No," he replied, "on cookin'."

They'd had a few, and when he retired to the toilet, she invited me to dine some evening at her restaurant free of charge. While I deliberated, me man returned. He might have relieved his bladder, but not his bad humour as he slumped sullenly into a seat. They left soon after. I never did dine at their restaurant, and regretfully, gave the Greeks a miss on Thursdays.

I'd met Gary the taxi driver a couple of times coming and going from the apartments, but he always seemed to be in a hurry. And I had noticed his worried or reticent demeanour. Coming from the Greeks one night we met at a junction with only a five-minute walk ahead of us. He looked terrible. "Yeah," he smiled, "I'm on about a hundred pills a day just to get by. I lost my job and my cab licence. Anything doin' out at your place? I'll do anything," he pleaded. I could do nothing but give him a twenty-dollar bill.

My farewell drinks with Gerry, Butch and his wife in Bluz Bar, Littleton Colorado in 1993/4.

Gerry and Butch invited me to Bluz for a farewell drink. Bluz was a bar in Littleton – a district I passed each day on the bus, the same place where a few years later a student ran amok in his school and shot about a dozen of his fellows. This was the same bar where the electricians and framers spent their time. Bluz had a special offer available every Friday evening, including a free roast beef with a cold salad.

When we arrived in the wreck that Butch called his car, a queue had already formed. The place was huge and three-quarters full. Four snooker tables were surrounded by a shouting, noisy mob. TVs turned up full blast created a terrible din. Most of the clients were like us, straight from work. Others came in and grabbed food and furtively left without buying anything. We got our plates and three jugs of Miller, and found seats near the mob from our site who were already well on. There were no South American framers present; apparently this type of boozing was not part of their culture. During the evening the electrician and framer would disappear for a few minutes, and return in a euphoric mood. I commented to Gerry about the flour around their nostrils. "Coke," he said with disgust. We had a good evening, at least the bits I remember.

Counting my money next morning, I concluded that parties given in your honour are best to be avoided.

The conclusion I came to is that in the US, man is the sum of his parts. Anyone can make it, but not overnight. A college course (for a price) and the subsequent proof of your capabilities in any of the trades will convert a four-dollar PUS to a twenty-four-dollar man. On Monday, October 3rd, I closed my account at the bank. It was snowing again – sixty-three inches is the seasonal average. I phoned the airport and booked a flight to New York where again I broke my journey to visit my niece Emer, a student in Fordham University. Next morning, the aircraft rose into a clear sky, banking away from the mountains and the city. It would be six months before I saw it again.

Psalm 88

I survive Lord, but there are those who wish me harm

And fit by hook or crook to have my head

But the life force is still with me and with you I am well armed

And so endure though my life hanging by a thread.

Chapter 8: A Winter of Discontent

You meet them in the street but you never know,

See them on their knees as they feign to pray.

But you never know the evil they conceive,

Evil they conceal with outward show.

In the spring of 1994, I unwisely returned to Denver for at that time my hip began to give me trouble. Nevertheless, when I arrived my apartment was available, though on inquiring, Gary had gone. One of the other guests said he'd gone into rehab. I hope things worked out for him. After moping around for a week, I rented a car and among the sites I visited was Mineral. The Ryder Corporation, my previous employers, were still involved, but down to a skeleton staff. I didn't approach Jeff but I met a friend, a guy who was second-generation Irish and in charge of a house maintenance company, and who offered me a job. After a few months my hip became very painful. I made enquiries through my health cover; Denver offered me a new hip for thirty thousand dollars. I was told cheaper deals were available but I declined. Jesus, it sounded too much like an abattoir. Anyway, it shocked me into deciding to return to Dublin. On the way I broke my journey in New York, and visited my niece Emer.

My family was surprised to see me which made me feel a failure, or like an old dog that had strayed and had found its way home again. But sensitivity not being my stronger emotion, I continued to plonk myself at any table that might offer me a meal.

At my home in the village only Eamonn remained, living in the apartment. A problem had begun to emerge. The village pub had acquired a late-night disco licence, this caper operating at weekends. The disco closed at two o'clock in the morning and those with transport left promptly. But our village being off all bus routes left quite a few of the clientele without transport. Bleary eyed and aimless, like fireflies they would congregate under the street lights. After a while some would wander off walking in the hope of hitching a lift. Others entertained themselves with sing-songs or knocking the crap out of one another. When spent, they would, weather permitting, sleep off their euphoria on the grassy banks of the roadside. While they gave us no hassle, the potential was there.

I recall a melee one morning at three o'clock, the racket so intense it roused me from my bed to the garden wall. I could see the surging group going this way and that. The contenders with coats flung off and sleeves rolled up, signalling murder by moonlight. In the middle of the throng was this big, gangly, red-headed fellow with a half dozen hanging out of him. After a while the activity abated and was reduced to a bunch on either side of the street hurling threats and insults. Usually this signalled the end of hostilities. Fun over, I retired to the house.

I was only in bed ten minutes when the furore erupted again. I heard giant footsteps rapidly approaching. Through my bedroom window I saw Ginger passing in full flight; behind him were the pursuers who ran out of puff opposite my window. One blocky fellow of nineteen or twenty thumped his bare chest, howling, "Come on, Ginger… you an' f***in' me." Apparently, the humour had gone off Ginger for without pausing he clumped into the dark hinterland.

I smiled to myself as I settled, but blue murder broke again. I lay awake because with Ginger at large, anything could happen. Within thirty minutes I heard big footsteps and a heavy thump as something was dumped into our garden. Next morning, I had a gander and found a heavy wooden post, about four feet long – obviously a cudgel he'd acquired while in hiding. Later, a neighbour told me that when Ginger's pursuers returned, they found somebody had nicked their coats.

I must add that by this time and due to Dublin Airport expansion, most of the village dwellings had been abandoned and no complainers were among those left. After some deliberation I decided to sell the house and subsequently the Airport Authority offered a reasonable price, and that was that.

There was no heartbreak in leaving, other than nostalgia for the fun I had with my sister's children, in particularly Gráinne, born with a congenital heart condition and whom I, pretending to be a madman, shoulder-backed her around the garden. Poor Gráinne, a wife and mother of two girls, died in 2013 at the age of forty-five. Anyway, I bought a semi-detached house in the city suburbs – nothing fancy, but it suited, it being quite near my sister and Lorcan's. As events turned out, it was the second biggest mistake of my life.

My niece Grainne and my brother-in-law Michael, taken at home when she was in her prime. Sadly, both are no longer with us today. RIP.

It so happened that a few old workmates, Paddy Delaney, Jimmy Tyrell and Billy Murphy plus a couple of other airport production mechanics, also lived in the area. With them and another neighbour, Joe O'Brien, we gravitated together at least once a week to make sense of our world. Of course, during the rugby season and Euro qualifiers we'd assemble in a pub, and on quite a few occasions finish up in my joint with some of them still there when I got up in the morning. I didn't mind because I had a history of similar behaviour.

Among my routines was visiting my sister's house at around quarter to seven of an evening. It was just to see her children, and (for opinionated me) to advise my brother-in-law on the developing problems of his trucking business.

My sister and her daughters whom I loved to visit, taken when they were on their summer holidays in Kerry c.1975.

It was a three-minute walk to their house, and I noticed Titch and his daughter, usually with her driving the car. They must have noticed me since I was meeting them so regular. Perhaps I, now being insignificant in their world just didn't register. It was on two evenings per week that I met them, a Tuesday and Friday if my memory serves.

It was an evening in March 1995, around the time Steve Collins beat Eubank when I met them, she was driving his car. Momentarily, her eyes caught mine before she turned to him and passed some remark. Both instantly turned toward me with mouths agape in helpless laughter. I was embarrassed. I felt humiliated as a normal person would and dismissed them with a glance of disgust. Their still open mouths sagged into mirthless disappointment.

Next morning, which was a Saturday, I met a relative of Titch's, a person I knew and respected. To my amazement he cut me short. From then on, people I had known to be friendly would avoid me. It did not worry me, but it was puzzling.

A few months later in a local public bar a friend shocked me when he told me that Titch had complained that I had embarrassed his daughter, their poor innocent child, a mere school girl! Her now driving the car?

This characterisation, embellished and elaborated to destroy. One would rather be accused of murder.

My informant didn't know where and when the situation was supposed to have taken place, and to this day, I don't know either. As for the daughter? I never met, spoke to or recall ever seeing this creature since she was seven or eight years old. Though I did see her twice after their accusation. Once at a neighbour's funeral where on seeing me in church she bolted, knocking mourners aside in her haste to escape. The second time was exactly where the original episode occurred. She was now driving her own car and on seeing me rolled her tongue in embarrassment while trying to squirm under the console. Not the outraged reaction of a victim.

I made an appointment with a solicitor. It was the first of four on the same subject. He advised me to get a witness, and that would be that. Though I tried several times to convince those who warily agreed that they had heard the rumour, none would agree to testify, not wanting to be involved in neighbour's petty wrangles or disputes. I was given the same legal advice on all my visits, "Get a witness," because if we charged him without a witness, their solicitor would bin the accusation. I had checked the local Garda station and there was no complaint. I then opted for dignified silence in the hope of the rumour dissipating, and people forgetting.

During this passage of time I wondered why Titch reacted. I was aware he complained of arthritis, though I had presumed it was psychosomatic, but pain real or imagined is pain and in that moment when I dismissed him his utter rage, pain and frustration were kernelised into making me his cursing stone. A petulant childish act and one I feel he later regretted, but once he set that rumour in motion there could be no denying it.

One day I saw him with a companion walking toward me and I accused him of denigrating me. I invited him to repeat it with his companion present so that we could solve his complaint. His only response was a gulp and a fart. I did call him a few rude names before departing.

As my mother would say, it never rains but it pours. No, the rumour did not die, but became pandemic when it was passed on to a couple of weirdos. A pair of pernicious half-wits never done quarrelling among themselves. A pair who without censure I afforded respect, consideration and excessive generosity yet they too found distraction and temporary accord in using me as their cursing stone. The rumour now furnished with the cant "nobody is to talk to him" instruction. No one bothered to accuse or complain to me or the Gardaí. I kept checking the Garda station for complaints, but none were recorded.

Has their campaign of vilification affected me? I am utterly dismayed by the events. As for people not speaking to me – I couldn't care less. Being regarded as a criminal and ostracised as a leper? I weep for my family. I have come to accept the event as one of life's vicissitudes.

I suspect the edict that, "Nobody is to talk to him," originated in the parish around 2014. This was after I wrote a letter to His Reverence with my address and phone number included. In the letter, written when I was drowning and in desperation, I alerted him about two of my most vicious persecutors who were daily communicants in his church. I appealed that he might suggest in a homily or confessional that repeated sin of slander negates redemption. It seems the fatwah was his reply, though he hardly delegated my personal letter to a committee. I shudder at the thought, because I was told church committees were the last resort of failed wannabes. Anyway, whoever issued the "don't talk to him" fatwah was a beaut, malice passed on through a mass of poisonous veniality. As Terry Thomas would say, "What a shower!"

My conscience is clear, for I have led a blameless life, and before God and all those who are precious to me I swear, other than to defend myself I have hurt no man, woman or child, either physically or psychologically in any way.

Within these pages my life is revealed and every address in parish, county, shire, country and continent I have lived in is there to be scanned for the slightest misdemeanour.

Psalm 7

Lord, deliver me from distress
Free me from their lying lips and duplicitous tongues
Bless me with the rejuvenating peace your presence is
So I may live to give as I have ever done.
I looked into my heart to find that which arouses hate
And truth was stark for only love and kindness do it know
So, what see'st mine enemies in me that so abominates
And are disposed to sow their covert sordid lies.
At times their manic hatred of me hurts
As they vie to poison me in neighbour's eyes
And in their contempt would have me held as dirt
While they themselves invent the victim's role.

Chapter 9: A Review of My Love Life

Our paths have yet not crossed, this I know
Nor have I seen your face among the teeming crowds.
And while I watch and search expressions as they come and go
None have matched the image I have of you.

Allow me to escape into the wonderful periods of my life; confine myself to the confraternity, comradeship, and affection I enjoyed.

Life has not been loveless, though only once did I experience true love – that adoration, that pure surrendering of oneself to another, that state of grace of love without demands. For me, it could not be requited. Let me begin at the beginning.

I cannot ever remember my mother cuddling or kissing me. Though on the other hand, while I never felt rejected, I never felt in need of cuddles. I now ask myself, why was this so? She was well educated by the standards of the time. From 1916-20 she was a boarder in Ramsgrange College, County Wexford. This is where she earned a diploma for home economics and animal husbandry. She had two elder brothers who were wonderful, kind-hearted, caring men, and I was always warmly accepted whenever we met. My mother's sister, Kitty, was likewise endearing, though she did not have a privileged education.

Our father was not formally educated above hedge school level, though he was well read and quite intelligent, retaining a logic and wisdom that impressed all who knew him. Above all the names I heard my mother accuse our father, I never heard her call him an eejit. During the earliest days of my childhood, my pre-school years, I recall her carrying me through the woods and out into the back field where cows grazed. She placed me on a clean spot in the cow shed floor where she had the job of milking the eight or ten cows – a condition of our father's employment. But I cannot remember cuddles. She'd sing through the chores while I bawled, because both her singing and her songs ('The Spinning Wheel' and 'The Three Lovely Girls from Banyon') were not very melodic.

This cow shed was an early type of Nissan hut, with its roof curved and corrugated. The whole building seemed to be sinking into the ground. It was seldom mucked out, though I remember my mother on occasions cursing under her breath while forking dung into a large wooden wheelbarrow as she cleared a space for the milk churns.

I recall those events and scenes, but no cuddles or kisses. And I never remember looking for them. At home in the house, our parents were united and I cannot recall nastiness. The odd row, yes, with our mother's language never going beyond, *Amadan*, *Leatherim*, or *Eullian*. And I remember our father silently getting to his feet and heading for the garden, a refuge he loved beyond everywhere else on earth.

I never saw an intimate moment between them. That business was obviously confined to the bedroom, with six of us proof of some sort of communion. Our father, a wonderful provider, was emotionally warm but demonstrably remote, never violent, never intimate. I have often wondered, was it a reflection of the times?! Indeed, the odd occasion when you saw a man out walking with his wife he'd be embarrassed, even annoyed that you had noticed him that you'd now tell everybody. Perhaps he only kissed his wife in private, if he kissed her at all? Maybe it wasn't manly to cuddle your children or push the pram (if you had one). That was your woman or your mott's job.

My first experience of love was when I was about five. Her name was Rose Hamilton. Their bungalow was a half mile upriver from ours in our wooded glen. We'd pass that way most evenings on our firewood expeditions, with Rose skipping out and taking my hand. I truly loved her, because she loved me. She demonstrated it by waiting when I would stop to tie the lace of my runners, or when I was picking up a pebble to take a pot-shot at a bird. I would often remain in their garden playing with Rose and their pet rabbit, while Lorcan, Bobby Dow and Jimmy McGrath, carried on down the wooded path.

The biggest test of our mutual love was when the Dooley girls, wearing their silly pixies that left them looking like gnomes, would tease us with their giggling, "Aren't they lovely!" and singing, "Da-han loves Ro-say." I didn't care, nor was I annoyed. I held onto

Rose's hand as if I owned her. Alas, her Scottish father Gerry – the head lad in the racing stable – decided to return to Scotland. I believe his decision was based on the need for him to move his family to another bungalow situated in the stable yard. As a man of principle, he declined and Jack McGrath filled the vacancy. Anyway, so ended my love affair. Happy days.

I clearly recall my first cuddle. It was my first day at school and, having been abandoned on the school step by our mother, the unfortunate Miss Tighes lifted me up in her arms whimpering endearments while trying to console this snotty-nosed bawling creature. This cuddling business felt so bloody alien, I wriggled free and headed full pelt toward the yard gate in an attempt to escape. The result was that I spent my first three weeks of school in third class, sitting beside my elder brother Lorcan.

That was the one and only cuddle I experienced until I was eighteen years old, as an employee of Yates, a wine merchant in Manchester. The embrace was a gesture by a girl to entertain her workmates, me being so shy. Of course, it wasn't love. Though love, as the song goes, 'is a many splendour thing'. I had, and still have, a love of my life – to this day I'm euphoric in the consciousness of being alive.

Funnily, I have never felt that way about a girl. I respected them yes, kissed them and made love to them. I absolutely adored them for the giving of themselves. But then I would walk away as if we were aliens with different dreams. Romance probably didn't fit in with the adventurous life I now dreamed about. Perhaps I possess an inherent brutishness. It was definitely not a rejection of female company. It was certainly not a longing for any other kind of love. For I have shared billets, digs and apartments, with fellows like myself, but the very thought of any kind of homosexuality nauseates me. And contrary to modern values, I am frightened of those who participate in it.

As I mentioned earlier in this journal, having left Bolton Street Tech at the age of fifteen, I worked for a Cecil Rathbourne, a local dairy farmer. They had a house maid called Marie – a beautiful girl around the same age as myself. I used to see her the odd morning arriving on a crock of a bicycle. I think she waved to me one or two mornings. Not an arm wave, but a little gesture with her hand. I believe she was just as shy as me. Anyway, I never returned her wave in case I'd make a mistake and look a right eejit. And so ended my romance that had never began.

I resigned from Rathbourne's after about a year, and found employment with another dairy farmer. This was the year of 1950 – the year I left home to live on a farm, they needed me every night at ten o'clock to check on the housed animals. I would be free two nights a week, Thursday and Sunday nights. Those nights I would catch the bus into the city and go to the cinema. Halfway on the journey to town, and coming to steep Kelly's hill, I began to notice a girl getting on our bus... a girl who I knew from my Bolton Street days. Nora was her name. She was quite friendly, taking the initiative by sitting beside me and querying as to where I was going. Nora was six inches taller than me, a blonde, and good-looking in a bulky, florid kind of way. She was aggressively friendly.

When I thought about inviting her into my dreams or a romance, I knew I'd be dumped as soon as something better turned up. I did bring her to the Regal Rooms cinema on a couple of Sunday nights, but she was too noisy; laughing during tense scenes when everybody else was silent, talking when I was trying to see the picture, and jumping up to look for the ice cream girl during emotional scenes. This behaviour drew attention and I detested people muttering and looking at me.

Anyway, to get rid of her I devised a plan. On the bus into town I always used to sit upstairs, and when she got on she would race up the stairs and plonk herself beside me. To throw her off my scent I remained downstairs in the bus, and when coming near her stop I found a reason to duck down and remain in hiding in case she came down searching for me. The plan worked and she got the message, though afterwards whenever we met she'd just grimace and roll her eyes and turn away as if she had come into range of a particularly odious fart.

It was on one of those Thursday nights that I had an experience that resulted in me finding my one and only true love. It was a film in the Capitol cinema called 'An American in Paris' starring Gene Kelly, Maurice De Chevalier and the adorable Leslie Caron. She was beautiful, so fragile and vulnerable, so innocent and youthful. There was a freshness and animation about her that made me glow. She remained on my mind, though I never dreamed about her. And I never saw myself as her lover. However, I never forgot her because the role she so brilliantly played exemplified innocent love – true love. I have often seen the film advertised, but I was never tempted to see it again, happy to retain my original vision. Actually, the only film I never grew tired of watching was 'Moby Dick', starring Gregory Peck as Captain Ahab and Leo Genn as first mate, Starbuck, a film which I have enjoyed three times.

In Manchester in 1952, I lived in the digs of Mrs. Ambrose at 51 Livesey Street, off the Oldham Road. A couple of local girls used to hang around the corner shop of our street. One of the girls was on friendly terms with Chris, a bus conductor from County Meath and my roommate. He introduced me to the spare girl, a lovely, dark-haired girl called Dympna. I brought her to the pictures a couple of times before she gave me the push. The grapevine recorded I was too quiet. It was humiliating being rejected. I felt everybody was laughing at me.

Later, there were one or two dates with different girls, but they showed little enthusiasm for my attentions. A year later I left Manchester and headed for a small town in Yorkshire called Selby. I had been promised that this was the town that would be the making of my fortune. For the first few months it was very disappointing due to the worst paying employment I'd ever encountered. And only for the care and attention of the landlady's niece Vera, who lived next door, I could have easily gone off somewhere else.

She was a nice girl, about five feet four inches with lovely brown eyes and shoulder-length brown hair. Her face was angular with a determined square chin and she had great teeth. She dressed sensibility, and by that, I mean plainly. That suited me fine because she didn't attract the attention of other wolves. Personality wise? I'm afraid it was flat and placid; a damp squib. She never lost her temper, nor did she hold individual opinions or tastes. Maybe it was the result of working in a vegetable canning factory?

She overcame those drawbacks with intimate little suppers, usually of fish and chips what with the rationing still in force. She was also cunning, never inviting me indoors without having her ten-year-old sister present. Vera needn't have worried because I was too shy for playing tiddly winks. Oh, I forgot to mention her parents were divorced. The mother was now living with someone else and the father was a long-distance lorry driver. Very long-distance... for I only saw him once. Where Vera was quiet, her vamp of a sister was a noisy pain, forever demanding attention. When I got a better job and moved into the hostel on-site, the romance fizzled out. A few years later Ned Madden told me she had married, had two children and had divorced her husband.

After ten months I left Selby and arrived in Scunthorpe. Without going into details, in my second digs I twice went out with the landlady's daughter. To her it was a novel experience, and a culture shock. In this rural part of Britain, a native didn't do this kind of thing. Whenever we'd meet someone she knew she'd grimace and become taut with embarrassment. I made excuses and left the digs, though altogether I remained in the area for about a year before heading for Sheffield.

Derby is a nice town. I had a good job and workmates who were compatible, so life was good there. I used to go dancing at the weekends, meet a girl, leave her to the bus and never see her again. Or if I did, I didn't recognise her having been drunk. I changed tack and began to visit the international club on the London Road. As far as I could make out, the clientele were all DP (wartime displaced persons, men and women, mostly Polish and Ukrainians). The girls were gorgeous, and of all ages. The blokes could have been lovely too, but I wasn't watching them. The band was great. The dances were waltzes, foxtrots and quick-step, but language difficulties prevented me from making any romantic headway. Then, in frustration I'd return to the church hall, back to the jumpin' and leptin' of the céilí and old-time. And afterwards, make the fruitless walks to and from the bus.

At that time I was living in Long Eaton, a village outside Derby where, by the way, the crafty old landlady used to rook us each night playing rummy. I arrived home one evening from work to find my brother Lorcan in the digs. He and Anna (his wife-to-be) were on a short holiday. He also told me that the wedding was in August, a couple of months away, and that I had been nominated to be best man. Come August I arrived home having been away for four years. I was reassured by people telling me I had no accent, as this was seen at the time as being Englified. The wedding was fun – the Cronin brothers-in-law were great singers, and were good neighbours.

After a week, Mick Markey (a good friend and neighbour) got me a job as a scaffolder on a building site. My workplace was in Coolock, on Dublin's northside. The job was the building of a factory for Cadbury's. With cash flow secured, I became a patron of the dance halls of the city in my new suit and bicycle. The four Provinces was an arid desert. Moran's Hotel was downmarket. Metropole was too upmarket. In the Francis Xavier Hall, I met Mollie, a gas character. She was shapely, very witty, good-humoured and great company. I made a date to meet her the following Friday evening outside the Carlton cinema at eight o'clock.

On Friday I caught the bus into town, and strolled up to the cinema where there was about a hundred girls waiting for their fellas. I felt a right eejit staring into so many expectant faces. Anyway, I saw no male faces among them. It appears it was the custom at the time for a lad not to be seen waiting.

Mollie was missing, and though I tried to appear nonchalant, I was already set on seeing a film. At a quarter past eight, I was on my last parade and there she was with many apologies. I was relieved, for I had begun to reflect on past experiences where identity was the problem. Anyway, we strolled around to the Adelphia cinema in Abbey Street where there was a good programme advertised. I immediately became engrossed in the film. After about five minutes a noise distracted me, like somebody groaning. I turned to Mollie and realised it was her with her mouth hanging open, snoring and a distinct smell of Guinness off her breath. When I woke her and we left the cinema, she told me she was employed in a shop where every Friday evening they would go to a nearby pub for a few bottles of stout.

That was how the romance began. It was an enjoyable interval in my love life which lasted for a couple of months before I noticed she was not as careful about her appearance as before. The conclusion I reached after much speculation – there was more than one Friday in her week. Our dates became less frequent, and there were no rows or arguments... just a drifting apart. After four months at home, I took the boat again. A couple of years later I was told she was having an affair with a married man, a chap from Swords who I knew from my school days.

It was 1956 when I returned to Derby where I found a job as a rigger with Babcock and Willcox, an engineering company. They were building a coal-fired power station in a place now known as

British Midlands. In my time it was Castle Donnington. I lived with a couple of hundred others in a hostel on-site. It was fine, with no way to spend your money other than save it or gamble it at the toss schools or poker sessions.

On Saturday evenings, myself and a couple of others would catch the bus into Nottingham, an hour bus ride away. We'd have the few jorums, go to a dance, then at ten thirty, run like the hammers for the last bus. It was a dead loss, but world events intervened.

It was 1956, and the era of the Hungarian revolution with thousands of people fleeing that country. Babcocks very generously offered one of their billets to house some refugees. About eighty of them arrived by bus. All male. All fine, big fellows, though minus the drawn, worn, scarred faces of bloodied defenders. Within twenty-four hours the invasion began – hordes of young women from Derby and hordes from Nottingham, some with their own motor cars. There was a surplus... so many that the disappointed left tearfully. Myself and a couple of other hopefuls, just trying to be sympathetic, offered ourselves as second prize. But it was the same old story, a disdainful, "On yer bike, Paddy!"

Avonmouth is a lovely area by the sea in Somerset. I was now employed by an engineering company called Grant Lyons, a Manchester company whose speciality was laying railway tracks. There were eight of us in the gang, all great fellows and mostly Irish. The nightlife was abysmal – no dancing, no clubs. It was a town of estates with the manhood involved in mining or in the huge dock area. At the weekends we would take the ferry across the Severn to visit a village called Pill, the reason being the pub stayed open an hour longer. Mostly, we went to Bristol by bus, but that meant getting taxis home. And that meant queuing for an hour. Still, I persisted, because there was pride at stake. At a dance I got away with a young Welsh girl and, having achieved a bond with her, I had to tell her the journey was too far.

I was in digs close to the dock gates in a very small estate originally built for the emergency services such as firemen and security personnel. A bunch of girls used to cycle round and around the estate every evening, probably for exercise. We'd stand or sit outside the digs smoking and making ourselves available. Two of the lads clicked, then I clicked. Joan Frazer was her name – smallish, great head of hair, good-looking and very jovial. She was a fireman's daughter and was employed in a garment factory. We used to go to the cinema regularly, and sometimes to the Lido; she certainly whetted my appetite when she appeared in a bathing suit! She was fun to be with, forever relating the goings on in the factory and in her home. Our friendship was inclusive, and intimate in the fact she naively told me all her secrets. Anyway, she made me feel privileged to be somebody she could trust. I was a person who was important in her life. But then she was only seventeen. I must say it was an experience I had never had before, and gave me a sense of maturity.

There was a Scotsman in our band of brothers. His name was Jock. He was about thirty-two and a horny bastard, and he made no secret of his lust. When out with Joan we ran into him, him taking the opportunity to crack all his double-meaning jokes which made Joan laugh. A few evenings later, Joan cycled up to our digs and asked to see me. Without a greeting she blurted, "I don't want to go out with you anymore, but we can still be friends." That said, she flew off. I was stunned, but what could I do? The lads in the digs consoled me with the notion that I'd have more time for the beer.

Two days later I meet Jock. "I was out with Joan last night," he grinned. I forced a laugh. "I'm getting there," he sniggered with a wink. I was astounded, but knowing Jock, he always went straight for the throat.

An evening or two later, Joan was on her bike doing the rounds with a couple of friends. And the next evening, and the next. I got one of the lads to query Jock. Apparently, what he got up to with Joan wasn't kosher, and that was the end of Jock. Through that summer of 1956, I saw Joan every evening. If she came near I'd go inside. She had one of her friends to intercede, but I declined. Why? The initial shock still hurt, my confidence had vanished and my self-esteem was dented. I swore I would never let it happen again.

Coming near the end of the summer, myself and a couple of the lads were in the Lido and I saw Joan with a couple of her friends. She waved and I waved back. In the pub next door, we made up, but the romance had gone. Was it love? I loved the pedestal she had placed me on – the trust, the warmth, the affection. And I enjoyed the paternal role. But to give me the boot after one encounter? And with squealy Jock? That was extreme disloyalty. No, it was not love.

Three months later I left for London, with somebody having told me there was money to be made in the East End. With my suitcase, I emerged from the underground onto the Whitechapel Road. Instinctively, I turned left and proceeded along the Bethnal Green Road. In the window of a grocery, a hand-written note declared there was accommodation nearby.

I found a job the next day in an Algate sugar refinery, about a mile and half from the digs. The hours were long but rewarding. After about a month I reluctantly left the digs because of my roommate's nocturnal habits. He was a grand young fellow who was too fond of the beer, seven nights a week. Not only that, he'd also bring his tipsy drinking companions along with their carry-outs. I was always invited to partake, but I always declined because of having to be at work at six in the morning.

Living over a Maltese café just opposite the refinery gates was where I now resided. It was a kip. The landlord was a nice enough guy, but it was his clientele that bothered. They were Maltese and what is known as Ponces, i.e. living off the immoral earnings of their girls. Girls who, on returning around three and four in the morning, created a racket. Also, when Maltese gather to talk, a high-pitched hollering match develops which is never-ending.

Good fortune got me established in a council flat in Sussex Street. After a week or so I discovered my next-door neighbours were Greek. The father had a stall in the nearby Spitalfields fruit and veg market, and their daughter, the poker-faced Maria, was a large, black-haired, fine-featured girl of about nineteen. She gave me the come-on signal, so I proposed a date. Her parents didn't seem to favour my attentions, for I'd occasionally meet them on the stairs, with them responding to my hello with stony, unrecognising stares.

I wasn't very adventurous in my selection of places to go. It was the cinema at night or the park on a Sunday afternoon. She always insisted on the film we saw, the park we frequented or the café where we had tea and a bun. The romance lasted for about four dates because, as familiarity grew, so did her bullying. She reminded me too much of my mother. That too was when her parents began to smile and say hello.

There were three Wicklow lads employed in the refinery, all around my age. We gelled immediately, especially one fellow, John

269

Healy from Rathnew. John had a girlfriend. She was a second-generation Irish girl who hunted with a bevy of other birds. Rachel was one of them. She too was nineteen years old.

We had now entered the beehive, basket, and mini-skirted era, with all the young men parading as Teddy boys (though of course, one didn't risk calling them Teddy boys). Rachel was five feet tall, had wild black hair, a big, generous mouth, and was always smiling with devilment. She was always perfectly turned out and in fashionable clothes. Never before had I enjoyed such company – wild, outlandish laughter, brilliant wit… most times at her own expense. The other girls were totally the opposite with their plucked eyebrows and false eyelashes, their bellies tortured with corsets to accommodate the mini and high heels which left them tottering about. They all depended on Rachel's personality to attract potential game.

I went out with Rachel for a while until she suggested I wasn't enamoured with her friends. I made excuses, but I still got the push. I often met her afterwards and had a laugh and a joke. But she was looking for someone else. I hope she found him.

I had by now found my way around the Hammersmith Palais, with its three or four Paddy wagons parked outside awaiting the unsuccessful lovers, the frustrated, and the drunks who would try to settle old scores or make a name for themselves by creating mini riots. New Cross was another, as well as Camden town and Leytonstone.

Now dressed to the nines and in the Blarney on Tottenham Road, I found a rich source of consolation, rarely leaving without a girl on my arm. There was this girl from Southampton who was older than me, and more experienced. After two dates I began to fear her voracity and checked out. I told her I was leaving town for a while.

Mary from Tipperary was a looker, and I was lucky to get her for in 1958 prime beef was at a premium. She was going out with this chap, also from Tipperary who worked as a camera man for a television station. I recall Mary saying something about the advertising end of things. I used to see him come in to the dance at eleven, a tall, well-dressed fellow wearing glasses. He'd be with a few other inebriated friends, all heading straight for the bar. Mary told me he was an alcoholic. She also told me when she had been ill, he'd been wonderful toward her.

There was a background to the chap's alcoholism. His father had been a manager of an Irish Government installation, and had fiddled the books to gamble. He was caught and jailed for a period, and all over a matter of a couple thousand pounds. In shame, they all had emigrated. God, these days you'd be still walking around after stealing a couple of billion. One could have nothing but sympathy for them.

Anyway, Mary was my girlfriend on and off for about six months. She was dark-haired and had a Spanish look about her with her small, slightly hooked nose, sharp chin and dark features. There was one disturbing feature – she bored me. She never commented on a film, a book or read a newspaper. She held no opinion on a court case that filled the pages at the time, which was all about ten Rillington Place and those murdered there. Mary was employed as a nanny; a one-child nanny, a role that wasn't very challenging. Two factors brought our romance to an end. One, she wanted a permanent relationship and I didn't. The other, her ex was continually pleading for her to go back as he missed her. I saw her several times afterwards in the Blarney. She'd smile, and at times we'd dance. That was when she was waiting for her fellow to appear. I had no regrets because it just wasn't love.

I then began to frequent a dance hall in Leytonstone, a twenty-minute bus ride away. I met a Scots girl there, a beautiful little redhead, a nurse in the nearby hospital. A couple of dates saw the end of that due to her losing interest.

It's funny the way one's needs ebb and flow. I'd get a girl to boost my stock, which was false and unfair on her. For I imagine that when we go to dances it's the same as going to market. You go to find the partner you want, be that a close friend, a lover and perhaps eventually a wife. Though I was a dunce at dancing, I enjoyed it, but I was seeing it as wasting their and my own time. This mood would last for months at a time. Anyway, I was probably a bore or too opinionated. I left London in 1962 and returned home to join the ranks of the unemployed for six months until I found employment with Aer Lingus.

Over the years I had many innocent affairs ending my search for her, that special one who would recognise that I was class. A Mayo man interpreted my dilemma with, "Her mother's not born yet and her father is dead."

Chapter 10: Reflection

How am I today? I ask myself. Well, I'm good! Though my physical and mental abilities are not at the lightning level of a few years ago. My ambition when I wake up in the morning is no longer to climb Everest but to climb out of bed, aching joints being constant companions. It's amazing how one's mind does not age, leaving you with the notion that the two are separate. A glance in the mirror hurts but proves the point. I still retain a curiosity about our world and its people. It leaves me braking my car whenever I see an old ruin where I can have a gander.

I used to take off in my van for a week or so and drive west or south and like the traveller, pull into any old site or old graveyard particularly around County Meath where there are few without the still well-tended graves of young, upper-class sons of the parish, officers who were lost in the Great War; mostly Church of Ireland sharing the graveyard with Catholics. This reminded me of Parramatta, NSW, where I found an overgrown and abandoned graveyard outside the town and discovered the majority of headstoned graves were Irish. There was a particular one with the message, 'Here lies our David aged three years who drowned in a well, its cover having been removed by a careless servant.' I felt their anguish.

I'm definitely being left behind in this tech age of computers and iPhones, gadgets that have made human memory redundant. You ask somebody a question and he or she must consult his or her phone. Since their introduction I detect a human insularity. People seem to have an incestuous relationship with the phone, the same phone that has all but cancelled that wonderful experience of meeting a smiling someone on the street. Seldom can one enjoy the utter graciousness of a smile, that inclusive, welcoming smile, though you know it's only perfunctory. Stony distracted glares are in. Smiles are out.

Happiness can exhilarate for a spell but in the long-term being reasonably content is enough. To be succinct I try not to be a self-absorbed whinger sitting around waiting to die.

My day begins around six o'clock, by eight I have purchased the newspaper – an English one. It costs ninety cents and is well worth it. I get world news and sports, and am kept abreast of medical, archeological and scientific discoveries currently being exploited. This allows me to mentally innovate, explore and to develop the possibilities of the product. Let me give you a few examples.

In January of this year I read about this fellow who calls himself Nigel W. Watson from Essex who is making a wonderful contribution – to who or what I still don't exactly know, though it could be science, medicine or sport. Anyway, it's in this sperm donation racket where he said he's fathered eight hundred children in fifteen years. Isn't that marvellous? Taking into account that over fifty percent of inseminations are negative... Nigel, so quintessentially English, states he is going to produce even more fresh sperm. What a gesture! Isn't it tremendous news?! Indeed, his efforts are worthy of a mention in the honours list, perhaps a knighthood. I wonder, do Nigel's clients ever consider the gene make-up of the progenitor, this compulsive masturbator and most probably a porn addict? Doesn't his middle name intrigue? Nigel does seem very excited with his exposure to the world. That is why he allowed himself to be interviewed. He visualises the game shows, the quiz programs and, of course, the inevitable book with its tear-jerking episodes of him making love to himself.

In March this year I read about a fellow announcing his discovery of a stomach gene which signals to the brain that the gut is full. Now, that is real science. Along with his discovery he has designed a pill that can fool that gene. The pill signals the brain that the gut is full when there's nothing in it.

That was the full statement. That is a tremendous discovery; the potential is stupendous. Indeed, on first glance this innovation puts the microchip in the shade. Let's consider a few of the obvious... Gluttony is kaput. No more heart attacks for those killing themselves jogging. The ladies can have the body beautiful in a couple of weeks with no sweat.

This pill will be a boon for hospitals with their perennial problem of more patients than beds; beds full of old codgers with nothing wrong with them except their families do not want them back. Let's face the facts, these beat-up, down-at-heel old codgers are no longer fit for purpose. Wouldn't it be a blessing to put them on the pill for a week and painlessly allow them to go to sleep? His or her absence would leave a vacant bed for someone else and save themselves the anxiety of being neglected in their own homes. It would probably take a couple of weeks for the hospitals to put this unique procedure on tap thereby saving the government and taxpayers millions. Isn't that what it's all about!? There would probably be an extra financial cost for the signing of death certificates, if they could find anybody to sign them.

Take the meals on wheels charity – that function so beloved of those housebound old nuisances is a charity that must be tackled. I'm referring especially to those cranky, disrespectful old bastards, male and female, never done moaning and groaning about the grub being too hot, too cold, or there's not enough of it due to them feeding their cats and dogs with the surplus. The service providers must be alerted to this new pill as a means of shortening their rounds and for once, let them experience the euphoria of a job well done. Prison authorities too should be able to offer this service to those doomed to spend their lives in captivity. Indeed, it would be a marvellous humanitarian gesture.

I noted other articles worth mentioning and perhaps I'll computerise my findings later.

'Kindliness is Godliness', so sayth Lord Buddha, and although that has always been my instinct, being kind is not as simple as it sounds. I don't know how many times I've been rebuffed when my attempts to be kind were misinterpreted, like the time when attending Bolton Street Tech. I saw a weedy eight-year-old lad waiting for his chance to cross the busy street.

"D'ya want me to see you across?" I said.

"Fuck off with yerself," was his reply as he darted across by himself.

It hurts to be rejected. So many friendships have been shattered by an unthinking, bad-tempered reply to a genuine offer of aid, though later some will apologise. I suppose balance and discretion must be your first instinct.

Our mother was a great one for helping out, and never lost a friend by it. She possessed the reserve of a nurse – intimacy without intrusion. Our father too was very kind, his unobtrusive manner and tone having a calming influence on all he met. Isn't that the kind of person you need to meet before going berserk? Lorcan, our eldest brother, would go to any lengths to help a neighbour or a friend. The only time he wasn't friendly was when he put on a football jersey. It was then he was very unfriendly. Our sister Margaret is also exceptionally kind, as are Frank and his wife Bridget, and Jack and Rosemary.

I encountered hundreds of very compassionate people when working in Britain. Jack of International Combustion who gave me a good job without even asking my name. Mrs. McLoughlan of Buller Street, Selby, who gave me a bed near midnight. Paddy Mooney's pound note. My Polish landlord in Manchester. Wally, my Russian workmate in London. I really appreciated the kindness of Mick Markey who, without me asking, fixed me with a job when I returned to Dublin, a Dublin with thousands of unemployed. The world is full of kind people, some with their kindness buried beneath layers of stress and dissatisfaction, but still capable of spontaneous kindness. There are plenty of the opposite among us – not bad, just thick.

I recall hearing an interview on the radio last year with a young man explaining an embarrassing temporary condition he had. This condition caused him to collapse without warning, leaving him twitching on the street. He described an incident in Rome where he took one of his turns. A passer-by with his wife concluded he had overdosed on drugs, but helped him to his feet and gave him twenty euro before sending him on his way. This young fellow laughed as he recorded the incident. I was disgusted with his attitude. Number one, he didn't need the money, yet took it. And number two, he only saw the funny side without mentioning the spontaneous kindness of a passer-by, or as our mother would say, 'from a black stranger'.

Sometimes I think that exceptionally decent, kind people were at some time in their early lives the recipients of compassion which tripped a switch, awakening a conscience that left them ever alert and responsive in times of need. I have met and known thousands of decent people in Aer Lingus and elsewhere and along with their peculiarities had the characteristics that make human beings beautiful, and left me the better for it. In these latter years I was more than kind to some of my neighbours, though never intimately friendly for I feared them, and as time passed my fear was justified.

SOME ADDITIONAL FAMILY PHOTOS
PAST AND PRESENT

My sister Margaret (third from right age 15 and a half) at work as an apprentice in FM Bakery, Dublin, c.1959/60.

Jack & Robert Monks, c1960.

Jack, Frank, and Lorcan (L to R) on best man duty.

Peadar Connor & his wife Phyllis, and Lorcan, Miley, Anna, Mick, and Margaret at St Margaret's GAA dinner-dance in Skerries c1966/8.

My father, Mick, Frank, Lorcan, Anna, Brigid and Margaret.

A rare photo of my parents and siblings together, taken on Mick and Margaret's wedding day, June 7, 1965.

My brother Jack Redmond and his wife Rosemarie, Tramore c.1964.

Jack, Margaret and my brother-in-law Mick, Tramore c.1964.

My brother-in-law Mick and my sister Margaret, Tramore Beach, c.1964.

Fr. O'Leary along with my brother Frank and his wife Brigid on their wedding day, August 10 1961.

My mother and niece Grainne in Jersey.

Me and Mick with my grandnephews Josh, Shane, and Ryan, July 2001.

Me with my brother in law Mick Howard after a night at the Autobahn pub, circa Christmas Eve, 2008.

Me with Margaret's girls, 2011.

Windsor Forest with Rufus & Seamus, 2012.

Jack, Margaret and myself at the Clann Mhurie GFC funday in the Naul, June 2014.

Me and my brothers Jack, Frank, Lorcan (L to R) and sister Margaret, December 2014.

Night out in town with Margaret's family, 2015.

In the Scottish Highlands in August 2015 with my niece Emer and her husband Matt.

Me with 'the aul dog' Rolo on South Beach, Rush, Co Dublin, July 2015.

GLOSSARY

Bate – Beat, assault

Bousey – Loutish

Bushman – Rough-cut hand saw

Butts on ye – Give me the core

Clane – Clean

Coffer – A reserve for a body of water

Corky – From Cork

Crook – Ill or sick (Australia)

Culchies – Country people

Dray – A four-wheel, horse-drawn cart

Eejit – An idiot

Ekker – Exercise, homework

Era – 'Have you got one?' or, 'Have you got one on you?'

Feckin' – A mild swear word

Gobshite – A foolish person

Hoor – Nuisance

Mott – Girlfriend or wife

Pissin wires – Red ants

Poteen or **Póitín** – Illegally made whiskey

Quare – Unusual or queer

Screech – A token or a small amount of money

Tanner – Sixpenny coin

The lump – A sub-contract

Thirty bob – One pound and fifty pence

Thruppenny bit – Three penny coin

Wan – One

Printed in Poland
by Amazon Fulfillment
Poland Sp. z o.o., Wrocław